Heirloom Cooking

WITH THE

Brass Sisters

Queens of Comfort Food™

Recipes You Remember & Love

MARILYNN BRASS & SHEILA BRASS

Photographs by ANDY RYAN

BLACK DOG
& LEVENTHAL
PUBLISHERS
NEW YORK

Page 1: Jelly and aspic molds, 19th-early 20th century; Page 2: Curry of Lamb with Saffron Rice; Page 5: Split Pea Soup; Page 6: Adventures; Page 15: Dot's Tuna Crescents; Page 29: Mrs. Yaffee's Pirogi; Page 32: New England Brown Bread; Page 35: Helen's Cheese Balls; Page 133: Aunt Ruth's Dilly Casserole Bread; Page 157: New England Brown Bread; Page 268: Toasted Almond Butter Cookies; Page 269: Mrs. Carter's Baked Stuffed Onions; Page 271: Cheese Bread

Published by
Black Dog & Leventhal Publishers, Inc.
151 West 19th Street
New York, NY 10011

Distributed by
Workman Publishing Company
225 Varick Street
New York, NY 10014

Manufactured in China

Cover and interior design by Susi Oberhelman
Photographs by Andy Ryan
Food Styling by Catrine Kelty
Kitchen Antiques by Marilynn and Sheila Brass

ISBN-13: 978-1-57912-784-8

h g f e d c b a

Library of Congress Cataloging-in-Publication Data is available on file.

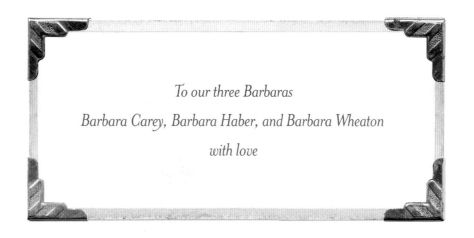

To our three Barbaras

Barbara Carey, Barbara Haber, and Barbara Wheaton

with love

CONTENTS

CHAPTER 4

Soup of the Day   109

CHAPTER 5

Staff of Life   131

CHAPTER 6

Home Plates

CHAPTER 7

SWEET FINALES 235

PREFACE

We are two roundish bespectacled women who have a combined total of 114 years of home cooking experience. We have always felt comfortable in the kitchen because we learned to cook at a very early age. Our mother, Dorothy, was an inspired home cook, and the meals she produced when we lived on Sea Foam Avenue, in Winthrop, Massachusetts, more than sixty years ago are still memorable.

Working at the black cast iron stove with its green enamel trim, we learned to ignore its idiosyncrasies to produce the soups and stews of our childhood, recipes we still make with pride today. We believe that there is nothing more comforting than the smell of a thick vegetable soup simmering on a back burner, a glistening brisket braising in the oven, or a dish of macaroni and cheese with its golden crust of buttery crumbs. We still relive the glories of the appetizers, vegetables, salads, and main dishes that came out of

Sheila, third grade, 1943; Marilynn, first grade, 1948

that sunny kitchen to become satisfying home-cooked meals. When we want to replicate these precious family recipes, we go to Mama's first cookbook, *All About Home Baking*, fragile now, but priceless, with her handwritten recipes on the front and back pages.

We couldn't have written *Heirloom Cooking* without consulting our manuscript cookbooks, those treasured notebooks of personal recipes compiled by home cooks. It is these living recipes, these notes handwritten on crumbling scraps of paper or the pages of old, well-worn cookbooks that inspire us to interpret the lost recipes and family stories of others. We continue to find these recipe collections, gathered together in bundles or in small boxes at yard sales, in used bookstores, or on the pantry shelves of friends.

Our personal collection of manuscript cookbooks has grown from 85 to 150 over the past two years. Because we are women of the twenty-first century, we have launched our own Web site (www.thebrasssisters.com) to communicate with our new friends, exchange recipes and family stories, and answer culinary questions.

In *Heirloom Cooking*, we give you the choice of planning and serving an entire heirloom meal or preparing a special heirloom dish from primary sources, the recipes handwritten by home cooks from all over the United States and Canada. The recipes we present are culturally diverse and tempting, from a German sauerbraten recipe from Ohio to a sophisticated liver paté from New York City. Discover Arline Ryan's Swedish Meatballs with Sour Cream Sauce from Indiana, Sweet Potato Pudding from North Carolina, Elinor's Shrimp Creole from Florida, and Danish Roast Goose Stuffed with Apples and Prunes and served with Red Cabbage and Caramelized Potatoes from Minnesota. Scottish baps appear as well as sweet and sour cabbage rolls and French-Canadian *tortière*. Mrs. Fredman's Coleslaw, from our childhood, is represented right along with Southern Icebox Pickles. For dessert we present a colorful choice of Red Velvet Cake, Green Tomato Pie, and a New England Blueberry Buckle, as well as other classic home-baked desserts.

We also pay tribute to the inexpensive vegetarian meals that utilized and celebrated the bounty of backyard gardens—those dumplings, frittatas, and pancakes that often served as main dishes in families that had more love in their kitchens than money in their purses.

Heirloom Cooking contains chapters on appetizers, soups, salads, vegetables, breads, and main dishes, as well as a respectable number of pies, cakes, and cookies. We have interpreted these handwritten recipes so that you can reproduce them in your own home kitchen, and we've tried to simplify the ones that once took hours or days to put together. To do this, we've turned to the culinary tools of twenty-first-century America—the mixer, the food processor, and occasionally, the microwave oven. Some recipes, such as those for bagels, have been scaled down and reinterpreted so that you will be able to prepare a home version of something that was usually produced in large quantities commercially. Not only have we kept it simple, we've also given you the freedom to adjust the seasonings, the size of the portions, and the cooking times. Please remember that the more exotic dishes, such as curries and patés, are interpretations of how an heirloom cook would have prepared these dishes in her own home kitchen. The recipes for roast goose and sauerbraten require more time to prepare and would have been served on special occasions.

What has influenced our appreciation of heirloom cooking the most has been the culinary journey we've taken across America. We've traveled through the South, the Midwest, and New England meeting old friends and making new ones. It was a sentimental journey because these visits with home cooks all over America have reinforced our belief that every family has a story and a recipe to document its own personal history. Sometimes the stories are sad, sometimes they are funny, but all are touching.

For us, traveling across America was a movable feast. We shared chicken pot pie in St. Louis, and we ate pierogi and stuffed cabbage in Ann Arbor. We learned about a Danish-American boy from Minneapolis who, upon losing his mother when he was fifteen years old, learned to cook the substantial meals needed to sustain his construction worker father. We were told of a young girl who, married at age fourteen to a Russian Orthodox priest, fed her five children her delicious cheese and farina dumplings between entertaining the bishop and ironing the church linen. There was the sprightly white-haired woman in Philadelphia, with a no-nonsense haircut and merry blue eyes, who advised us to add brewed coffee to our soups and gravies to give them a richer color. Later, we found the same advice in a Southern cookbook from the 1870s.

These encounters were precious, but the message was always the same. Cooking is the way we show our love for others. It's the way we nurture and support our family and friends. Heirloom cooking is just another definition for comfort food.

We have provided you with a keepsake envelope in the back of *Heirloom Cooking* as well as a special chapter of blank lined pages on which to transcribe the stories and recipes of your own family. We encourage you to listen to each story, write down the recipe, and make the book your own. Have fun cooking!

MARILYNN AND SHEILA BRASS
Cambridge, Massachusetts
2008

HOW TO USE THIS BOOK

We hope you will enjoy using this book. We have tried to make the recipes easy to understand and the ingredients easy to find. We'd like you to be so inspired by the recipes that you go into your own kitchen and start cooking.

Nearly all of the ingredients for the recipes in *Heirloom Cooking* are those found in most home pantries. You probably won't have to make a stop at your local gourmet shop to stock up on special spices, herbs, flours, or extracts. If you do find that some ingredients prove to be elusive, we have included a short list of suppliers (see Sources on page 269) whom we suggest you contact to order what you need. Most of the recipes will make four to six servings; several of them can be successfully halved or doubled. Some of the soup recipes make more than four to six servings. We suggest freezing leftover soup. What constitutes a serving size is often subjective, and open to interpretation, so for some recipes, we have tried to give you measurements in cups or slices for each serving. Decreasing or increasing the recipes may result in adjustments to cooking times.

➤➤ SOME SUGGESTIONS ◄◄

BEFORE YOU BEGIN

- Read each recipe several times. Make sure you understand the directions, know what ingredients are needed, and note how many servings the recipe will yield.
- Adjust oven racks before turning on the oven.
- Have all ingredients at room temperature, unless otherwise stated.
- Prepare pots and pans, and set out racks for cooling.
- Assemble your ingredients and utensils.

COOKING TIPS

- Combine ingredients in the order they are listed.
- Set a timer when a dish is in oven or special timed directions are given, such as "boil for 2 minutes."
- Allow completed dishes to cool completely, unless otherwise noted.
- Store cooked dishes in appropriate containers and refrigerate.

INGREDIENTS

BRANDY, SHERRY, AND WHISKEY

We bought small amounts of good-quality brandy, sherry, and whiskey to have on hand when making heirloom recipes. We use them to flavor recipes, plump raisins, and season fruitcakes.

BUTTER

For the recipes in this book, we use unsalted or sweet butter, softened at room temperature. Some recipes call for butter that is refrigerator-firm or melted before it is combined with other ingredients. We used generic store brand butters and found them to perform as well as commercial brands. If you do not have unsalted butter on hand, you can use salted butter for cooking, but do not use salted butter when baking because its moisture content can affect your results. We suggest that you reduce the amount of salt when cooking if you use salted butter. Do not use whipped butter in any of the recipes.

CHOCOLATE AND COCOA

Chocolate was often a luxury ingredient in the kitchens of the women whose recipes we tested. Occasionally, we introduced a gourmet chocolate when testing a recipe and noted a subtle enhancement of flavor, but we also found that familiar commercial brands of chocolate and cocoa produced good results. We discovered that by judiciously adding small amounts of bitter or baking chocolate to semisweet chocolate, we could achieve the complexity of flavor we were seeking. When a recipe requires baking chocolate, we use bitter chocolate. We were vigilant about using the correct cocoa, either American-style or Dutch, depending on the rising agents used in the recipe. Store chocolate and cocoa in a cool dry dark place. Milk chocolate candy bars can be used for Milk Chocolate Pound Cake (page 242).

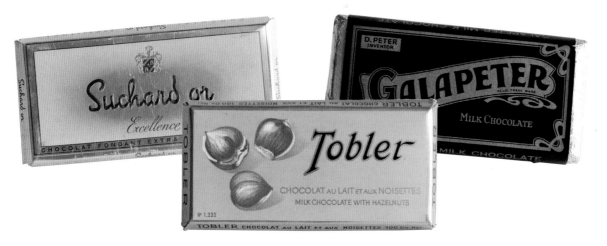

Tin advertising displays for candy bars, 1920s–1930s

DAIRY PRODUCTS

The recipes in this book use homogenized milk, not skim milk, and cultured nonfat butter-milk. We used whole-milk ricotta. We do not use reduced-fat cream cheese or nonfat sour cream. For cream, we use heavy cream, whipping cream, or half-and-half. We use farmer cheese or pot cheese instead of dry curd cottage cheese. We do not use reduced fat cheese or products referred to as cheese food.

EGGS

For consistency, we used only U.S. graded large eggs. Unless otherwise noted, the eggs should be at room temperature. Some recipes call for beating the eggs before adding them to the other ingredients. Egg whites should be at room temperature before being beaten. Eggs added directly to a warm or hot mixture run the risk of cooking too rapidly. To temper the eggs, stir a small amount of the hot mixture into the eggs before adding the eggs to the recipe.

Toy milk jugs, 1930s

EXTRACTS AND PURE FLAVORED OILS

Vanilla is the most popular flavor in the recipes we tested. We use only pure vanilla, lemon, and almond extracts. Pure citrus oils, when substituted for extracts, resulted in some very true flavors, and we provide a source for ordering them (see Sources on page 269).

FLOUR AND GRAINS

Use all-purpose bleached or unbleached flour unless the recipe calls for a specific type, such as bread flour, cake flour, or pastry flour. Some recipes require graham flour or rye flour. We also use yellow and white cornmeal interchangeably. Even though most large grocery chains carry specialty flours, you can order these items by mail or on the Internet (see Sources on page 269). For smooth gravies, we suggest that you use quick-mixing flour, which is finer than regular flour. It is available in grocery stores under the brand name Wondra. We tested several recipes with well-known commercial brands of flour but we found that using store brands produced the same results.

Measure flour by scooping a cup of flour and leveling it with a knife. If a recipe calls for "1 cup sifted flour," sift the flour and then measure it. If a recipe calls for "1 cup flour, sifted" measure the flour first and then sift it.

Measuring spoon, 1930s; bowl, American, 1930s

FRUIT—FRESH, DRIED, AND CANNED

We use the fruit called for in the original recipe whenever possible. Most of the manuscript cookbooks call for raisins, currants, prunes, cherries, dates, figs, and candied peels such as orange, lemon, or citron. When we did make substitutions, such as dried fruit for fresh or fresh for dried, we noted it. We use fresh fruit when it is in season and buy dried fruit in small quantities. Often, we found that plumping dried fruit in orange juice, tea, or brandy before using added another level of flavor.

We used canned fruit when it was appropriate to the recipe, such as canned pineapple and mandarin orange sections for Dot Luke's Hawaiian Jellied Salad (page 78) or the cranberry sauce for Aunt Ida's Apple Cranberry Noodle Pudding (page 229).

LARD AND SALT PORK

We buy only commercial brand lard for use in recipes that call for lard. Old pastry recipes often call for a combination of lard and butter. We found that some cookies and pie crusts were particularly flaky and tender when made from lard or a combination of lard and butter. We also found that using lard gave an old-world flavor and texture to finished dishes. We use commercial brand salt pork to add flavor to heirloom dishes. Salt pork is remarkably salty. Since it might be necessary to remove the tough skin and blanch the salt pork, we suggest that you substitute bacon or pancetta (Italian bacon), when appropriate.

Roseville Pottery bowl, American, 20th century

HEIRLOOM COOKING

⤖ THE HEIRLOOM PANTRY SHELF ⤛

We keep certain ingredients for preparing heirloom recipes on our pantry shelf. These items (listed below) have a long culinary history, and in one form or another they continue to be helpful in reproducing the recipes we find in manuscript cookbooks: garlic powder, onion powder, dehydrated onion flakes, tomato ketchup, tomato sauce, tomato paste, mayonnaise, Worcestershire sauce, dry mustard, prepared mustard, Tabasco sauce, canned green chilies, chopped hot peppers in brine, pimentos, chili sauce, curry powder, cayenne pepper, cream of mushroom soup, cream of celery soup, packaged or canned broth, creamed corn, canned clams, clam broth, soda crackers, common crackers, Crown Pilot crackers, ginger jam, apricot jam, chocolate syrup, maraschino cherries.

Substitutions can be made when preparing heirloom recipes in your own home kitchen, such as fresh garlic and onion for garlic powder, onion powder, or dehydrated onion flakes.

LEMON, ORANGE, AND LIME JUICE AND ZEST

We use medium-sized lemons and oranges, as well as regular-sized Persian limes, with firm, unblemished skins. Use a Microplane zester/grater or a traditional grater to remove the zest or colored part of the rind, leaving behind the bitter white pith. We roll the fruit on a flat surface to break up the juice pockets first. Then cut the fruit in half and juice it on a reamer; strain the juice to remove any seeds. A lemon weighing $4\frac{1}{2}$ ounces yields approximately 2 teaspoons grated zest and 3 tablespoons lemon juice. An orange weighing $6\frac{1}{4}$ ounces yields approximately 2 tablespoons grated zest and 4 tablespoons orange juice. A $3\frac{1}{2}$-ounce lime yields approximately 2 teaspoons of grated zest and approximately 5 tablespoons lime juice.

NUTS

Our choice of nuts depended on the original recipe. Walnuts, pecans, peanuts, and almonds were typically found in the larders and pantries of the women whose recipes we tested. Buy nuts in small quantities and store them in sealed and dated plastic bags or covered plastic containers in the freezer to preserve their freshness.

SALT AND PEPPER

We generally use freshly ground black pepper in our heirloom recipes because its flavor is more assertive than white pepper. However, white pepper has the added advantage of not being visible in white foods. We use table salt as well as kosher salt in our recipes. Kosher salt has larger crystals, and it draws more fluid out of protein when sprinkled on its surface. This is part of the koshering process. Because table salt has finer crystals, 1 teaspoon of table salt contains more than 1 teaspoon of kosher salt. Specialty salts sold in gourmet shops should be sprinkled on top of dishes to add a burst of saltiness and to enhance the flavor of the dish. We've adjusted the salt and pepper in recipes according to our own taste, but we suggest that you taste and adjust seasonings to your taste.

SPICES AND HERBS

Cinnamon is the most popular spice in our recipes, followed by nutmeg, ginger, cloves, and allspice. For those who wrote these living recipes, spices were not easily accessible and were often expensive. Some cooks were creative and mixed small amounts of different spices or herbs to achieve multiple levels of flavor. Buy spices in small quantities and store them in a cool dark place.

Early heirloom recipes called for herbs that were readily available, such as parsley, sage, thyme, and rosemary. Basil, oregano, dill, summer savory, and saffron were introduced with the arrival of immigrants from the Mediterranean, Eastern Europe, and India. Spice blends such as curry powder, garam masala, and red curry powder have gained in popularity as America's cuisine becomes more diverse.

Vintage spice tins, American and English

SUGAR

Use white granulated sugar unless a recipe calls for a specific type, such as light brown sugar, confectioners' sugar, or sanding sugar. We generally do not use dark brown sugar because we think the flavor is too assertive for most of the recipes, but you may prefer it. If you use dark brown sugar, use the same amount as light brown sugar. Brown sugars should always be firmly packed in a measuring cup. Store in a tightly closed plastic bag to prevent it from hardening. We tried store-brand and commercial-brand sugars and found that both provided successful results. Sweeteners with additional flavors include maple syrup, molasses, honey, and light and dark corn syrup. Store confectioners' sugar in a sealed plastic bag so that it is easier to measure. Sift it after measuring to remove any lumps. Sanding sugar, also known as decorating or sparkling sugar, is coarser than table sugar and is found in the baking sections of grocery stores.

VEGETABLE OIL AND OLIVE OIL

We use a pure, unflavored vegetable oil such as corn oil or canola oil for deep-frying and baking. We always use fresh oil when we deep-fry. We use extra-virgin olive oil for pan-frying and for some of the salad dressings. It's worth the extra cost because of the superior flavor it adds to finished dishes.

VEGETABLE SHORTENING

Solid vegetable shortening can be used for some of the recipes in *Heirloom Cooking*. We buy it in small containers to ensure its freshness and store it according to the manufacturer's instructions. Whenever we had a choice, we used butter instead of shortening.

VEGETABLES—FRESH, CANNED, AND FROZEN

We used fresh vegetables when they were in season. We used canned vegetables only when we wanted to replicate the flavor and appearance of an heirloom recipe because most cooks used their own home-canned vegetables. We also substituted frozen vegetables, when available, for out-of-season fresh vegetables or canned vegetables.

YEAST

We used active dry yeast in baking the recipes that called for a raised dough. We used a quick-rising yeast only when we found the recipe benefited from its use. We did not use cake yeast. We proofed our yeast in water that had been heated to 115°F.

UTENSILS, STOVES, AND APPLIANCES

BAKING PANS

We are specific about noting the size, weight, and material of cooking and baking ware and always try to use standard sizes. We use only 9-inch ovenproof glass pie plates, not the ones with handles or ruffles. Manufacturers of glass baking products often suggest lowering the baking temperature when using their products. We suggest that you follow the instructions that come with any product you use. However, the temperatures we state for ovenproof pans are the ones we used for these recipes. No one knows your stove and baking equipment better than you do. Many of our baking pans and utensils are more than thirty years old. We are used to working with them. Several were purchased at yard sales for a few dollars. If you need to buy kitchenware, we suggest that you explore all the options, buy brand names, and keep instructions on how to use them in a file folder in a handy place.

MIXERS AND FOOD PROCESSORS

We used a KitchenAid standing mixer for most of the recipes because one of our goals was to save home bakers as much time as possible. We used the dough hook for easy kneading. A handheld mixer will also work for many of these recipes, as will a wooden spoon or a whisk, but it will take more time and effort, and the texture and result may vary. We are careful to note that certain recipes such as those for muffins and quick breads benefit from gentle hand mixing.

Toy steamer and pots, 1890s–1900s

HEIRLOOM COOKING

POTS AND PANS WE FIND USEFUL

- 9-inch by 13-inch by 1-inch jelly roll or half-sheet pan
- 14-inch by 17-inch metal baking sheet
- 17-inch by 11-inch by 1-inch metal jelly roll pan
- 8-cup and 10-cup Bundt pans
- Metal springform pan
- Round cake pans
- 9-inch by 5-inch by 3-inch metal loaf pan
- 10-inch by 4¼-inch angel food cake or tube pan
- 8-inch by 8-inch by 2-inch pan for bar cookies and brownies
- 9-inch by 9-inch by 2-inch pan
- Muffin tins
- Round jelly mold
- 9-inch by 13-inch by 2-inch metal or glass pan
- 9-inch ovenproof glass pie plate
- 9-inch, 10-inch, and 12-inch quiche dish
- 1½-quart ovenproof glass or ceramic baking dish
- 2 quart overproof rectangular glass dish
- 8-inch round tart pan
- Large metal roasting pan for water bath
- 8-inch and 10-inch nonreactive stainless steel heavy-bottomed frying pans
- 5-quart nonreactive stainless steel heavy-bottomed saucepan
- Cast iron and enamel Dutch oven
- 8-quart nonreactive stainless steel stockpot
- 12-quart nonreactive stainless steel stockpot
- Ovenproof custard cups
- Set of nonreactive glass or stainless steel mixing bowls
- Double boiler
- 8-inch round soufflé/casserole dish

Cast iron baking pan, American, early 1900s

✈ COOKING AND BAKING AIDS ✈
WE CAN'T LIVE WITHOUT

- Standing mixer with paddle, whisk, and dough-hook attachments
- Food processor with metal blade and grating and shredding blades
- Microplane zester/grater (to grate zests)
- Offset spatulas (to smooth batters and frost cakes and cookies)
- Tongs
- Turkey lifters
- Turkey baster
- Potato ricer
- Thermometer to check oven temperature
- Candy thermometer to test sugar syrup and oil temperature
- Instant-read thermometer to test water temperature when proofing yeast or checking temperature of roasts

- Scale (for weighing ingredients)
- Disposable gloves
- Disposable piping bags
- Strainers (for sifting, removing seeds from juice, and dusting with confectioners' sugar)
- Cooling racks in a variety of sizes
- Parchment paper
- Wax paper
- Silicone baking liners
- Set of stainless steel measuring cups for measuring dry ingredients: ⅛ cup, ¼ cup, ⅓ cup, ½ cup, ⅔ cup, ¾ cup, 1 cup
- Set of stainless steel measuring spoons for measuring dry and liquid ingredients: ⅛ teaspoon, ¼ teaspoon, ½ teaspoon, 1 teaspoon, 1 tablespoon. Spoons with a rectangular bowl are easier to dip into narrow-necked spice jars.

We use a 7-cup Cuisinart food processor, usually with the metal blade attachment. Using a food processor for mixing pastry or cookie dough and switching to alternate blades for grating or shredding saves time and provides uniform results. For many recipes, a blender can be used in place of a food processor, and we've noted where that substitution is applicable.

STOVES

We used a gas stove to test the recipes. Since every stove is different, we suggest that you honor the idiosyncrasies of your own stove and use an oven thermometer. Turn cookie sheets halfway through baking if you have any hot spots in your oven. We usually bake one sheet of cookies at a time, but if you do multiples, be sure to switch them from rack to rack and front to back halfway through baking.

Miniature molds, American and English, 1870s–1920s

The Essence of Heirloom Cooking

There is nothing that tastes as good as something cooked by someone who loves us. It is the memory of these comforting meals that sustains us in a world that constantly changes. People need a place where they feel safe, even if it is constructed from the ephemeral aromas and tastes created in the kitchens of their past.

As we look through our collections of manuscript cookbooks, we realize that everything old is new again. In the twenty-first century we see a return to cooking with local seasonal ingredients and an interest in taking from the earth the best it has to offer. We also find a continuing commitment to maintaining the earth as a healthy and bountiful resource.

It is important to celebrate the heirloom kitchen in our own home kitchens by re-creating those meals and memories and honoring that commitment. We want to preserve the flavor, taste, and value of heirloom recipes, but we must listen to the stories of the people who created them. We have to understand their daily obligations to provide and maintain a home. We have to learn about the types of foods they raised or bought, and the amount of time it took to harvest or secure those foods and prepare them for their family's meals. People have always had to confront the challenges of hard times when just surviving was a victory, but to survive while making a family feel loved and protected was heroic.

We are fortunate that handwritten recipes still exist. They may be fragile and crumble as we touch them, but they are, nevertheless, living recipes. They will never be lost if we assume their stewardship by cooking them in our own kitchens. We are grateful that our grandmothers, mothers, aunts, and friends had the foresight to jot down their personal recipes in old notebooks, sometimes attaching fragments of even older recipes to the pages with safety pins or bent nails. Through these, often multigenerational, documents, they have bequeathed to us what they valued most—their own personal histories illustrated by the meals they cooked every day. They have taught us that we have much to learn about food and how it's prepared to appreciate its value. We must never forget that these women were not just home cooks, they were "homemakers," a title which was hard-won and worn with pride.

For some, cooking is a challenge. To others, it is as natural as walking through the kitchen door. Cooking is intuitive; it is not as specific as baking because there is usually room for interpretation. It is not uncommon for the home cook to adjust seasonings, substitute ingredients, or change cooking times and still achieve essentially the same result as

the original. We want to re-create the foods we ate as children, the food our mothers and grandmothers wrote and talked about. Heirloom cooking, like most home cooking, should be simple and economical. It should use ingredients readily available from the home pantry or the local grocery store. Above all, it should be enjoyable to eat. The dumplings, stews, and soups of yesterday should still taste good when made in today's kitchens.

Because women came together socially at church or temple gatherings, at holiday celebrations, or through something as universal as sharing a cup of tea or coffee, they were able to exchange recipes and advise each other on how to make the best corned beef hash or bake the best refrigerator rolls. These formal and informal get-togethers provided an opportunity to educate each other in how to run a household, feed a family, and, more importantly, how to create a home. They also provided a universal meeting place for women to support and celebrate one another when they talked about their fears and joys. Not to be forgotten are the men who found themselves maintaining their homes by going into the kitchen to cook family meals.

Developing a self-image has always been important to women. Except for the years that America took part in World War II, when women's skills and labor were needed in manufacturing, most women did not work outside the home after marriage until just after the middle of the twentieth century. One of the few ways a woman could individualize herself, whether she was formally educated or not, was by creating and personalizing a recipe admired by others. More than one husband urged his wife to ask

Cooking pamphlets, American, 1950s

for the recipe for brisket or macaroni and cheese served by their hostess so that she could prepare it in their own kitchen.

Because so many women were honorable in crediting the creator of a recipe, more than fifty years later, we are able to acknowledge a recipe for Lemon Chicken, authored by Anna Morse. This was one of the recipes she shared with the members of "The Railroad Club," the group of women who met morning and evening when commuting from the North Shore of Massachusetts to Boston. Anne Kemelman, a member of the club, at age ninety-eight still remembers Anna and the other women who loved to exchange recipes, discuss the stock market on their commute, and eventually form an investment club.

We found that heirloom cooks were clever at substituting ingredients and judging how much was needed from large ingredients such as heads of cabbage or sweet potatoes. The guidelines for recipes were more permissive, and with the introduction of standardized measurements by The Boston Cooking School, and its zealous director, Fannie Merritt Farmer, the burden of replicating the amounts of ingredients was lessened. No longer was a teacup, a tumbler, a gill, or butter the size of an egg a mystery.

In comparing heirloom recipes, we found that a woman established her own guidelines for selecting and purchasing the major ingredients for the meals she cooked in her kitchen. When buying fish, she would often ask, "What's fresh today?" If it didn't pass her scrutiny, she turned to canned tuna and canned salmon with very good results. Women were comfortable cooking with commercially canned foods because most women had

Cooking pamphlets, American, 1920s–1950s

learned to preserve foods at home to feed the family when times were lean or when food was out of season. However, home-canned food was only as good as the skill of the person who canned it. In a farm society with no refrigeration, heirloom cooks kept food in cold places such as icehouses or cellars. Sausage meat was highly salted and kept in crocks and covered with a layer of lard. This sometimes led to spoilage. Most home cooks eventually switched to commercially canned foods because it was convenient and more dependable.

With refrigeration came the choice of frozen foods, and women who were now working outside the home in increasing numbers took advantage of this new way to reduce time-consuming repetitive chores like washing and cutting up vegetables and fruit. Women still buy canned tomato sauce and cream soups because their mothers used them or because they enable the modern home cook to quickly prepare casseroles and meat-loaves with a traditional taste.

The campaign slogan of Herbert Hoover in 1928 promised a chicken in every pot, but during the Great Depression, the home cook sometimes found herself struggling to pay dearly for that chicken and searched for ways to make it go further. Chicken soup and chicken pot pie were two good ways to stretch a poultry purchase. If a woman lived on a farm and raised chickens herself, she served them only for special occasions because she needed the chickens to provide the eggs she sold. It was traditionally accepted that women could keep for themselves the money they made by selling eggs. Often, Mother's egg money became a nest egg for emergencies or special treats for the children.

During the nineteenth and early twentieth centuries, veal was described as a budget meat. It was less expensive than chicken. Veal was particularly favored for Italian dishes, but it also found its way into recipes such as Mock Chicken Salad and Swedish Meatballs. Veal was a lean meat and responded well to periods of long moist cooking, making it an economical choice to feed the family.

Beef was the standby of the home kitchen. Even the more challenging cuts of beef could be transformed into appealing home plates such as sauerbraten, meatloaf, and corned beef. These culinary challenges resulted in leftover favorites such as corned beef hash and meatloaf sandwiches. The creative heirloom cook could use her skills in braising, stewing, and roasting to tenderize the less expensive choices, and there was always ground beef, the versatile ingredient that found its way into soups, sauces, and casseroles.

Pork has always been the salvation of the kitchen budget, whether utilized for stuffing cabbage leaves, making a ham loaf, or baking beans. Hearty and satisfying, pork dishes fed many for very little. Most American women lived on farms during the nine-teenth century, and some still did up until the middle of the twentieth century. Most farm families raised their own pigs and learned to utilize them "from tail to snout."

Heirloom cooking often used generous amounts of cheese and eggs. Although dishes such as frittatas and macaroni and cheese may not have met all of the requirements of vegetarianism, they were still able to satisfy the culinary needs of those who refused to eat meat, fish, or poultry. An added bonus for the home cook was that eggs and cheese were both available and inexpensive.

Living recipes made use of familiar spices—cinnamon, nutmeg, cloves and ginger—for savory dishes as well as sweet. As transportation improved, the price of spices declined, and it was often worth spending money for small amounts of spice to enhance the flavor of home cooking. Women sought to prevent their cooking from becoming repetitive or dull. Two recipes—our mother's Romanian Stuffed Cabbage made with tomato sauce and Bunny Slobodzinski's Polish Stuffed Cabbage with Salt Pork Gravy—taught us that two home cooks could prepare a recipe using the same primary ingredients, but still end up with two very different dishes, each reflecting her ingenuity and her cultural heritage.

With the coming of immigrants from the Mediterranean and Eastern Europe, herbs such as thyme, oregano, dill, and basil were put to good use as homemakers duplicated the dishes they had first learned to make in their homelands. The home cook could grow herbs on a kitchen windowsill. Because living recipes continuously used the same ingredients—cabbage, cheese, eggs, ground meat, macaroni, potatoes—home cooks found it necessary to personalize them with their own combinations of spices and herbs. A few adventurous women learned to cook with the exotic spices of India, and curries of chicken, lamb, and shrimp were included in their repertoire.

Home cooks have always known how to make something out of nothing. They learned to turn stale bread into puddings and frittatas, and crumbs into pie crusts. By supporting brand loyalty with sometimes three generations of women buying products with encouraging names such as Reliable Flour and Blue Ribbon Mayonnaise, they learned how to perform culinary magic in the kitchen.

Heirloom recipes provide us with valuable information about who these home cooks were, how they lived, and what they prepared in their kitchens. Because they belong to the past, they can teach us so much about what life was like then and what they hoped life would be like for those who came after them. We cannot go into our kitchens without thinking of these generations of women who honored their responsibility to feed their families and preserve their homes. These are the women who knew how to banish tears with a slice of homemade bread and butter or calm fears with a bowl of hot soup and a hug. When we reproduce their recipes, which have lain forgotten on shelves or in boxes, in our own kitchens, we are filled with expectation, remembrance, and joy.

CHAPTER 1

IN THE BEGINNING

Appetizers and first courses have always been an important part of every meal. They are the first act, the prelude to what is coming next. If the appetizer tastes good, than chances are the rest of the meal will be delicious. • Almost every language has a word for appetizers. In our family, we used the Yiddish word *farschpais* to refer to herring salad or chopped liver prepared to pique our appetites—we interpreted its meaning as something to spice up the meal. Italian families referred to their caponata (an eggplant-tomato spread) as the *antipasto*—something served before the rest of the meal. If we want to be fancy, we can call the recipe for savory Mystery Stuffed Mushrooms an *hors d'oeuvre*. These days, we often refer to these tempting first bites as something to whet or sharpen our appetites.

Reading through our growing collections of manuscript cookbooks filled with handwritten recipes, we've found a bounty of intriguing starters with interesting stories about the women who created them.

While not all starters are created equal, they should be simple and inexpensive to make and use easily obtainable ingredients. Some of the recipes in this chapter use similar ingredients such as cheese, eggs, or chicken livers, but they are used in very different ways. For example, the chopped liver of our childhood is very different from Ione Ulrich Sutton's sophisticated liver paté, with its buttery texture and hint of chopped sweet gherkins.

We found the recipe for Ione's paté as we leafed through a pile of faded handwritten recipes, late at night, in a New York bookstore. Ione Ulrich Sutton was a Renaissance woman. She was the Financial Officer of the Museum of Modern Art in the 1930s, and she worked on Wall Street in the 1940s and 1950s. Above all, she was a creative hostess who generously passed on her recipes for paté and zucchini pie to those who asked for them, often jotting them down on her own business stationery. We found that her recipes are as good today as they were when she served them at gatherings for her socially prominent friends.

Mrs. Yaffee's pierogi are meat-filled treasures in a crust rich with chicken fat. Baked, rather than boiled, these crusty starters came from the mother of our next-door neighbor, Thelma Hankin. Stopping by to visit on Sea Foam Avenue after a trip to Mexico, Mrs. Yaffee graciously shared her recipe with the women sitting on beach chairs in her daughter's driveway. We still have her recipe transcribed in our mother Dorothy's handwriting. Mama used to serve two or three pierogi with a bowl of homemade chicken soup, but we've made these smaller pierogi as appetizers.

A local yard sale provided Libby Corkery's Spicy Ribs with Barbecue Sauce. Our agent, Karen, gave us Libby's file of handwritten recipes. The telephone operator for the Town of Groton, Massachusetts, for thirty-five years, Libby was a formidable home cook. These ribs are juicy, succulent finger food and a perfect start to a festive party.

Browsing in an antique store in Marblehead, Massachusetts, we found the recipe for Helen's Fried Cheese Balls, tasty little bites that are wonderful dipped in a Chili Mayonnaise. As we handled the fragile pages of this manuscript cookbook, we found a precious love letter, written from Charles to Helen and dated June 27, 1897. In it, we read about the hopes the young couple had for a life together now that her father had given his blessing to the engagement. When Charles wrote his love letter, he had no idea that his "own darling little girl" would turn out to be such a gifted home cook and capable hostess.

Our friend Nick Malgieri provided us with the recipe for a savory cheese cracker that tasted very much like the ones Grandpa Katziff brought us from the family grocery store years ago. We adapted the recipe to include an extra level of flavor by substituting blue cheese for cheddar and adding the crunch of chopped walnuts. The taste of these crackers comes as close to the waffled cheese treats of our childhood as we can get.

We hope that you will enjoy reading the stories and preparing the recipes in this chapter, and that in making them your own, you will re-create the good times they represent.

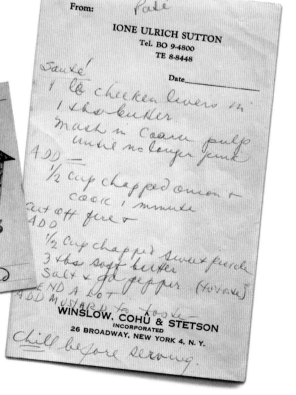

Libby's Spicy Ribs with Barbecue Sauce

{ 1960s }

YIELD: 20 RIBS, 6 APPETIZER SERVINGS

4 lbs. pork baby back ribs, separated

1¼ cups chopped onion

1 tablespoon salt

1 tablespoon pickling spice

1½ cups water

1 cup ketchup

¾ cup chili sauce

¼ cup firmly packed brown sugar

2 tablespoons Worcestershire sauce

1 tablespoon celery seed

¼ teaspoon garlic powder

⅛ teaspoon hot pepper flakes

1 teaspoon ground mustard

Tabasco sauce (optional)

Tips & Touches

- For a more spicy sauce, add more Tabasco sauce.
- Remove some of the cinnamon sticks from the pickling spice to reduce the cinnamon taste of the sauce.

SOME APPETIZERS JUST BRING A CROWD TOGETHER. *People don't stay strangers long when they're wiping barbecue sauce off their chins. Maybe that's what Libby Corkery, of Groton, Massachusetts, planned when she entertained—comfort food that was actually "finger-licking" good. This is a home cook's interpretation of barbecue. There are lots of pantry shelf ingredients in this recipe, so break out the ketchup, celery seed, and garlic powder.*

1. Place ribs in a heavy 8-quart pot. Add onion, salt, and pickling spice. Add water to cover ribs. Cover pot and bring to a boil. Reduce heat and simmer 1 hour, occasionally stirring with a wooden spoon and checking to make sure water doesn't evaporate. Replenish water if needed.

2. Set the oven rack in the middle position. Preheat the oven to 325°F. Coat a 9-inch by 13-inch by 2-inch ovenproof glass baking dish with vegetable spray.

3. In a small saucepan, combine water, ketchup, chili sauce, brown sugar, Worcestershire sauce, celery seed, garlic powder, hot pepper flakes, mustard, and Tabasco sauce, if using. Bring to a boil, reduce heat, and simmer 5 minutes. Place ribs in prepared dish, pour sauce over ribs, and turn ribs once in sauce to coat. Bake 1 hour, or until ribs are tender and falling off the bone. Turn ribs at least twice during baking. To serve, spoon sauce on top and pass extra sauce on the side.

MRS. YAFFEE'S PIEROGI

{ 1940s }

YIELD: 20 PIEROGI

FOR DOUGH

2 cups flour

2 teaspoons baking powder

½ teaspoon salt

½ cup chilled chicken fat or shortening

2 eggs, beaten

2 tablespoons ice water

1 egg, beaten, for glaze

FOR FILLING

¾ lb. ground beef

2 tablespoons chicken fat or olive oil

1 cup finely chopped onion

1 cup finely chopped boiled potatoes

½ teaspoon salt

¼ teaspoon coarsely ground black pepper

THIS IS ONE OF THOSE GREAT RECIPES *that women exchange when visiting. We lived next door to Thelma Hankin, who held court with the ladies of Sea Foam Avenue during spring and summer afternoons in the 1940s. Her mother, Mrs. Yaffee, a talented home cook, could talk a good recipe. These meat and potato–filled pastries are like Jewish baked empanadas. The chicken fat in the dough gives these tender little savories a satisfying flavor. Originally made with shredded leftover pot roast or brisket, we use ground beef.*

1. To make the dough: Combine flour, baking powder, and salt in the bowl of a food processor fitted with the metal blade. Add chicken fat or shortening and pulse until mixed. Add eggs and ice water. Process until dough pulls away from the sides of the bowl. Remove dough from bowl, divide in half, and shape each half into a disk. Place each disk in a plastic bag. Chill until firm enough to roll, at least 2 hours.

2. To make the filling: Sauté ground beef in a large frying pan over medium heat until no trace of pink remains. Transfer cooked meat to a large bowl. Do not drain fat from meat. Add chicken fat or olive oil to pan and return pan to medium heat. Add onions and sauté until translucent, 5 to 7 minutes. Add onions to bowl with meat. Add potatoes, salt, and pepper and stir to combine. Let cool.

➤➤ THE HISTORY OF PIEROGI ◄◄

Pierogi are small pastries filled with meat, onions, and potatoes. They are first cousins to *piroghi* (from Slovakia), *piroshki* (from Armenia), and *pelmeni* (from Russia). Mrs. Yaffee's Pierogi are baked, not boiled or fried. Not quite a dumpling, more of a small pie, the singular of *pierogi* is sometimes referred to as a *pierøg* or a *parog*. Pierogi have existed in some form since the sixteenth century and trace their origin to Russia and possibly to China. Pierogi can be filled with shredded cabbage, mushrooms, or farmer's cheese.

SOME THOUGHTS ON CHICKEN FAT

Chicken fat gives pierogi dough and chopped liver their distinctive flavor and texture. Traditionally, small amounts of chicken fat were collected from several kosher chickens. The raw fat was tightly wrapped and frozen. When enough fat was collected, it was defrosted and rendered with chopped onions on top of the stove.

Chicken fat is essential to many Jewish recipes. What lard is to Christian cooks, chicken fat is to Jewish cooks. Rendering chicken fat can be dangerous, but there is an alternative to simmering a large amount of fat on a hot stove. After roasting chickens, pour off the hot cooking liquid that collects in the pan and chill it in the refrigerator. Harvest the thick layer of golden fat that collects on the surface of this gravy, store it in an airtight container, and freeze it for future use. Small amounts of rendered chicken fat keep in the freezer for about three months and are available when needed. Rendered chicken fat can also be purchased at kosher markets.

3. Set the oven rack in the middle position. Preheat the oven to 375°F. Line a 14-inch by 16-inch baking sheet with foil, shiny side up, and coat with vegetable spray, or use a silicone liner.

4. On a lightly floured work surface, roll out one dough disk to a $\frac{1}{16}$-inch thickness. Cut into circles using a 4-inch round cookie cutter dipped in flour. Combine scraps and reroll to cut at least 10 circles total. Work remaining dough disk in the same way to cut 10 more circles.

5. Place a heaping tablespoon of the meat mixture in the center of each dough circle. Using your finger, moisten edges of each circle with water and fold over dough to form a half-moon. Use the tines of a salad fork to crimp the folded edge. Place on prepared baking sheet and brush with beaten egg. Bake about 20 minutes, or until golden brown. Remove from oven, place baking sheet on rack, and cool 5 minutes. Serve immediately. Store leftover pierogi in a covered container in the refrigerator.

Tips & Touches

- Because pierogi are made with chicken fat, the dough is fragile. Handle it with care to prevent tears. Patch tears with thin pieces of extra dough.
- Baked pierogi can be frozen, defrosted, and reheated in a 375°F oven for 5 to 7 minutes.
- Pierogi can be served hot, warm, or at room temperature, as an appetizer or on the side with a bowl of chicken soup.

Mixed Olives with Lemon and Rosemary

YIELD: 6 SERVINGS   { 1970s }

THIS IS ONE OF THOSE RECIPES WE MADE, *when we were sweet young things, to take to parties in Cambridge, Massachusetts. It became Sheila's signature appetizer, and years later, there are those who still remember the mix of olives, the touch of citrus, and the use of the then exotic herb, rosemary. The caper berries are an optional addition, enhancing the crunchy texture. This recipe uses olives very different from the canned black or bottled green ones we grew up with.*

1. Bruise rosemary sprigs with the bottom of a small metal saucepan and remove leaves.
2. Place rosemary, olives, olive oil, lemon juice, lemon zest, capers, red pepper flakes, caper berries, and garlic in a large nonreactive bowl. Mix thoroughly and cover with plastic wrap. Refrigerate for at least 2 days before serving.

2 sprigs fresh rosemary, each 5 inches long

1½ lbs. assorted brined olives

¼ cup extra-virgin olive oil

1 tablespoon lemon juice

2 teaspoons grated lemon zest

1 tablespoon brined capers (not salt-cured)

¼ teaspoon red pepper flakes

½ lb. caper berries (optional)

3 cloves garlic, smashed

TIPS & TOUCHES

- We used a mix of Manzanilla, Kalamata, Sicilian, and Bella Cerignola Rosa olives for a good range of color and texture. Picholine and Calabrese olives can also be used for this recipe.
- We don't add salt because the olives are brined, but the seasoning can be adjusted.
- Olives can be garnished with thinly sliced rounds of lemon and sprigs of rosemary.

45

Auntie Dot's Chopped Liver

{ 1930s }

YIELD: 2½ LBS. CHICKEN LIVER

½ cup flour

2 lbs. chicken livers, rinsed and patted dry

2 tablespoons chicken fat or olive oil, plus extra, if needed (see "Some Thoughts on Chicken Fat" on page 43)

2 cups chopped onion

1 teaspoon salt

½ teaspoon coarsely ground black pepper

4 large eggs, hard-cooked, 1 yolk reserved for garnish, balance chopped

THIS IS THE CHOPPED LIVER THAT OUR MOTHER, *Dorothy, made when we were growing up. She always used a hand chopper and a wooden bowl and lots of homemade chicken fat. We use a food processor with excellent results but don't expect a smooth buttery paté. The variation in texture is what makes this appetizer so special. Chopped liver is delicious spread on a piece of rye bread, topped with a slice of raw onion. Marilynn was always responsible for the sieved egg yolk mimosa garnish.*

1. Place flour in a plastic bag. Add chicken livers and shake until lightly coated. Shake floured livers in a strainer over sink to remove excess flour. Set aside.

2. Heat chicken fat or olive oil in large heavy frying pan over medium heat. Add onions and cook until just translucent, 5 to 7 minutes. Remove to a bowl and set aside. Working in batches, fry livers in chicken fat remaining in the pan until bottoms are brown and crunchy, about 5 minutes. Turn and cook until the second side is browned, another 5 minutes. Remove one liver from the pan and cut into it. Livers are done when no pink remains in the interior when you cut into the liver. Add more fat during frying if the pan gets dry.

3. Place onions and livers in the bowl of a food processor fitted with the metal blade. Pulse until mixture is combined, but still coarsely textured. Remove half of mixture and set aside. Pulse remaining mixture to a texture that is slightly coarser than paté. Combine two liver mixtures and fold in chopped eggs. Add more chicken fat if the texture is a little dry. Add salt and pepper; taste to adjust seasonings.

4. Refrigerate chopped liver in a covered container until 15 minutes before serving. Serve in a mound on a platter surrounded by crackers and celery stalks. Press reserved yolk through a fine sieve and scatter resulting mimosa on top of mounded liver. Do not leave out at room temperature for long periods of time.

TIPS & TOUCHES

- Fry chicken livers in batches to avoid crowding the pan, which will result in uneven cooking.
- Use a metal egg slicer to save time chopping eggs.

NEW YORK PATÉ

YIELD: 8 TO 10 SERVINGS

{ 1930s }

WE FOUND THIS LIVING RECIPE *for a sophisticated chicken liver paté on the personalized notepaper of Ione Ulrich Sutton, who was affiliated with the brokerage firm of Winslow, Cohu & Stetson, in New York. Further research told us that the personal papers of Ione, a career woman, writer, and active Republican, reside in the Eisenhower Library, in Abilene, Kansas. Just as important, Ione knew how to cook and entertain by preparing simple, but memorable, appetizers. Her guests often requested these recipes.*

1. Heat 2 tablespoons butter in a large frying pan over medium heat. Working in batches, add as many chicken livers as will comfortably fit in the pan and cook until well browned on one side, about 5 minutes. Turn with a spatula and cook until the second side is browned, another 5 minutes. Add more butter if needed. Remove pan from heat and mash livers with a fork in pan. Return pan to heat and continue cooking until livers are no longer pink, about 2 minutes more. Add chopped onion and cook an additional 2 minutes.

2. Place liver mixture in the bowl of a food processor fitted with the metal blade. Process until smooth. Add remaining 6 tablespoons butter, gherkins, mustard, salt, and pepper and pulse until blended. Line small molds or custard cups with plastic wrap with a 1-inch overhang, spoon paté into molds, and chill until firm. Unmold 15 minutes before serving by lifting plastic wrap and placing paté on plates.

8 tablespoons butter, softened to room temperature, divided, plus more if needed

2 lbs. chicken livers, rinsed and patted dry

1 cup finely chopped onion

1 cup finely chopped sweet gherkins

1 tablespoon prepared yellow mustard

¾ teaspoon salt

½ teaspoon coarsely ground black pepper

TIPS & TOUCHES

- Always rinse chicken livers and pat dry on paper towels before frying so they don't sputter.
- Chicken Liver Paté can also be served in a large communal mound accompanied by toast rounds or savory crackers.

HOW TO SELECT AND PREPARE CHICKEN LIVERS

Buy chicken livers from a reputable butcher to insure freshness. Always choose livers that are free of green spots or discolorations. To clean, remove membranes and any fat adhering to livers and separate the lobes. Chicken livers should be rinsed and patted dry with paper towels before frying.

Nick's Savory Blue Cheese and Walnut Crackers

{ 1940s — 1990s } YIELD: 40 CRACKERS

1 cup all-purpose flour

½ teaspoon salt

1 teaspoon coarsely ground
    black pepper

4 oz. blue cheese

½ cup cold butter, cut into
    8 pieces

1 cup toasted walnuts, coarsely
    chopped

OUR GRANDPARENTS, CELIA AND JOSEPH KATZIFF *ran a mom-and-pop grocery store on Shirley Street in Winthrop, Massachusetts, and when Grandpa Katziff wasn't taking Sheila to East Boston to buy hair ribbons or toys, he was bringing home special treats like waffled cheese crackers from their store. Our friend Nick Malgieri's recipe for Peppery Cheddar Coins comes the closest to replicating the taste of those treats from the 1940s. We substituted the blue cheese and walnuts, but you can make them with the original cheddar.*

1. Combine flour, salt, and pepper in a bowl and set aside. Combine blue cheese and butter in the bowl of a food processor fitted with the metal blade. Pulse five or six times to combine. Add flour mixture and pulse until mixture forms a ball.

2. Remove dough from bowl of food processor, form into a log 1½-inches wide, and wrap in wax paper or plastic wrap. Refrigerate until firm, about 2 hours.

3. Set the oven rack in the middle position. Preheat the oven to 350°F. Line three 14-inch by 16-inch baking sheets with foil, shiny side up, and coat with vegetable spray, or use silicone liners.

4. Cut dough into ¼-inch-thick slices. Place slices on baking sheets, no more than 16 crackers to a sheet. Sprinkle crackers with chopped walnuts. Cut a 4-inch by 4-inch square of wax paper. Place wax paper on top of each cracker and press gently with the bottom of a glass to flatten. Bake 15 to 17 minutes, or until crackers are a light golden color. Transfer to a rack and let cool. Store between sheets of wax paper in a covered tin.

Tips & Touches

- This recipe is adapted from Nick Malgieri's Peppery Cheddar Coins from *Cookies Unlimited.*
- Blue cheese and walnuts give this cracker more of a bite, as well as a crunchy texture.

Ione's Zucchini Pie

YIELD: 6 TO 8 SERVINGS

4 cups grated zucchini

1 cup coarsely chopped onion

½ cup chopped fresh parsley

1 teaspoon salt

½ teaspoon coarsely ground black pepper

¼ cup butter, softened to room temperature

2 large eggs

9-inch pie shell, baked and cooled (see Sheila's Savory Pie Crust on page 248)

2 teaspoons mustard

TIPS & TOUCHES

- Be sure to stir eggs vigorously into hot vegetables so they don't pre-cook.

WE DECIDED TO CALL THIS A ZUCCHINI PIE, *rather than a zucchini quiche, because there is no milk or cheese in the recipe. Painting the crust with mustard gives this simple, but sophisticated, pie a special zing. Easy to assemble, it's the type of elegant appetizer a New York career woman such as Ione Sutton would have prepared before leaving for work in the morning.*

1. Set the oven rack in the middle position. Preheat the oven to 375°F.
2. Squeeze excess water out of zucchini and place in a bowl. Add onion, parsley, salt, and pepper and stir to combine. Melt butter in a large heavy skillet over medium heat. Add zucchini mixture and cook until vegetables no longer taste raw, 4 to 5 minutes.
3. Whisk eggs in a bowl until yolks and whites are combined. Gradually pour into skillet with hot vegetables, stirring rapidly.
4. Paint bottom of pie shell with mustard. Spoon mixture into prepared pie shell and smooth the top. Bake 25 to 30 minutes, or until a tester inserted into middle comes out clean. Serve slices of zucchini pie on individual plates. Garnish with a tablespoon of sour cream and a sprig of fresh parsley.

✈ USING HERBS ✈

Fresh herbs should be stored in a container with their stems in water in the refrigerator. Fresh parsley and other flat-leaved herbs can be chopped and frozen in a metal ice cube tray. Frozen cubes can be transferred to a plastic bag, dated, and stored in the freezer for up to three months. Add herb cubes to stews and soups during cooking, as needed.

Dried herbs have a more concentrated flavor than fresh herbs. Dried herbs should be kept in a cool dark place, not near a source of heat such as a kitchen stove. Date the containers used for storing dried herbs and replace the herbs after one year.

SUBSTITUTIONS: 1 teaspoon of dried herbs = 2 tablespoons of fresh herbs

MYSTERY STUFFED MUSHROOMS

YIELD: 6 TO 8 SERVINGS   { 1 9 6 0 s }

THERE IS A REAL HONEST-TO-GOODNESS *mystery here. We found this recipe in our Aunt Ida Katziff's recipe box, but we don't know where she found it. Ida once confessed to us that she was "an old-fashioned girl" and didn't use fancy seasonings like basil or oregano. So, we can only guess that she tasted these mushrooms, thought very highly of them, and requested the recipe. Someday, we hope to find who the originator of this recipe is.*

1. Set the oven rack in the middle position. Preheat the oven to 375° F. Coat a 9-inch by 13-inch ovenproof glass baking dish with vegetable spray.

2. Finely chop mushroom stems. Heat 5 tablespoons of the butter in a skillet over medium heat. Add chopped stems and onion and cook until softened, about 4 minutes. Do not let vegetables burn. Add bread crumbs and continue to cook until bread crumbs are lightly browned, 2 to 3 minutes. Remove from heat. Add basil, salt, cayenne, and walnuts and stir to combine.

3. Place mushroom caps in prepared dish. Use spoon to stuff with bread crumb mixture. Press down on stuffing gently to be sure caps are completely filled. Sprinkle filled caps with grated Parmesan cheese and dot with remaining tablespoon of butter. Bake until filling bubbles, 20 to 30 minutes. Serve immediately. Store leftover mushrooms in a covered container in the refrigerator.

1 lb. large white mushrooms suitable for stuffing, caps and stems separated

6 tablespoons butter, softened to room temperature, divided

1 cup chopped onion

½ cup fine bread crumbs

½ teaspoon dried basil

½ teaspoon salt

¼ teaspoon cayenne pepper

¼ cup toasted walnuts, finely chopped

½ cup grated Parmesan cheese

TIPS & TOUCHES

* If you want a slightly different flavor, oregano can be substituted for the basil.
* Mushrooms can be prepared ahead of time and refrigerated. Let them come to room temperature before baking. They may have to stay in oven a little longer if refrigerated.
* Leftover mushrooms are also good eaten cold with a splash of red wine vinegar.

Stuffed Mushrooms

1 lb. large mushrooms   ½ slice bread, crumbled
1 small onion, minced   pinch cayenne
5 tbsp butter   pinch salt
¼ tsp sweet basil   ¼ cup chopped walnuts
                               grated fresh Parmesan cheese

Chop mushroom stems finely and sauté with the onion in the butter. Add the bread and toss until browned. Add spices and nuts. Stuff caps with mixture and top each with parmesan cheese. Dot with butter. Refrigerate until needed.

51

SALMON MOUSSE

{ *1950s* }

WE FOUND THIS RECIPE FOR SALMON MOUSSE *on one of those cards that tells us "what's cookin'.... from the kitchen of" but neglected to tell us whose kitchen. The underlining of the word,* blender, *seems to point to the 1950s when using a blender was very innovative. Don't let the use of canned salmon deter you from trying this creamy appetizer. It's simple and delicious.*

1. Coat a 9-inch by 5-inch by 3-inch loaf pan with vegetable spray or line bottom and sides of pan with plastic wrap; or lightly coat a 4½-cup mold with vegetable spray.
2. Pick through salmon to remove skin and bones. Place salmon in a bowl, flake with a fork, and set aside.
3. In a glass measuring cup, sprinkle gelatin on top of lemon juice. Whisk to combine. Let stand 5 minutes. Add boiling water, let stand 2 minutes, and whisk again.
4. Place salmon, onion or scallions, mayonnaise, dillweed or dill, paprika, salt, cayenne pepper, and gelatin mixture in the bowl of a food processor fitted with the metal blade. Process on high until smooth. Add cream and process to combine. Place mousse in prepared loaf pan or mold and chill for at least 2 hours, or until firm.
5. To unmold, dip bottom of pan or mold into a bowl of warm water for few seconds to loosen mousse. Invert a serving plate over mousse. Quickly turn plate and mousse over. Mousse should slide out easily onto plate. Store covered with plastic wrap in the refrigerator until ready to serve.

1 (12¾-oz.) can pink salmon

1 (¼-oz.) envelope unflavored gelatin

3 tablespoons lemon juice

½ cup boiling water

¼ cup finely chopped onion or scallions

½ cup mayonnaise

1 teaspoon dried dillweed, or 1 teaspoon chopped fresh dill

1 teaspoon paprika

Salt to taste

⅛ to ¼ teaspoon cayenne pepper

1 cup heavy cream

TIPS & TOUCHES

- Draining salmon and removing the skin reduces the strong flavor.
- Sprinkle mousse with paprika, garnish with fresh dill, and serve with crackers or toast fingers.

HELEN'S FRIED CHEESE BALLS WITH CHILI MAYONNAISE

{ 1900 }

YIELD: 12 BALLS, 1¼ CUPS CHILI MAYONNAISE

FOR CHEESE BALLS

1 cup grated sharp cheddar cheese

½ cup fine bread crumbs

5 drops Worcestershire sauce

1 egg, beaten

Vegetable oil, for frying

FOR CHILI MAYONNAISE

1 cup mayonnaise

6 tablespoons chili sauce

1 teaspoon lemon juice

½ teaspoon salt

½ teaspoon cayenne pepper, or brined hot chopped peppers

THESE LITTLE CHEESE BALLS REMIND US OF *crunchy little crab balls, but without the crab. We found this recipe in a manuscript cookbook whose pages crumbled as we touched them. We added the perky Chili Mayonnaise dipping sauce. The cookbook contained a love letter from Worcester, Massachusetts, written from Charles to Helen on June 27, 1897. Conservative by today's standards, the letter reflected the joy of a young couple looking forward to their marriage.*

1. To make the cheese balls: Cover a cooling rack with three layers of paper toweling. In a bowl, combine cheese, bread crumbs, Worcestershire sauce, and beaten egg. Roll dough into balls about 1 inch in diameter. Set aside.

TIPS ON DEEP-FRYING

- Always use an electric fryer, following the manufacturer's instructions, or a deep flat-bottomed heavy pot on a level surface.
- Do not use plastic utensils when frying.
- Use fresh oil every time you fry.
- Heat oil gradually and in an uncovered pot. The pot should be only half-filled with oil to allow for foaming that may occur when items are lowered into it.
- Use a thermometer to gauge the temperature of the fat at all times.
- Keep the temperature of the fat constant. Allow time for the temperature to adjust after each batch.
- If appropriate, dry items on paper towels before immersing in hot fat.
- Keep items the same size so they will fry uniformly.
- Do not crowd items in the pan.
- Have a bowl of ice water handy for spatters and burns. Never leave the frying area unattended.
- Let oil cool completely in pan before discarding.

2. To make the chili mayonnaise: Combine mayonnaise, chili sauce, lemon juice, salt, and cayenne pepper in a bowl and mix well. Cover and chill until ready to use.

3. Heat 1½ inches of oil to 375°F in a heavy, deep, flat-bottomed pan or electric fryer. Use a slotted spoon to transfer balls, one at a time, into hot oil. Fry balls in batches of four (to keep oil temperature from dropping), turning once, until both sides are golden brown, about 2 minutes on each side. Remove with slotted spoon to prepared rack. Cover with additional paper towels and allow to drain. Serve immediately or keep warm in a 200°F oven until ready to eat. Serve with Chili Mayonnaise.

TIPS & TOUCHES

- We often use commercially brined chopped hot peppers because they can be kept refrigerated and ready for use.
- Crowding cheese balls during frying will result in lowered oil temperature.

Corn Pancakes with Sour Cream and Chives

YIELD: 16 MINI PANCAKES

1 cup flour

2 teaspoons baking powder

¾ teaspoon salt

¼ teaspoon coarsely ground
  black pepper

2 eggs, separated

½ cup milk

1 tablespoon butter, melted

1 cup canned or cooked corn

2 tablespoons butter, softened to
  room temperature

1 cup sour cream

¼ cup snipped chives

Tips & Touches

- Corn pancakes are best day they are made.
- These pancakes are also good served with fresh snipped dill on top instead of chives.
- Serve pancakes on a warmed platter.

We found this handwritten recipe *on a faded index card in the file of The Church Lady of Mansfield, Ohio. These savory corn pancakes are meant to be served with chicken or pork, but we decided to make them silver dollar–size and garnish them with sour cream and snipped chives. This is one of the earliest recipes from The Church Lady's collection, which spanned the early 1900s through the 1950s.*

1. Place flour, baking powder, salt, and pepper in a mixing bowl and set aside. Beat egg yolks in another bowl. Beat in milk and melted butter. Add dry ingredients and stir gently to combine. Fold in corn.

2. Beat egg whites until stiff in the bowl of a standing mixer fitted with the whisk attachment. Fold egg whites into batter.

3. Melt 2 tablespoons butter in a large frying pan over medium heat. Spoon 1 tablespoon batter into pan for each pancake, pressing down gently on pancakes once they are formed to make them thinner. Cook pancakes until the tops begin to bubble around the edges, about 2 minutes. Turn and cook until the undersides are golden brown, about 2 minutes more. Serve immediately, topped with sour cream and chives, or keep warm on a tray in 200°F oven for not more than 15 minutes. Store leftover pancakes in a covered container in the refrigerator. Reheat in frying pan with melted butter over low heat.

CHICKPEA AND POTATO CHOLAY

{ 1970s }

YIELD: 4 SERVINGS

1 (19-oz.) can chickpeas

1 (28-oz.) can whole tomatoes

2 medium potatoes, boiled

1 tablespoon butter, softened to
    room temperature

2 tablespoons vegetable oil

1 teaspoon cumin seeds

1 teaspoon garam masala

1 teaspoon curry powder

¼ teaspoon red chili powder

1 cup chopped onions

1 large clove garlic, minced

½ teaspoon salt

2 tablespoons lemon or lime juice

THIS IS THE CHICKPEA AND POTATO CHOLAY *that our friend Katy first tasted as a young girl in England, where she was raised. Katy learned how to cook from her mother, Viru, who is an expert in Indian cuisine. Although sometimes thought of as a vegetable stew, cholay is very adaptable, and is a good appetizer when served with untoasted wedges of pita bread.*

1. Drain chickpeas in a colander and rinse with cold water. Transfer to a bowl and set aside.

2. Drain tomatoes in colander, cut into ½-inch dice, and set aside in another bowl.

3. Peel and cut potatoes into 1-inch pieces and place in third bowl.

4. Melt butter with oil in a saucepan over low heat. Add cumin seeds. Turn heat up slightly and stir with wooden spoon until cumin seeds sizzle. Add garam masala, curry powder, and chili powder and stir to mix. Add onions and garlic and continue cooking until softened, 2 to 3 minutes. Stir in diced tomatoes. Add chickpeas, potatoes, and salt and cook, stirring, until chickpeas and potatoes are heated through, 4 to 5 minutes. Remove cholay to a serving dish and let cool to room temperature. Pour lemon or lime juice on top before serving.

➤➤ GARAM MASALA ◄◄

Garam masala originated in the kitchens of India, where it varies by region. It has a sweeter, hotter, more assertive taste than curry powder. Although Indian cooks prepare their own blends of garam masala, a good commercial blend can be found in the spice sections of grocery stores or food markets carrying international foods. Garam masala is a strong spice mix, and a little goes a long way. One of the advantages of cooking with garam masala is the wonderful aroma that scents the kitchen. Although curry powder may contain some of the same spices as those found in garam masala, substituting curry powder will not give the same depth of flavor as using garam masala. Reddish brown in color, it is suggested that it be added toward the end of cooking.

ROSE AND NATALIE'S CAPONATA

YIELD: 6 CUPS

{ 1960s }

WE FIRST TASTED THIS RECIPE AT A GATHERING *fifteen years ago. We loved the sour-sweet eggplant spread and discovered that it had been passed down through the D'Ambosio-Peluso family from Ozone Park, Queens. As a child, Rose Peluso Slobodzinski recalls her aunts competing for the best caponata recipe at family gatherings, but she always voted for the version made by her mother, Natalie D'Ambosio. Rose taught her youngest child, Natalie Pangaro, how to make her caponata, and thus this recipe continues through three generations of a Neapolitan-American family.*

1. Wash eggplant and pat dry with a paper towel. Cut into ½-inch cubes (you should have about 6 cups).

2. Heat ½ cup of the olive oil in large frying pan over medium heat. Add eggplant and sauté until tender and golden brown, 5 to 7 minutes. Remove eggplant and set aside. Add remaining 2 tablespoons oil to pan. Add onion and celery and sauté until tender, about 5 minutes.

3. Return eggplant to pan. Stir in tomato sauce, tomato paste, and raisins. Bring mixture to a boil. Lower heat, cover, and simmer for 15 minutes. Add vinegar, salt, pepper, sugar, capers, and olives. Simmer, covered, stirring occasionally, for 20 minutes more. Cool to room temperature. Refrigerate overnight in a covered container to allow flavors to marry.

1 large eggplant, unpeeled

½ cup plus 2 tablespoons olive oil, divided

1¼ cups diced onion

1 cup diced celery

1 (15-oz.) can tomato sauce

1 tablespoon tomato paste

½ cup golden raisins

¼ cup red wine vinegar

½ teaspoon salt

½ teaspoon coarsely ground black pepper

1 to 2 tablespoons firmly packed brown sugar

2 tablespoons capers, drained

20 pitted, brined black olives, cut in slivers or quartered

TIPS & TOUCHES

- Be sure to use red wine vinegar, not balsamic vinegar.
- The addition of brown sugar balances the flavor.
- Caponata can be served on top of pasta, but should be thinned with a little tomato sauce before being heated.

Toy enamelware colander, early 1900s

36
WAYS
to Serve
Recipes
SALADS and SANDWICHES
Being a collection of
150 tested recipes
for home cookery
arranged by months
ORIGINATED AND PUBLISHED BY
CHICAGO, U.S.A.
Wesson
Oil
One Quart Net
For Making
Good Things to Eat
Saladtime
with 615 Recipes
Lutes
990 Kilocycles

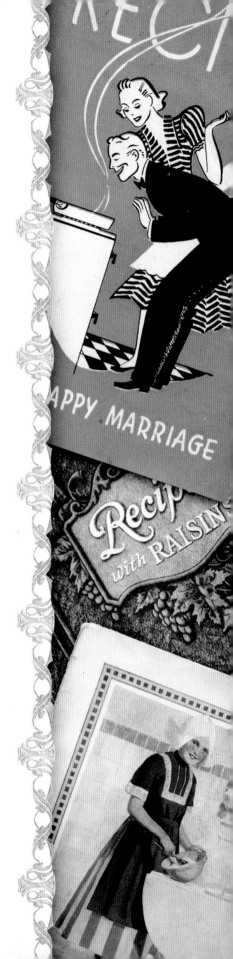

CHAPTER 2

SALAD DAYS

There's something bright and breezy about the title "Salad Days." It reminds us of spring lunches on front porches with the scent of lilacs in the air, or backyard Victory Gardens with their bounty of homegrown greens. We grew up in a community where the best vegetables were hand selected for us at the local market or presented to us by local gardeners. As budding home cooks, we learned early that salads should be crisp and colorful, pleasing to both the eye and the palette. ● When we browsed through our collection of manuscript cookbooks, we found that home cooks treated their salad plates as if they were canvases, creating a picture of what was seasonally appealing as well as what tasted good. We learned that with a few deft passes of a knife, these women could make carrots into pennies and radishes into roses. Tomatoes picked off the vine, while still warm from the sun, could be cut into wedges or generous slices.

We found that salads could be light or substantial—a jellied tease full of fruit and marshmallows could serve as a first course for a bridge party; or a hearty bowl with an abundance of chopped bacon, eggs, and vegetables could be put before the men in the family. Some of these home cooks practiced the tradition of their Mediterranean heritage and served a few greens dressed with oil and vinegar as palette cleansers after the main course and just before dessert.

When these women created their salads, they honored the changing seasons by selecting the best ingredients available. The lettuces and berries of summer gave way to the robust cranberries and yams of autumn, while winter salads using rice and nuts promised contentment, as did coleslaws of shredded cabbage, peppers, and onions. Spring brought its plates of Sunshine Potato Salad, golden with egg yolks, welcome after the dark days of winter, as well as offerings of early greens touched with fruited mayonnaise.

Salad dressing pamphlet, American

When making salads, home cooks had to be creative in the kitchen because they had to use what they had in their pantries or root cellars. What might be leftovers to some became a delicious, perhaps daring, salad plate to others. The boiled dressing, forgotten for so many years, can become an easy ally of today's home salad maker just as it added a touch of richness to Mrs. Julian's Shrimp Salad, a handwritten recipe from the 1920s. It seems that no one could forget the darling candle salads of the 1950s, which are just as fascinating to today's children as they were two generations ago.

Most of the salads we selected are memorable not just for their ingredients and creativity but because they have become the legacy of the women who served them. A colorful and significant chopped salad, prepared every October by a friend who held her annual Finally Fall Brunch to celebrate the cooler weather of the changing seasons, is as good today as when she first started making it twenty years ago. Although she has left us, we will always remember her when serving her signature salad.

A recipe called Mock Chicken Salad has become a tradition in the Paxton-Grigor-Hails Family, from Pennsylvania. Originally made from veal and pork because chicken was more expensive, this thrifty substitute became a family favorite for the picnics that accompanied swimming parties.

The secret of Mrs. Fredman's Coleslaw has finally been revealed, and her achievement can now be shared with all of the customers who ate at her Shirley Street delicatessen, in Winthrop, Massachusetts, more than fifty years ago. Her friendly culinary rivalry with Mrs. Nat of Nat's Delicatessen is still remembered fondly, with a nod of respect to both ladies, as is the memory of Mr. Fredman, in his slippers and cap, smoking a cigar and reading a Yiddish newspaper while his wife dished out coleslaw and corned beef sandwiches to generations of young Winthropites.

We hope you'll try Dot Luke's Hawaiian Jellied Salad with its pineapple and mandarin orange slices. Now, hostesses can serve this creamy pale green salad at their own family picnics, even if they don't eat it with chopsticks the way everyone did on the Island of Oahu in the 1950s.

And finally, we praise a winter salad made with rice, honey, and walnuts, which is still remembered almost forty years after a young resident brought it to a Sunday potluck supper at the Cambridge, Massachusetts, YWCA.

Mayonnaise maker, mixer, American, 1920s–1930s

Sunshine Potato Salad

YIELD: 6 TO 8 SERVINGS

6 waxy potatoes (about 3 lbs.)

½ cup extra-virgin olive oil

¼ cup apple cider vinegar

1 tablespoon water

2 teaspoons salt

½ teaspoon coarsely ground black pepper

⅓ cup diced red bell pepper

⅓ cup diced green bell pepper

1 cup finely chopped celery

1½ cups finely chopped onion

3 large eggs, hard-cooked and coarsely chopped

⅓ cup coarsely chopped dill pickles

½ cup mayonnaise

1 tablespoon prepared yellow mustard

Red and green bell pepper rounds, for garnish

We have to give two home cooks credit for this recipe because their versions of it were so similar. Constance Etz Ferdon, from our collection of Martha's Vineyard living recipes, and Elizabeth Corkery, from Groton, Massachusetts, came up with virtually the same recipe for a marinated potato salad, made golden with mustard and egg yolks. This is the first potato salad we've ever made that uses both an oil and vinegar marinade and mayonnaise. Diced red and green peppers make the potato salad crunchy.

1. Place potatoes in a steamer basket over simmering water, cover, and steam just until tender when pierced with a small knife, 15 to 20 minutes. Do not overcook. Remove to a large bowl. Peel when cool enough to handle. Cut into 1-inch cubes.

2. In another bowl, whisk together oil, vinegar, water, salt, and black pepper. Pour dressing over warm potatoes and stir gently to coat. Cover and place in refrigerator to marinate at least 6 hours, or overnight. Stir and shake occasionally for even marinating.

3. Pour off any excess marinade. Add red and green pepper, celery, onion, eggs, and dill pickles and toss gently to combine. In a small bowl, stir together mayonnaise and mustard. Add to salad and toss to coat vegetables. Cover and refrigerate until ready to serve. Serve garnished with rounds of red and green pepper. Store leftover potato salad in covered container in refrigerator.

Tips & Touches

- Cook potatoes only until tender.
- Toss ingredients gently to prevent potatoes from falling apart.

Mrs. Fredman's Coleslaw

YIELD: 8 CUPS

8 cups shredded cabbage
  (about 2 lbs.)

2 cups shredded carrot
  (about 3 large carrots)

1½ teaspoons kosher salt

3 tablespoons apple cider vinegar

¾ cup Miracle Whip salad dressing

¼ cup sugar, or as needed

Salt and coarsely ground
  black pepper

MRS. FREDMAN WAS KNOWN FAR AND WIDE *for the coleslaw she served at Fredman's Delicatessen on Shirley Street, in Winthrop, Massachusetts. She and Mrs. Nat, of Nat's Delicatessen, a few doors down, had a friendly competition over who made the best coleslaw and potato salad. Both coleslaws were superior, but customers were fiercely loyal to one or the other. Larraine Byne Yaffee was able to provide this recipe because her aunt, Alice Ceder, worked for Mrs. Fredman during the 1950s.*

1. Combine cabbage, carrots, and salt in a large nonreactive glass or stainless steel bowl and mix thoroughly. Add vinegar, salad dressing, and sugar and mix to combine. Cover bowl with plastic wrap and refrigerate overnight.

2. Drain off any liquid collected in bottom of bowl. Season to taste with salt and pepper. Store leftover coleslaw in a covered glass container in the refrigerator.

Tips & Touches

- The original recipe made a large amount of coleslaw.
- We added more carrots in proportion to cabbage because we like a colorful coleslaw.

Food choppers, American, early 1900s

SWEET POTATO SALAD

YIELD: 8 SERVINGS   { 1960s }

THIS COLORFUL, TASTY SALAD IS PERFECT *for autumn gatherings. We suggest that you start this salad early in the day so that the flavors will come together. Steam the sweet potatoes the night before. The sweet potatoes should still be a bit firm when you make the salad.*

1. To make the salad: Place sweet potatoes in a steamer basket set over simmering water. Cover and steam about 20 minutes (see Tips & Touches). Remove to a large bowl and allow to cool.

2. When cool enough to handle, cut potatoes into ¾-inch dice and return to bowl. Add orange marmalade, apricot jam, and red pepper and toss to coat.

3. To make the vinaigrette: Place oil, vinegar, orange juice, and mustard into a container with a cover. Cover and shake to combine. Remove cover; add salt, black pepper, garlic or garlic powder, hot pepper flakes, and orange zest. Replace cover and shake to combine.

4. Pour vinaigrette over salad and stir gently with a wooden spoon. Mound salad on a platter or place in a large bowl, cover with plastic wrap, and refrigerate for at least 4 hours to allow flavors to marry.

5. Remove salad from refrigerator 15 minutes before serving. Serve sprinkled with pecans. Store leftover salad in a covered container in refrigerator.

FOR SALAD:

3 lbs. sweet potatoes, peeled and cut into 2-inch chunks

¼ cup orange marmalade

¼ cup apricot jam

1 cup diced red bell pepper

1 cup toasted pecans, coarsely chopped

FOR VINAIGRETTE:

¼ cup extra-virgin olive oil

1 tablespoon apple cider vinegar

⅓ cup orange juice

1 tablespoon prepared mustard

½ teaspoon kosher salt

¼ teaspoon coarsely ground black pepper

2 cloves garlic, minced, or ¾ teaspoon garlic powder

⅛ teaspoon hot pepper flakes

Grated zest of 1 orange

Food chopper, American, 1890s

TIPS & TOUCHES

- Steaming sweet potatoes for 20 minutes is an arbitrary amount of time. The best way to know when they're cooked is to test them: They should still be a bit firm. If you overcook them, they will fall apart.
- Do not use baked sweet potatoes for this salad.
- Do not mix pecans into salad or they will be come soggy.

Barbara Carey's Chopped Salad

YIELD: 4 TO 6 SERVINGS   { 1970s }

THIS IS THE CHOPPED SALAD RECIPE *our friend, Barbara Carey, used when she held her annual Finally Fall Brunch. Barbara loved the colder weather, and after a hot New England summer, she gathered family and friends to celebrate the coming of autumn. This is a great salad because the ingredients and their amounts can be adjusted for the number of people you will be serving. Barbara always finely chopped or shredded the ingredients.*

1. Place romaine and iceberg lettuce in bottom of a 10- to 12-cup clear glass bowl with a generous diameter (ours is 8 inches in diameter and 4 inches high) and set aside.

2. Finely chop bacon and eggs. Layer bacon, eggs, and onion separately over shredded greens. Add a layer of peas and a layer of carrots. Mix mayonnaise and sour cream together and spread on top of salad. Top with Swiss cheese and serve. Store leftover salad covered with plastic wrap in the refrigerator.

2 cups shredded romaine

2 cups shredded iceberg lettuce

4 oz. cooked bacon

4 large eggs, hard-cooked

1 cup chopped red onion

1 cup fresh or frozen peas, boiled until tender

1 cup grated carrots

1 cup mayonnaise

1 cup sour cream

½ lb. shredded Swiss cheese

 PUTTING TOGETHER A CHOPPED SALAD

Chopped salad is a wonderful choice for a gathering because you can tailor it to the season or to the tastes of your guests. You can omit the bacon, cheese, and eggs and go for a lighter dish or you can leave them in for a more substantial one. Always choose a large-diameter bowl to accommodate the layers of chopped ingredients and show them off nicely. The bowl should be shallow enough to allow guests to scoop through the layers of cheese and dressing on top to sample all the layers. You can also serve the salad layered in individual clear glass bowls or martini glasses.

CANDLE SALAD

YIELD: 4 SERVINGS

8 leaves of Boston lettuce

4 canned pineapple slices

4 bananas

4 strips green bell pepper

4 maraschino cherries, or 4 strips
(½-inch long) pimento

¼ cup sour cream, or ¼ cup
mayonnaise

THIS IS ONE OF THOSE 1950S FANTASY SALADS *that appeal to children of all ages. Growing up in a Jewish household, we were treated to the Jewish version of candle salad, made with sour cream and a maraschino cherry, for Sunday night supper. Our Christian friends enjoyed a similar salad made with mayonnaise and a piece of pimento for the flame. This was a pretty sophisticated salad for a seven-year-old.*

1. Arrange 2 leaves of lettuce on each of four plates. Place one pineapple ring on each plate. Peel bananas, cut off ends, and stand upright in center of pineapple rings to make "candles." Tuck strips of pepper into pineapple at base of candles to look like candleholders. Split cherries and place split-side-down on top of bananas to simulate flame (or use pimento strips).

2. Drizzle sour cream or mayonnaise down sides of bananas to represent melted candle wax.

TIPS & TOUCHES

*   It can be a bit tricky to get a banana "candle" to stand up in the middle of a pineapple ring. Try a dab of cream cheese "glue" or fill part of the hole with torn lettuce.

Blue milk glass salt; glass Liberty Bell cherry jar, American, 20th century

Mock Chicken Salad

{ 1875 }

Mock chicken salad does not contain *any chicken. This recipe, found in a tattered manuscript cookbook, calls for chopped roast pork. Laced with some good quality mayonnaise or boiled dressing, this salad filled the need for a quick, tasty, yet inexpensive meal.*

Combine roast pork, celery, bell pepper, olives, mayonnaise or boiled dressing, salt, and black pepper in a large bowl. Cover and refrigerate for at least 2 hours before serving. Store leftover salad in a covered container in the refrigerator.

4 cups coarsely chopped roast pork

1 cup chopped celery

¾ cup chopped red bell pepper

½ cup pimento-stuffed green olives (about 6 olives)

½ cup mayonnaise or boiled dressing

½ teaspoon salt

½ teaspoon coarsely ground black pepper

HOW MOCK CHICKEN SALAD WAS INVENTED

It's always a challenge to make "mock" anything because you have to have a reliable substitute in your home kitchen. Mock chicken salads were made from cubes of roast pork or roast veal, both of which were less expensive than chicken, which was a source of eggs for the farm family. Some heirloom cooks ground their roast pork or veal and bound it with mayonnaise to make their mock chicken salad sandwiches. Preparing mock chicken salad allowed inventive homemakers a way to conserve the hens that lay the eggs, which they often sold to supplement their income.

Barbara's Rice Salad with Cumin and Walnuts

{ 1 9 7 0 s }

FOR SALAD

2½ cups cooked wild rice, cooled (cook according to package directions)

3 cups cooked long grain white rice, cooled (cook according to package directions)

1 cup toasted walnuts, coarsely chopped

FOR VINAIGRETTE

¼ cup extra-virgin olive oil

¼ cup vegetable oil

1 teaspoon salt (omit if rice is salty)

¼ teaspoon coarsely ground black pepper

¼ cup plus 1 tablespoon honey

¼ cup plus 2 tablespoons lemon juice

2 teaspoons ground cumin

¼ teaspoon cinnamon

WE FIRST TASTED THIS SALAD *when Marilynn was living at the YWCA in Cambridge. The Y did not serve a supper on Sunday nights, so the girls would get together and do a communal meal. Marilynn's friend, Barbara, had lived on a kibbutz in Israel, and she put this salad together using a hot plate in the resident kitchen to make the rice. We added the wild rice, and this salad is as good today as it was when we first tasted it.*

1. To make the salad: Combine wild rice, white rice, and walnuts in a large bowl. Stir together with a wooden spoon.

2. To make the vinaigrette: Whisk together olive oil, vegetable oil, salt, if using, pepper, honey, lemon juice, cumin, and cinnamon in small bowl. Pour vinaigrette over salad and toss with two serving spoons. Cover bowl with plastic wrap and refrigerate for at least 2 hours to mellow flavors. Serve at room temperature. Store leftover salad in a covered container in the refrigerator.

TIPS & TOUCHES

- To cook wild or white rice, use water or low-sodium chicken stock and follow the cooking instructions on the rice package.
- Coat measuring cups and measuring spoons with vegetable spray before measuring honey. It will be easier to add to a recipe.

Silver nut cups, American, 20th century

Mrs. Julian's Shrimp Salad

Here's another recipe from the manuscript cookbook *of the lady who brought us Mock Chicken Salad (page 71) and Crispy Norwegian Potatoes (page 103). A grand home cook, this lady handwrote her recipes in an unassuming little composition book whose tattered pages have inspired us in so many ways.*

1. In a large bowl, combine macaroni, shrimp, onion, celery, pimento, parsley, salt, pepper, and eggs.
2. Add mayonnaise and toss until all of the ingredients are well coated. Chill before serving. Store leftovers in a covered container in the refrigerator.

3 cups cooked macaroni, cooled

3 cups cooked shrimp, cut into ½-inch dice

½ cup finely chopped onion

1 cup chopped celery

1 cup chopped pimento

3 tablespoons chopped fresh parsley

1 teaspoon salt

½ teaspoon coarsely ground black pepper

3 large eggs, hard-cooked and coarsely chopped

¾ cup mayonnaise

⋗ QUICK SALAD DRESSINGS ⋖

Almost all manuscript cookbooks have recipes for boiled dressing, mayonnaise, and French dressing. Several of these dressings take extra time to prepare and call for the use of a double boiler and eggs. Others suggest that you add whipped cream just before serving. For generations, home cooks have taken the easy way out by working with their favorite commercial brand of mayonnaise, enhancing its taste and texture with pureed fruit, ketchup, mustard, jam, capers, chopped pickles, or relishes. A dash of lemon juice or a bit of orange zest is often helpful, combined with a touch of sugar, to balance the flavor of these inventive dressings.

 Tips & Touches

- The ingredient amounts can be adjusted to make the salad your own.
- Any salad containing eggs and mayonnaise should not remain unrefrigerated for long periods of time.

BOILED SALAD DRESSING

YIELD: 2 CUPS

¼ cup sugar

2 teaspoons salt

¼ cup sifted flour

1 tablespoon dry mustard

⅛ teaspoon cayenne pepper

3 tablespoons white vinegar

1½ cups hot water

2 large eggs or 4 yolks

2 tablespoons vegetable oil or heavy cream

THIS IS THE SALAD DRESSING RECIPE *we found with the Mock Chicken Salad. This is very much like a homemade cooked mayonnaise. It's worth the effort to make and serve this creamy salad dressing. The manuscript cookbook also had the recipe for Crispy Norwegian Potatoes (page 103).*

1. Combine sugar, salt, flour, mustard, and cayenne pepper in the top of a double boiler. Add vinegar and whisk. Gradually whisk in hot water.

2. Bring about 1 inch of water to a simmer in the bottom of double boiler. Set top of double boiler over bottom, and cook, stirring constantly with a wooden spoon, until mixture is thick and smooth, about 3 minutes.

3. Remove top of double boiler from heat. Whisk eggs or yolks lightly in another bowl. Add a little of the hot mixture to the eggs, whisking briskly to temper. Then whisk eggs back into top of double boiler with hot mixture. Place top of double boiler on bottom and cook 1 minute, stirring with wooden spoon. Transfer dressing to clean bowl. When cool, thin with oil or cream.

➤ ➤ HOW TO USE PREPARED AND DRY MUSTARD ◄ ◄

When we refer to "prepared mustard," we are talking about a condiment made from ground mustard seeds, salt, and vinegar. Dry mustard is a powdered spice made from pulverized mustard seeds. Heirloom cooks often added prepared mustard to their dishes to enhance the flavor because it was an inexpensive, readily available ingredient. However, certain heirloom recipes call for dry mustard, which has been milled from mustard seeds and sold commercially for almost two hundred years.

SUBSTITUTION: 1 tablespoon prepared mustard = 1 teaspoon dry mustard

FRUIT "MAYONNAISE"

YIELD: APPROXIMATELY 2 CUPS

{ 1920s }

We found that this heirloom recipe *for a fruit mayonnaise based on pineapple and orange juice was wonderful with Dot Luke's Hawaiian Jellied Salad (page 78). It's light and fruity, and the addition of whipped cream at the end makes it soft and cloudlike.*

2 large eggs

¼ cup sugar

¼ cup pineapple juice

¼ cup orange juice

1 teaspoon orange zest

2 tablespoon white vinegar

3 tablespoons water

½ cup heavy cream, whipped

1. Whisk eggs in a bowl until lightened. Gradually whisk in sugar and set aside.

2. Combine pineapple juice, orange juice, orange zest, vinegar, and water in the top of a double boiler. Bring about 1 inch of water to a simmer in the bottom of double boiler. Set top of double boiler on bottom, and cook, stirring with wooden spoon until heated through. Add small amount of hot liquid to eggs and whisk briskly to temper. Return egg mixture to hot juice and continue to cook, stirring until mixture thickens and coats the back of a spoon, about 2 minutes more.

3. Remove mayonnaise to another nonreactive container and allow to cool for 5 minutes. Place plastic wrap on the surface of the mayonnaise and refrigerate. Fold in whipped cream just before serving. Store mayonnaise in a covered container in the refrigerator. Leftover mayonnaise may deflate slightly.

Dorchester Pottery mixing bowl, American, early 20th century

Dot Luke's Hawaiian Jellied Salad

{ *1950s* }

YIELD: 10 SERVINGS

2 (3-oz.) packages lime gelatin

1 cup pineapple juice, heated

Juice of 2 limes

Juice of 1 orange

1 cup canned pineapple chunks, drained and diced

1 (11-oz.) can mandarin orange slices, drained

6 oz. cream cheese, softened

1 cup heavy cream, whipped

½ cup mayonnaise

1 cup mini marshmallows

½ cup toasted pecans, chopped

Iceburg lettuce, shredded, for serving

Tips & Touches

- This salad is very good with Fruit "Mayonnaise" (page 77).

THIS RECIPE CAME FROM DOT LUKE, *the mother of our friend Liane Welch. Liane grew up in Honolulu, on the Island of Oahu. Dot passed away in 2006, at the age of eighty-four. When Liane went through her mother's papers, she found her recipe for a jellied lime salad, which brought back fond memories of a refreshing treat on hot afternoons. Dot often made it for potluck picnics and large family gatherings. Family and friends always ate this salad with chopsticks.*

1. Coat a 10-cup mold with vegetable spray.
2. Dissolve gelatin in hot pineapple juice in a 2-cup measure. Add lime juice, orange juice, and enough water to equal 2 cups of liquid. Pour gelatin into a bowl, stir well, cover, and chill until nearly firm.
3. Lightly whisk chilled gelatin mixture. Fold in pineapple chunks, orange slices, cream cheese, whipped cream, mayonnaise, mini marshmallows, and pecans. Pour into prepared mold and chill 3 to 4 hours, or until firm.
4. To release, dip bottom of mold in bowl of hot water for few seconds. Invert a plate on top of the mold, then turn plate and mold over. Salad should unmold easily. Arrange lettuce on individual salad plates and place slice of jellied salad on top.

Mary Bradshaw's Egg and Gherkin Salad

{ 1880s }

YIELD: 4 SERVINGS

1 cup gherkins

6 large eggs, hard-cooked

1 teaspoon salt

¼ teaspoon cayenne pepper

2 teaspoons lemon juice

¼ cup butter, softened

Shredded iceberg lettuce,
  for garnish

Sliced radishes, for garnish

4 pieces toasted white bread,
  cut into fingers and
  generously buttered

THIS SALAD IS FROM THE MANUSCRIPT COOKBOOK *of Mary Bradshaw, an English woman, who recorded her personal recipes from the 1880s to the 1920s. Mary provides us with recipes for tea sandwiches, meat pies, comforting servings of milk toast, and dainty salads, as well as menus for Bible study groups and World War I knitting instructions.*
This is a very ladylike salad. We suggest that you double the recipe if you are expecting some gentleman guests.

1. Line four ½-cup ramekins with plastic wrap and set aside.
2. Place gherkins in the bowl of a food processor fitted with the metal blade. Pulse until finely chopped. Remove gherkins to a large bowl. Place eggs in food processor and pulse until finely chopped. Add eggs to bowl with gherkins. Add salt, cayenne pepper, and lemon juice and stir to combine. Add butter and mash to a soft paste. Divide mixture among prepared ramekins, smooth the tops, cover with plastic wrap, and chill at least 2 hours.
3. Run knife around inside of ramekin to loosen salad. Unmold salad from each ramekin onto a bed of shredded iceberg lettuce. Serve with thinly sliced radishes and buttered toast fingers.

Tips & Touches

- This salad has the consistency of an egg paste and is very delicate.

Mrs. O'Brien's Cranberry Delight Salad

YIELD: 10 SERVINGS   { 1950s }

THIS IS A RECIPE FROM *the manuscript cookbook of Geneva Bellevue O'Brien, of Belmont, Massachusetts. A lively woman of French–Canadian heritage, she and her mother held "baking days" twice a week during which they produced enough bread to feed Geneva's husband, Eugene, and their four children. Mrs. O'Brien always kept two tins decorated with circus carousals filled with cookies and cake on her kitchen counter. Cranberry Delight Salad was featured at Thanksgiving and Christmas.*

Juice and grated zest of 2 oranges

4 cups cranberries

1 cup raisins

2 cups sugar

½ cup toasted walnuts, coarsely chopped

10 Boston lettuce leaves, for garnish

Mandarin orange slices, for garnish

1. Pour orange juice into a measuring cup and add enough cold water to equal I cup. Pour into a heavy-bottomed saucepan. Add cranberries, raisins, and orange zest and mix with wooden spoon to combine. Add sugar and stir.

2. Place pan over medium heat, bring to a boil, and cook, stirring constantly, until mixture begins to thicken, about 13 minutes. Cool completely. Stir in walnuts. Spoon onto plates lined with Boston lettuce leaves and garnish with mandarin orange slices.

TIPS & TOUCHES

- Add a little more cold water to the cranberry mixture if needed.
- For a fancy presentation, hollow out half of an orange rind, fill with Cranberry Delight Salad, and serve on bed of lettuce.

Green Depression glass measuring cup, 1930s; tin advertising bank, 1920s

Banana Nut Salad

YIELD: 4 SERVINGS

6 cups chopped or torn lettuce

4 firm bananas

1 cup sugar

1 cup hot water

Juice of 1 lemon

¼ teaspoon salt

½ cup mayonnaise

1 cup toasted walnuts, coarsely chopped

THIS RECIPE CAME FROM THE MANUSCRIPT COOKBOOK *of the lady who provided us with the recipes for Mrs. Julian's Shrimp Salad (page 75), Mock Chicken Salad (page 71), and Boiled Salad Dressing (page 76). This lady loved her salads. This is a very simple dish to put together, great for those days when you have all that ironing to do.*

1. Divide lettuce among four salad plates. Peel bananas and cut into 1-inch-thick rounds. Cover with wax paper and set aside.
2. Place sugar and water in a heavy-bottomed saucepan. Bring to a boil over medium heat, stirring with a wooden spoon. Boil 5 to 6 minutes, stirring constantly until mixture thickens and becomes syrupy. Add lemon juice and boil 2 to 3 minutes more, still stirring constantly.
3. Remove pan from heat. Add bananas to pan, turning with a slotted spoon until bananas are evenly coated with syrup. Divide banana slices among prepared plates, setting slices on top of lettuce. Sprinkle bananas with salt and drizzle with remaining syrup. Add a dollop of mayonnaise to each and sprinkle with walnuts.

Tips & Touches

- Either iceberg or Boston lettuce can be used for this salad. Iceberg lettuce should be shredded, and Boston lettuce should be torn.
- Sprinkle salads with maraschino cherries or dried cherries for additional color.

Majolica lemon reamer, Japanese, 1920s–1930s

HERRING SALAD

{ 1 9 3 0 s }

CHOPPED HERRING IS THE TRADITIONAL APPETIZER *eaten during the Jewish holidays. Although other herring salads sometimes include chopped beets and sour cream, this simple savory salad uses only herring, onions, and apples. We've substituted diminutive pieces of herring in wine sauce for the large salty slices of herring that our mother had to repeatedly soak, skin, and bone. A touch of cinnamon enhances the slightly sweet flavor of the wine sauce. This salad is very nice served on a bed of Boston lettuce, garnished with slices of hard-cooked egg and dill pickles or sliced Granny Smith apples.*

1 (32-oz.) bottle herring tidbits and onions in wine sauce

8 soda crackers

1 large apple, peeled, cored, and grated

4 large eggs, hard-cooked

1 tablespoon sugar

⅛ to ¼ teaspoon cinnamon

1. Drain herring and onions in a colander, rinse under cold water, and place in a large bowl. Cover with cold water and soak for at least 3 hours, changing water at least once. Rinse in cold water and gently squeeze to remove excess liquid.

2. Place soda crackers in the bowl of a food processor fitted with the metal blade. Pulse until finely crumbed. Remove to a small bowl.

3. Place herring and onions in bowl of food processor fitted with metal blade. Process until well ground, but not to a paste. Remove to large bowl. Add cracker crumbs and grated apple and mix thoroughly. Chop hard-cooked eggs, reserving 1 yolk for garnish (refrigerate until ready to use). Add chopped eggs, sugar, and cinnamon and mix to combine. Refrigerate salad at least 2 hours or overnight in covered nonreactive container to allow flavors to blend.

4. Form salad into a mound on serving plate. Press reserved yolk through a fine sieve and sprinkle over herring.

TIPS & TOUCHES

- Cover bowl containing grated apple with plastic wrap to prevent discoloration.
- Chopped herring was originally made using a metal handheld chopper. To replicate the texture of the original recipe, save five pieces of herring, chop by hand, and add to processed herring salad.

400
Suggestions for
VEGETABLES
AND POTATOES

Giving correct cooking methods,
to help you harvest a full quota
of nutritional values — with
a section on Home Canning.

A "HOOK-UP"
COOK BOOK   No 7

DELL

The
VEGETABLE

Being a collection of ...
recipes of fresh and canned
...les—showing their dietet...
...nd giving sensible metho...
...y and service ...

AND PUBLISHED BY
...D MAGAZINE CO. INC...
..., U.S.A.

275 Recipes for
MEALS
WITHOUT MEAT

Now is the time — and here are
countless ways—to prepare substantial Meatless Main Dishes.

A "HOOK-UP"
COOK BOOK

DELL

No 6

Calendar of Dinners
615 Recipes
...arion Harris Neil

...ing Crisco

CHAPTER 3

SIDE DISHES

Just because side dishes, such as vegetables, are good for you, this doesn't mean they shouldn't taste good. There are even people like us who eat our vegetables before the main dish. Whether they're raw, chunky, pureed, or fried, we love them. The good news is that it's easier to learn to love vegetables when someone puts a little extra effort into bringing out their natural goodness. • We know that there are some of you who shun the thought of using canned vegetables, so we've tried to substitute fresh and frozen ones. However, canning is an accepted method of preserving food and was once a part of every home cook's repertoire. There are still some hearty well-organized souls who have the time and patience to home-can the bounty of their gardens or the

seasonal surplus of their local markets. For some, canning is still the middle step between growing and serving what one eats.

As the methods of commercial canning and freezing of vegetables became more advanced, and as we went from being members of farming communities to urban dwellers with larger freezers, the type of vegetables we served changed. Although there's a special joy in eating a firm flavorful tomato just off the vine, canned plum tomatoes can be the next best thing for some recipes when tomatoes are not in season. It's not always what one serves, but how one serves it. Frozen corn and lima beans, briefly steamed and seasoned with a squeeze of lemon juice and a touch of butter, taste almost as good as fresh. To be more specific, the home cooks whose recipes we feature here knew that when vegetables

Children's dishes, English, early 20th century

HEIRLOOM COOKING

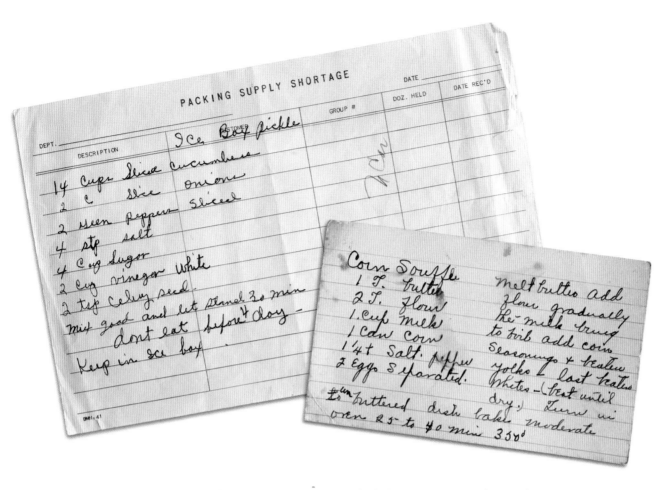

PACKING SUPPLY SHORTAGE

DEPT. _____
DESCRIPTION

Ice Box pickle

14 cups slice cucumbers
2 C slice onions
2 green peppers sliced
4 stp salt
4 cup sugar
2 cup vinegar white
2 tsp celery seed
Mix good and let stand 30 min
dont eat before 4 day —
Keep in ice box

Corn Souffle
1 T. butter
2 T. flour
1 cup milk
1 can corn
¼ t salt, pepper
2 eggs separated.

Melt butter add
flour gradually
the milk bring
to boil add corn
seasonings + beaten
yolks & last beaten
whites (beat until
dry) Turn in
un buttered dish bake moderate
oven 25 to 40 min 350°

are dressed up a bit—whether by sauce or marinade, baking au gratin, or frying—they are more appealing and memorable than those that are merely boiled until they become a pale sodden mass.

Exploring the vegetable recipes of home cooks has shown us the almost miraculous feats women could perform by presenting humble beans and squash with their own fanciful touches. A gratin of yellow summer squash turns into an almost ethereal dish with the addition of a rosy paprika sour cream sauce. A recipe for Baked Butternut Squash from Michigan, with its buttery brown sugar glaze, satisfies the traditionalists in us all.

We salute two Church Ladies—Jean Downey, the minister's wife, who achieved wonders with her Marinated Vegetables, and Louella MacPherson, for her Church Cauliflower, with its blanket of buttery bread crumbs and cheese.

We also acknowledge those who believe that a pickled cucumber is a green vegetable by sharing a recipe for crisp Icebox Pickles from North Carolina, an easy road to travel for almost instant pickle gratification. We can't say enough good things about the rosy goodness of Elizabeth Corkery's Stovetop Pickled Beets, whose color and taste brighten up any meal.

We invite you to think of these recipes as a movable feast, as you travel from Massachusetts to New York to Michigan to North Carolina, sampling the best of the harvest.

Jane Bullard's Yellow Squash Casserole

YIELD: 6 TO 8 SERVINGS

FOR CASSEROLE:

3 cups cut-up (¼-inch pieces) yellow squash

1 tablespoon extra-virgin olive oil

¾ cup chopped shallots

½ cup sour cream

4 tablespoons butter, softened to room temperature

1 teaspoon salt

½ teaspoon coarsely ground black pepper

1 tablespoon fresh thyme leaves

½ teaspoon paprika

¼ cup grated Parmesan cheese

¼ cup grated Romano cheese

1 egg, beaten

FOR TOPPING:

1 cup soft bread crumbs (see How to Make Soft Bread Crumbs on page 215)

2 tablespoons butter, melted

1¼ cups grated Parmesan cheese

THIS DISH IS ACTUALLY CALLED *Summer Squash Au Gratin, which means that it is a casserole with a top layer of buttered bread crumbs and cheese, browned in the oven. Whatever name it goes by, plain or fancy, it's delicious. The paprika-flavored sour cream sauce is outstanding. We found this recipe in a gift bundle of living recipes from our friend Bonnie Slotnick, who runs a cookbook shop in New York.*

1. Set the oven rack in the middle position. Preheat the oven to 350°F. Coat a 9-inch by 13-inch ovenproof glass baking dish with vegetable spray.

2. To make the casserole: Place squash in a steamer basket, set over simmering water, and cover. Steam just until tender, 10 to 12 minutes. Do not overcook. Cool and pat dry with paper towels. Set aside.

3. Heat olive oil in small frying pan over medium heat. Add shallots and cook, stirring with wooden spoon, until translucent, about 5 minutes. Set aside.

4. Combine sour cream, butter, salt, pepper, thyme leaves, and paprika in a large saucepan over medium heat. Cook, stirring, until butter melts and mixture is smooth, 3 to 4 minutes. Add Parmesan cheese and Romano cheese and stir until smooth. Remove from heat and whisk in egg. Fold in sautéed shallots. Add squash and gently stir to combine. Place in prepared dish and level the top.

5. To make the topping: Mix bread crumbs with melted butter and Parmesan cheese in a small bowl and sprinkle over squash. Bake about 30 minutes, or until bread crumbs are golden brown and cheese is bubbling. Serve hot. Store leftovers covered with wax paper in the refrigerator.

CARAMELIZED POTATOES
(Brunede Kartofler)

YIELD: 6 SERVINGS   { 1950s }

THIS IS A TRADITIONAL DANISH RECIPE *for preparing potatoes,*
which we received from Edward Steenberg. Ed prepares his specialty—
Danish Roast Goose Stuffed with Apples and Prunes (page 210)—for family
and friends at Thanksgiving and Christmas. He always serves these potatoes
and Red Cabbage (Rødkål) (page 104) as accompaniments.
Ed learned to cook when he was just fifteen years old, following the death
of his mother, Erma Horn Steenberg.

2 lbs. small new potatoes (about 12)

2½ teaspoons salt, or to taste, divided

¼ cup sugar

¼ cup butter, softened to room temperature

¼ teaspoon coarsely ground black pepper

1. Place potatoes in saucepan with 2 teaspoons of the salt. Add water to cover potatoes by about 1 inch. Bring water to a boil, reduce heat, and simmer 15 to 20 minutes, or until tip of knife can be inserted into potatoes easily. Do not overcook.

2. Drain potatoes in a colander, rinse under cold water, and peel. Cut potatoes into quarters, or wedges, if potatoes are large.

3. Place sugar in a heavy frying pan over low heat and cook, stirring constantly with a wooden spoon, for about 3 minutes, or until sugar turns golden brown (not black). Add butter and stir until smooth. Add as many potatoes as will fit easily in one layer. Using spoon, roll potatoes in sugar and butter mixture until coated and golden. Cook about 6 minutes, or until small particles of brown caramel adhere to the potatoes.

4. Remove potatoes to a heatproof bowl. Repeat to caramelize remaining potatoes. Sprinkle potatoes with remaining ½ teaspoon salt (or to taste) and the pepper and serve.

TIPS & TOUCHES

- You can use larger waxy potatoes, quartered.
- This a very rich dish, and it is a traditional complement to Danish Roast Goose Stuffed with Apples and Prunes.

LIBBY'S STOVETOP PICKLED BEETS

YIELD: 4 CUPS

{ 1950s }

THIS VERY SIMPLE RECIPE FOR PICKLED BEETS *from Elizabeth Corkery, of Groton, Massachusetts, helped us overcome our fear of beets. The cooking process prevents the bleeding usually associated with working with beets and is much easier than roasting beets in the oven and peeling them afterwards. These beets get better as they sit in the refrigerator. They look very pretty in a pressed-glass dish.*

6 medium beets

1 cup white vinegar

2/3 cup water

1/2 cup sugar

1/4 teaspoon salt

1/4 teaspoon whole cloves

1 cup sliced onion

1. Wash beets. Trim any long stems, leaving about 1 inch of stem. Do not trim tails. Bring a pot of water to a boil over medium heat, add beets, and return to a boil. Cook about 35 minutes, or until blade of a small knife can be inserted into beets easily. Remove beets from pot and let cool. Peel and cut into 1/4-inch-thick rounds.

2. Combine vinegar, water, sugar, salt and cloves in nonreactive heavy-bottomed saucepan. Bring to a boil, reduce heat, and simmer 5 minutes, stirring with a wooden spoon. Add beets and onion and simmer another 5 minutes. Remove from heat and place in a glass container. Cool completely, cover, and refrigerate overnight. Pickled beets are best served the next day. Store leftover beets in the refrigerator.

TIPS & TOUCHES

- Leaving part of the top stem and tail on beets prevents them from bleeding during cooking.
- Golden beets or Candy Cane Beets make a nice presentation with less bleeding.

➤➤ PICKLING SPICE ◄◄

Pickling spice is a mix of spices used to preserve vegetables such as cucumbers, tomatoes, and cauliflower or to flavor condiments such as chutneys. The main ingredients in pickling spice are bay leaves, peppercorns, cinnamon sticks, mustard seeds, and whole cloves. Pickling spice can vary as to composition and quantities of ingredients. It is also used for curing meats and cooking corned beef or pot roasts.

SIDE DISHES

91

Icebox Pickles

　　YIELD: 1 GALLON

14 cups pickling cucumbers,
unpeeled and sliced
¼-inch thick

2 cups sliced onions

2 green bell peppers, sliced

2 cups white vinegar

3½ cups sugar

4 teaspoons salt

2 teaspoons celery seed

⅛ teaspoon cayenne pepper

⅛ teaspoon ground cloves

2 bay leaves (fresh if possible)

WE FOUND THIS RECIPE IN A MANUSCRIPT COOKBOOK
*from North Carolina. It's simple and quick and produces a crisp pickle.
Don't hesitate to make half the recipe. These pickles keep for several
weeks in the refrigerator. The lady who created this recipe may actually
have used an icebox. Be sure to use glass or stainless steel containers
that will not react with the vinegar.*

1. Layer cucumbers, onions, and green peppers in a medium
   nonreactive glass bowl and set aside.
2. Combine vinegar, sugar, salt, celery seed, cayenne pepper, cloves,
   and bay leaves in a nonreactive stainless steel saucepan. Bring to a boil,
   pour over cucumbers, and let stand 30 minutes. Pack into a 1-gallon
   glass jar. When completely cool, place in refrigerator. Pickles will keep
   about 4 weeks stored in a glass jar in the refrigerator.

Tips & Touches

- Icebox Pickles are ready to eat
  within 4 hours, but for
  improved flavor, the original
  recipe suggests waiting 4 days.

SUGGESTIONS FOR PICKLING CUCUMBERS

- It's better to use small pickling cucumbers.
- If you use large cucumbers, peel them first. They won't be
  as crisp as pickling cucumbers, but they will taste good.
- Do not eat bay leaves.
- Pickled cucumbers can be transferred to smaller clean
  glass jars and refrigerated.
- A special pickling salt prevents pickles from turning dark
  and the pickling liquid from turning cloudy. This recipe
  uses table salt.

BAKED BUTTERNUT SQUASH

YIELD: 6 SERVINGS

2 lbs. butternut squash, peeled and cut into 1-inch cubes

4 tablespoons butter, softened to room temperature

2/3 cup firmly packed brown sugar

1 (20-oz.) can pineapple chunks (about 2 cups), drained

3/4 teaspoon salt

1/2 teaspoon coarsely ground black pepper

1 teaspoon dried ginger

1/2 cup toasted walnuts, coarsely chopped

THIS RECIPE WAS WRITTEN ON AN INDEX CARD *from the Midwest. We love the sauce made with butter and brown sugar, with its touch of ginger. Butternut squash is a favorite autumnal dish, especially in New England, but it's perfect for Thanksgiving dinner all over the country. The crunchy walnuts add balance to the tender squash.*

1. Set the oven rack in the middle position. Preheat the oven to 425°F. Line a 17-inch by 11-inch by 1-inch jelly roll pan with foil, shiny side up, and coat with vegetable spray. Place squash in a large bowl.

2. Melt butter in a saucepan over medium heat. Add brown sugar and stir with a wooden spoon until combined. Add pineapple, salt, pepper, and ginger. Bring to a boil, reduce heat to medium, and cook until mixture is syrupy, about 15 minutes.

3. Pour pineapple mixture over squash and toss to coat. Spread squash on prepared pan. Bake 20 minutes, shaking pan after 10 minutes for even cooking, until squash is soft when pierced with a small knife. Sprinkle with walnuts and serve immediately. Store leftover squash in a covered container in the refrigerator.

TIPS & TOUCHES

• Shake nuts in a strainer to remove nut dust.

Toy tin saucepan, German, 1890s

LOUELLA'S CHURCH CAULIFLOWER

YIELD: 6 SERVINGS

{ *1950s* }

LOUELLA MACPHERSON WAS A FRIEND OF *Mary Johnson, our agent Karen's mother. Mary and Louella attended The First Congregational Church in Kenosha, Wisconsin. Louella's recipe for cauliflower in a cheese sauce was a much-loved regular at the annual Harvest Home Dinner and became a staple in the Johnson home. Mary added the butter to the breadcrumb topping.*

1. Place cauliflower florets and I teaspoon of the salt in a heavy saucepan. Add water to cover. Bring to a boil, reduce heat, cover, and cook until cauliflower is tender when pierced with a small knife, 10 to 12 minutes. Drain and set aside.

2. Melt I tablespoon of the butter in a saucepan over low heat. Add bread crumbs and mix to combine. Set aside.

3. Melt the remaining ⅓ cup butter in a large frying pan over low heat. Add mushrooms, green pepper, remaining teaspoon salt, and black pepper. Cook 5 minutes, stirring constantly with a wooden spoon. Remove from heat, add flour, and mix thoroughly. Return pan to heat, increase to medium heat, add milk, and cook, stirring, until mixture begins to thicken. Remove from heat.

4. Set the oven rack in the middle position. Preheat the oven to 350°F. Coat a I½-quart round ovenproof casserole with vegetable spray.

5. Place half of the cooked cauliflower in prepared dish. Pour half of the mushroom-pepper sauce over cauliflower and sprinkle with half of cheese. Repeat to layer the remaining cauliflower, sauce, and cheese. Sprinkle with bread crumbs mixture.

6. Place baking dish on cookie sheet and bake 25 to 30 minutes, or until casserole is golden brown and bubbling. Serve hot. Cool any leftover cauliflower in the baking dish, cover with a paper towel and plastic wrap, and refrigerate. To reheat, remove paper towel and plastic wrap and place in a 300°F oven until warmed through, 10 to 15 minutes.

1 head cauliflower (1½ lbs.), cut into small florets

2 teaspoons salt, divided

⅓ cup plus 1 tablespoon butter, divided

½ cup fine bread crumbs (see How to Make Fine Bread Crumbs on page 178)

½ lb. sliced white mushrooms

¼ cup chopped green bell pepper

1 teaspoon coarsely ground black pepper

¼ cup flour

2 cups scalded milk

1⅓ cups medium-sharp cheddar cheese, grated

TIPS & TOUCHES

• Milk is scalded when small bubbles form around edges.

Zucchini Cheese Bake

{ 1940s }

YIELD: 8 SERVINGS

2 lbs. zucchini

1 cup finely chopped onion

¼ lb. butter, melted

1¼ cups fine bread crumbs
(see How to Make Fine Bread
Crumbs on page 178)

⅓ cup heavy cream

4 eggs, beaten

1¼ cups grated American cheese

1 teaspoon salt

½ teaspoon coarsely ground
black pepper

½ teaspoon chopped fresh dill

THIS WAS ONE OF THOSE LITTLE HEIRLOOM GEMS *we found while browsing through some scraps of paper late at night at our friend Bonnie Slotnick's cookbook shop in New York. This handwritten recipe made imaginative use of two popular inexpensive ingredients, zucchini from the garden and American cheese. We brought this recipe into the twenty-first century by using a food processor to grate the zucchini, but a handheld grater will do the job.*

1. Set the oven rack in the middle position. Preheat the oven to 350° F. Coat a 1½-quart ovenproof soufflé dish with vegetable spray or butter.

2. Wash and peel zucchini. Trim both ends. Grate with the metal grating blade of a food processor. Wring out grated zucchini in a dish towel over sink to remove as much liquid as possible. Squeeze zucchini again by hand to remove any remaining liquid. Set zucchini aside in a large bowl.

3. Squeeze chopped onion by hand to remove as much liquid as possible. Add to bowl with zucchini. Add melted butter, bread crumbs, and cream. Add eggs and mix thoroughly. Fold in cheese, salt, pepper, and dill until completely combined.

4. Spoon mixture into prepared dish and bake about 1 hour and 15 minutes, or until golden brown on top and bubbling around edges. If zucchini seems to be browning too quickly, cover with foil. Serve hot. Cover leftovers with a layer of paper towels and then wax paper and store in refrigerator. Pour off any liquid that collects before reheating.

TIPS & TOUCHES

- Squeeze as much liquid as possible from the zucchini and onion before assembling the casserole. The dish will be watery if you don't.

Jean Downey's Marinated Vegetables

YIELD: 6 CUPS

1 (15 ½-oz.) can cut green beans, liquid reserved (see step 1)

1 (15 ½-oz.) can cut wax beans, liquid reserved (see step 1)

1 (17-oz.) can lima beans, liquid reserved (see step 1)

1 cup finely chopped red onion

½ teaspoon coarsely ground black pepper

Pinch of salt

¼ teaspoon chopped, brined hot chilies

¼ cup extra-virgin olive oil

¾ cup sugar

¾ cup white vinegar

1 large clove garlic, finely chopped

¼ cup chopped fresh parsley

THE RECIPE FOR THIS MARINATED VEGETABLE SALAD *comes from Jean Downey, who served with her minister husband at churches in Indiana, Kentucky, and Massachusetts. An unflappable cook, Jean and her husband ran a summer church camp when they were newly married, and she made all of the meals for summer church youth groups. She also cooked for countless Unitarian Universalist teas, lunches, and suppers in Westford and Groton, Massachusetts.*

1. Set a strainer over a bowl and drain green beans, wax beans, and lima beans. Reserve ½ cup bean liquid; discard the remainder. Combine drained beans, onion, pepper, salt, chilies, and olive oil in a large bowl and set aside.

2. Combine sugar, vinegar, reserved bean liquid, and garlic in a saucepan over medium heat and stir with a wooden spoon until mixture starts to boil. Remove from heat and pour over bean mixture. Stir thoroughly. Add parsley and toss. Place in a nonreactive container and let cool. Cover and refrigerate overnight. Drain before serving.

Tips & Touches

- We use chopped chilies in brine to add a bit of bite to the salad.
- Be sure to drain salad before serving. Reserve liquid to store leftover salad.

Toy colander, American, 1920s

MARINATED FRESH BEAN SALAD

YIELD: APPROXIMATELY 6 CUPS

{ 2 0 0 8 }

THIS VERSION OF THE MARINATED VEGETABLE SALAD *uses fresh and frozen vegetables.*

1. Cook lima beans according to package directions and place in a large bowl.
2. Place green beans, wax beans, and salt in a saucepan. Add cold water to cover. Bring to a boil and boil 6 minutes, add mini corn and boil additional minute. Drain vegetables in a colander. Immerse beans in a bowl of cold water to stop the cooking. Let stand 5 minutes. Drain well. Add to bowl with lima beans. Add onion, pepper, chilies, and olive oil.
3. Combine sugar, vinegar, water, and garlic in a saucepan over high heat and stir with a wooden spoon until mixture starts to boil. Remove from heat and pour over bean mixture. Stir thoroughly. Add parsley and toss. Place in a nonreactive container and let cool. Cover and refrigerate overnight. Drain before serving.

1 (12-oz.) package frozen lima beans

9 oz. fresh green beans

9 oz. fresh wax beans

1 teaspoon salt

1 cup fresh mini corn, cut in rings

1 cup chopped red onion

½ teaspoon coarsely ground black pepper

½ teaspoon chopped chili peppers in brine

¼ cup extra-virgin olive oil

¾ cup sugar

¾ cup white vinegar

¾ cup cold water

1 large clove garlic, finely chopped

¼ cup finely chopped fresh parsley

Miniature baskets, American, 1920s–1930s

Mrs. Carter's Baked Stuffed Onions

YIELD: 6 SERVINGS   { 1905 }

This recipe comes from the manuscript cookbook *of the Carter Family, from Portland, Maine. Marion A. Carter was the originator of the manuscript cookbook, filled with heirloom recipes, covering three generations.*

1. Coat a 9-inch by 13-inch ovenproof glass baking dish with vegetable spray.

2. To prepare the onions: Peel and trim onions but do not cut off root ends. Slice off ½ inch from stem ends and set aside for stuffing. Bring a large saucepan of water to boil. Add whole onions, cover, and return water to boil. Reduce heat and simmer about 15 minutes, or until a tester inserted into onions penetrates easily.

3. Drain onions and allow to cool. Hollow out onions by first cutting around the interiors with a small knife, leaving a wall about ¼-inch thick (at least three layers of onion). Then scoop out insides with a spoon or melon baller. If an onion falls apart, reinforce with a layer of onion that has been scooped from another onion. Chop scooped-out insides and reserved slices from onion tops and set aside for stuffing. Place onions, root ends down, in prepared pan.

4. To make the stuffing: Heat olive oil in a large frying pan over medium heat. Add ground beef and cook until no longer pink. Remove to a bowl. Add salt, pepper, parsley, thyme, reserved chopped onion, bread crumbs, and 3 tablespoons of chicken stock and mix to combine.

5. Set the oven rack in the middle position. Preheat the oven to 375°F.

6. Spoon stuffing into hollowed out interiors of onions, pressing down gently to pack well and mounding stuffing over the tops. Add any leftover stuffing to bottom of pan. Add ½ cup of chicken stock to the bottom of the pan.

7. To make the topping: Mix bread crumbs and olive oil in small bowl. Sprinkle over onions. Cover with foil and bake 25 minutes. Uncover and bake 15 minutes more, or until onions are nicely browned on top. (Larger onions may need to bake a little longer.) Serve onions hot along with any extra stuffing from bottom of baking dish. Store leftover baked onions in a covered container in the refrigerator. Reheat in a low oven or microwave until hot.

FOR ONIONS:

6 large sweet onions

FOR STUFFING:

2½ tablespoons extra-virgin olive oil

¾ lb. ground beef, cooked and drained

¼ teaspoon salt

½ teaspoon coarsely ground black pepper

1½ tablespoons chopped fresh parsley

1 teaspoon dried thyme

¼ cup fine bread crumbs (see How to Make Fine Bread Crumbs on page 178)

3 tablespoons low-sodium chicken stock for filling

½ cup low-sodium chicken stock for bottom of pan

FOR TOPPING:

⅓ cup fine bread crumbs (see How to Make Fine Bread Crumbs on page 178)

¼ cup extra-virgin olive oil

Mrs. E. R. Brown's Corn Soufflé

YIELD: 4 LUNCHEON OR 6 SIDE DISH SERVINGS

½ teaspoon salt

¼ teaspoon coarsely ground black pepper

¼ teaspoon dry mustard

4 eggs, separated

4 tablespoons butter, softened to room temperature

¼ cup flour

1 cup milk

¼ cup half-and-half

1 cup fresh, frozen, thawed, or canned corn, drained

FOUND ON A TWO-CENT POSTCARD *sent to Susan Adams, Grand Central, New York, this fluffy but substantial corn soufflé is equally acceptable as a savory luncheon dish or as an accompaniment to a stew or braise. It really stars when paired with gravy. Another recipe from the file of The Church Lady of Mansfield, Ohio.*

1. Set the oven rack in the middle position. Preheat the oven to 400°F. Butter a 1½-quart glass or ovenproof baking dish or coat with vegetable spray.

2. Combine salt, pepper, and mustard in a small bowl and set aside. Place egg yolks in a medium bowl. Place egg whites in the bowl of a standing mixer fitted with the whisk attachment.

3. Melt butter in a heavy-bottomed saucepan over low heat. Remove from heat, add flour, and stir with wooden spoon until combined. Return pan to heat, increase to medium, and add milk and half-and-half, stirring, until sauce has thickened. Add salt, pepper, and mustard, and stir to combine. Remove sauce from heat and spoon into large bowl. Beat yolks with fork to combine. Pour small amount of sauce into yolks, whisking to temper yolks, then return yolk mixture to bowl with sauce, whisking to combine quickly. Fold corn into sauce mixture.

4. Beat egg whites until stiff peaks form. Fold egg whites into sauce mixture until completely combined.

5. Turn down oven to 350°F. Pour soufflé mixture into prepared dish. Bake 1 hour, or until soufflé rises, turns golden brown on top, and pulls away from sides of baking dish. A tester inserted into the center should come out clean. Soufflé will deflate within a few minutes, so serve immediately. Soufflé is best served the same day. Place any leftovers in a container, cover with plastic wrap, refrigerate, and eat as a personal snack.

TIPS & TOUCHES

- Using white pepper means no black flecks in your soufflé.
- Run your finger around the rim of a soufflé before placing it in the oven to form a "high hat" when baked.

CRISPY NORWEGIAN POTATOES

THIS RECIPE SHOULD PROBABLY BE CALLED *Norwegian Potatoes and Carrots because both vegetables have leading roles in this dish. The potatoes and carrots, flavored with nutmeg and onions, are actually twice baked, once in liquid, and once on a jelly roll pan, to produce crunchy buttery nuggets. We found this handwritten recipe tucked in among dessert recipes from the early part of the twentieth century.*

1. Set the oven rack in the middle position. Preheat the oven to 350°F. Coat a 9-inch by 13-inch ovenproof glass baking dish with vegetable spray. Set aside.
2. Bring 4 cups of water to a boil.
3. Melt ½ cup of the butter in a Dutch oven or heavy-bottomed casserole over medium heat. Add onion and cook until translucent, 5 to 7 minutes. Add potatoes, carrots, salt, pepper, and nutmeg. Cook 1 minute, stirring with a wooden spoon. Remove to prepared baking dish. Add enough boiling water to cover vegetables. Cover with foil and place in oven. Bake about 40 minutes, or until vegetables are tender when pierced with the tip of a knife. Remove from oven.
4. Drain vegetables in a colander.
5. Line a 17-inch by 11-inch jelly roll pan with foil, shiny-side up, and coat with vegetable spray. Arrange vegetables in an even layer in prepared pan. Melt remaining ½ cup butter and pour over vegetables. Return to oven and bake for 55 minutes, shaking pan every 15 minutes, until brown and crispy. Serve immediately. Store leftover vegetables in a covered container in the refrigerator.

1 cup butter, divided

2 cups coarsely chopped onion

3 lbs. potatoes, peeled and cut into ½-inch chunks (8 cups)

4 cups sliced (¼-inch rounds) carrots

2 teaspoons salt

1½ teaspoons coarsely ground black pepper

1 teaspoon nutmeg

Silver nutmeg grater, English, early 1800s

Red Cabbage (Rødkål)

{ *1960s* }

¼ cup butter, softened to room temperature

½ cup diced (½-inch) onion

20 oz. shredded red cabbage (about a 1½-lb. cabbage)

½ cup white vinegar

½ cup sugar

2 teaspoons salt

¼ cup currant jelly

THIS HEIRLOOM RECIPE FOR DANISH RED CABBAGE *is an accompaniment to Ed Steenberg's roast goose recipe (page 210). It is easy to make, and the red cabbage, red onions, and currant jelly turn the vegetables a glistening garnet color. The slight acidity of the red cabbage nicely balances the richness of the goose. Red cabbage should be made the day before because the flavor is even better when it is reheated.*

1. Brown butter lightly in a Dutch oven or heavy pot over low heat, stirring with a wooden spoon. Add onion and cabbage. Stir well. Add vinegar, sugar, and salt. Cover and simmer 1 hour and 20 minutes, or until cabbage is soft, stirring occasionally. Add currant jelly in last 10 minutes of cooking and stir to combine.

2. Cool cabbage to room temperature and refrigerate cabbage in a covered container overnight before serving. Rewarm over medium heat.

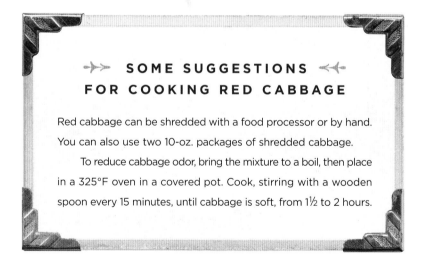

➤➤ SOME SUGGESTIONS ◄◄
FOR COOKING RED CABBAGE

Red cabbage can be shredded with a food processor or by hand. You can also use two 10-oz. packages of shredded cabbage.

To reduce cabbage odor, bring the mixture to a boil, then place in a 325°F oven in a covered pot. Cook, stirring with a wooden spoon every 15 minutes, until cabbage is soft, from 1½ to 2 hours.

Mrs. Hodges' Savory Sweet Potato Puff

YIELD: 6 TO 8 SERVINGS

3 eggs, separated

¼ lb. butter, softened to room temperature

½ cup firmly packed brown sugar

½ cup heavy cream

2 tablespoons sherry

½ teaspoon salt

½ teaspoon coarsely ground black pepper

½ teaspoon dried ginger

1 teaspoon grated lemon zest

2 tablespoons ginger jam

1 tablespoon grated fresh ginger

⅓ cup ricotta

1 cup cooked riced sweet potatoes (from about 3 medium sweet potatoes)

WE FOUND THIS HANDWRITTEN RECIPE *for a sweet potato puff in a copy of* Mrs. John G. Carlisle's Kentucky Cook Book, *owned by Mrs. Harriette G. Hodges. It was originally referred to as a sweet potato pudding, but we renamed it. This puff is both sweet and savory with three kinds of ginger. If you omit the pepper, it can serve as a dessert with whipped cream or vanilla ice cream. Both Mrs. Hodges and Mrs. Carlisle were true Southern cooks, and they both knew their stuff.*

1. Set the oven rack in the middle position. Preheat the oven to 350°F. Coat a 1½-quart ovenproof glass or china baking dish with vegetable spray or butter.

2. Place egg whites in the bowl of a standing mixer fitted with the whisk attachment. Beat until soft peaks form. Set aside.

3. Cream butter and sugar in the bowl of standing mixer fitted with the paddle attachment. Add egg yolks and mix thoroughly. Add cream, sherry, salt, pepper, ginger, lemon zest, ginger jam, and grated ginger. Mix until well combined. Add ricotta and sweet potatoes. Fold in reserved egg whites.

4. Pour into prepared pan and bake 45 minutes, or until a tester inserted into puff comes out clean. Serve immediately. Puff will deflate a little on standing. Cover any leftover puff with plastic wrap and store in the refrigerator. Warm in low oven before serving.

TIPS & TOUCHES

* To steam sweet potatoes: Peel 3 sweet potatoes, cut into 1-inch chunks, and place in the steamer basket over simmering water. Cover pot and steam for about 20 minutes, or until tip of knife can penetrate easily. Put sweet potatoes through ricer and measure 1 cup.

FRENCH RISOTTO
(White Rice)

YIELD: 6 SERVINGS

{ 1960s }

This dish is not a true risotto. It's just the way we make the white rice that accompanies many of the home plates in Heirloom Cooking. *Years ago, we discovered that Julia Child made her rice the same way, by coating the grains with oil. Since she called it "French Risotto," we did, too. This is one of the few recipes that we make with dried onion flakes, which absorb any extra moisture left after the rice has finished cooking. Although onion flakes are optional, they give the rice a bit of crunch.*

1. Heat olive oil in a saucepan over medium heat. Add rice and stir with wooden spoon until all of the grains are coated with oil, about 1 minute.

2. Add stock or water, salt, pepper, and parsley. Stir once or twice and bring to a boil. Cover, reduce heat to very low, and cook 18 minutes, or until rice is tender. Remove pan from heat, uncover, and stir in dried onion flakes. Cover rice and cool for 2 minutes. Remove cover, stir, and serve.

1 tablespoon extra-virgin olive oil

1 cup long grain white rice

2 cups low-sodium chicken stock or water

½ teaspoon salt

½ teaspoon coarsely ground black pepper

1 tablespoon dried parsley

2 tablespoons dried onion flakes (optional)

TIPS & TOUCHES

- You can use chopped fresh parsley instead of dried parsley.

Food choppers, American, 1890s–1920s

CHAPTER 4

SOUP
OF THE DAY

We've always had an intimate relationship with soup. It warms us when we're cold, cools us when we're hot. It feeds us when we're hungry, and most importantly, soup comforts us when the going is rough. • There is something very appealing and universal about that round steaming bowl placed before us. Growing up, it seemed that everyone's mother knew how to make soup, some better than others. Some home cooks had more ingredients to work with, including meat, fish, or chicken. For those who couldn't afford meat, there were always free soup bones from a generous butcher. Chicken feet and chicken backs were indispensable ingredients of choice by the thrifty, but they also made a darn good soup. Liquid masterpieces were also created from beans, corn, and root vegetables.

As we read through the handwritten recipes that we've gathered, we realized that every bowl of soup represents someone's story, whether it was the story of the person who made the soup or the person who ate it. It seems that everyone loves soup, even a person as awe-inspiring as the principal of our grammar school, Preston L. Chase, who made a cup of soup mixed with crumbled soda crackers his permanent choice for lunch at the local spa.

For us, there were the Friday morning aromas of our mother's chicken soup, with its abundance of celery, carrots, onion, and parsnips, which she made for the Sabbath. Our honorary aunt, Rose Levy, produced an admirable vegetable soup, made with dried split peas, barley, noodles, and big chunks of soup meat, while sharing her kitchen with an elderly white cat named Lucky.

On hot summer nights on Sea Foam Avenue, our mother used to make quick versions of cold soup for our father using canned tomato soup or glass jars of beets for her cream of tomato soup and her borscht. She mixed these handy ingredients with generous portions of old-fashioned sour cream and garnished them with a sprinkling of chopped green onions.

And so, we became acquainted with all manners of soup, both hot and cold. In time, we began to understand that soup was more than just a hearty main dish served in a thick crockery bowl. We learned that some soups were better served in delicate double-handled soup bowls, on damask tablecloths, laid with silver spoons. Soup could be a starter or even a dessert. The late Gloria Schleiger Story, a 91-year-old home cook from Nebraska, provided us with a recipe for *Schnit Suppe*, a soup from her German-Russian heritage made from dried prunes and apricots. This hearty sweet soup is served for dessert during the cold Nebraska winters.

Advertising bean crock, Durgin-Park Restaurant, American, 1950s

Although we traditionally relate the stories of inspired home cooks, in this chapter we also celebrate the story of our friend Arthur, who as a young Swedish-American teenager had to leave school in the middle of the Depression to help support his family. His culinary journey started as he waited in line outside the kitchen of the stylish Statler Hotel in Boston. Selected to work with the hotel chefs, Arthur started out by washing pots and pans and later was allowed to wash vegetables. Clever and industrious, he acquired kitchen wisdom and eventually became a chef at the hotel. Upon retirement, he brought his culinary talents to the kitchen of a prestigious women's college. We recently found, tucked away, a copy of his recipe for clam chowder made with minced salt pork and heavy cream, an example of the best of New England chowders.

Margaret Yarranton, transplanted from the Isle of Wight, brought her home cooking skills to Belmont, Massachusetts, where she replicated a very traditional English cream of parsnip soup for her young family. More modest than Arthur's Clam Chowder, Margaret's soup uses milk as well as cream. Accompanied by a green salad and homemade bread and butter, it makes a memorable meal.

We revisit the home kitchen of Virginia P. Lima, of Providence, Rhode Island. In this working class Portuguese household, Mrs. Lima produced her long-simmering red bean and chorizo soup. A flavorful meal in a bowl, her children still remember it today. Mrs. Lima sometimes simmered the chorizo in her soup and sometimes served it on the side.

And finally we pay tribute to some classic heirloom soups: Scotch Broth, Split Pea Soup, and Baked Bean Soup. We encourage you to make your bowl of soup even better by presenting some recipes for crisp White Hall crackers and buttery Homemade Croutons.

Scotch Broth

YIELD: 8 SERVINGS

4 tablespoons extra-virgin olive oil, divided

1 to 1½ lbs. lamb shanks

2 cups chopped onion

2 cups chopped celery

1½ cups chopped carrot

1 teaspoon kosher salt

½ teaspoon coarsely ground black pepper

9 cups low-sodium beef broth

2 bay leaves

2 teaspoons dried parsley

⅓ cup barley

1½ lbs. waxy potatoes, cut in quarters

2½ cups chopped frozen turnips

WE FOUND SEVERAL RECIPES FOR SCOTCH BROTH. *Simple, easy, and inexpensive, this is a lovely warm soup perfect for cold winter days and nights. Just a touch of lamb, a good helping of barley, and some aromatics make this comforting soup appealing.*

1. Heat 2 tablespoons of the oil in a large, heavy frying pan over medium-high heat. Add lamb shanks and cook until well browned on all sides. Remove to a large Dutch oven or heavy-bottomed pot.

2. Add remaining 2 tablespoons oil to frying pan and reduce heat to medium. Add onion, celery, and carrot and cook until onions are translucent, about 7 minutes. Scrape into pot with lamb. Add salt, pepper, beef broth, bay leaves, parsley, and barley. Cover and bring to a boil. Reduce heat and simmer 1 hour.

3. Add potatoes and turnips and cook until soft, another 30 minutes. Allow soup to cool. Remove and discard bay leaves. Remove meat from pot. Pull meat from bones and discard bones. Shred or chop meat and return to pot. To serve, bring soup to a simmer and ladle into warmed soup bowls. Store leftover soup in a covered container in the refrigerator.

Tips & Touches

- The potato and the turnips may fall apart and thicken the soup.
- Fresh turnips can be substituted for frozen, but they may take a little longer to cook.

Spongeware mixing bowl, American, early 20th century

Arthur's Clam Chowder

{ *1940s* }

WE FIRST TASTED THIS CLAM CHOWDER *more than 20 years ago. A rich milky chowder, loaded with clams and potatoes, it is simple to make and easy to serve. Arthur worked in the kitchens of the Statler Hotel, in Boston, as a teenager, during the Depression. He became a seasoned chef, who graciously shared his recipes. Arthur's recipe called for salt pork, but we suggest using bacon or pancetta. The butter and flour mixture is called a roux.*

1. Melt 2 tablespoons butter in a Dutch oven or heavy-bottomed 5-quart pot over medium heat. Add onions and cook, stirring with a wooden spoon, until translucent, about 5 to 7 minutes. Stir in bacon or pancetta and cook until fat begins to melt into onions, about 5 minutes. Turn down heat if bacon or pancetta begins to burn.

2. Add flour, reduce heat to low, and stir briskly to make a roux. Cook roux 1 minute. Add pepper. Add broth and reserved clam liquid to roux, continuing to stir until chowder begins to thicken. Add clams. Remove chowder from heat.

3. Heat milk and cream in a separate 1½ quart pot over medium heat until small bubbles form around the edges. Add to chowder, set chowder pot over medium heat, and bring to a simmer, stirring briskly. Stir in potatoes. Add remaining 2 tablespoons butter and cook, stirring gently, until melted. Do not allow chowder to boil. Serve in heated soup bowls, garnished with fresh parsley, crumbled common crackers, or Pilot crackers. Store leftover chowder in covered containers in refrigerator. Reheat gently. Do not boil or cream will curdle.

4 tablespoons butter, divided

2 cups coarsely chopped onions

4 slices bacon or 3 ounces pancetta, diced

½ cup flour

2 8 oz. bottles clam broth

3 10½-oz. cans chopped clams, drained and liquid reserved

¼ teaspoon coarsely ground black pepper

2 cups milk

2 cups cream

1½ lbs. potatoes, peeled, cooked, and diced (about 4 cups)

¼ cup chopped fresh parsley (optional)

Tips & Touches

- Serve with Souffléd Common Crackers (page 161)
- If you use salt pork, it is important to remove the tough layer of skin before dicing.
- Each can of clams will yield a little over 5 ounces of clam liquid which should be added to the bottled clam broth.
- If you like a thicker chowder, mix 2 tablespoons of flour with softened butter and whisk into chowder.

Katherine's Savory Tomato Peanut Butter Soup

YIELD: 4 SERVINGS

1 (28-oz.) can tomato puree

¾ cup creamy peanut butter

1 teaspoon salt

½ teaspoon coarsely ground black pepper

½ teaspoon paprika

1 cup low-sodium beef stock

2 tablespoons butter, softened to room temperature

Pinch of red pepper flakes

We found this recipe in a cunningly illustrated *recipe journal from the 1920s. This soup is good served either hot or cold. The peanut butter adds richness to the soup yet it is not readily identifiable upon tasting. This soup takes on a whole new personality when served cold.*

1. Combine tomato puree and peanut butter in a large heavy-bottomed pot and blend with a wooden spoon or whisk until smooth. Add salt, black pepper, and paprika.
2. Add stock and bring to boil. Reduce heat and simmer 10 minutes. Add butter. Add red pepper flakes and stir to blend. Allow to sit 5 minutes to marry flavors. Serve hot or cold. Store leftover soup in a covered container in the refrigerator.

Tips & Touches

*   Serve hot with buttered Homemade Croutons (page 148)
*   Serve cold with a touch of sour cream and a sprinkling of red pepper flakes or paprika.

Folding wire basket, American, early 20th Century

Fred's Creamy Potato Soup with Thyme

{ 1 9 2 0 s }

YIELD: 6 CUPS

4 medium boiling potatoes (2 lbs.), peeled and quartered

2 teaspoons salt, divided

½ cup chopped celery leaves

1 cup sliced onion

1 bay leaf

½ cup heavy cream

2 tablespoons butter, cut into dice

½ teaspoon coarsely ground black pepper

½ teaspoon dried thyme

½ teaspoon chopped chilies in brine

1 cup milk

Homemade Croutons, for garnish (page 148)

THIS RECIPE CAME FROM A MANUSCRIPT COOKBOOK *given to Katherine and Fred by Ceil and Betty. This little treasure was loaded with recipes, including Tomato Peanut Butter Soup, Corned Beef Hash, and Shepherd's Pie—all hearty heirloom recipes designed to please a husband. This soup is thick and satisfying and can be enjoyed either hot or cold. It's great hot with the buttery Homemade Croutons (page 148) or with finely chopped chives or some fresh thyme leaves if served cold. We suggest using fresh thyme for the potato soup if you have some.*

1. Place potatoes in a large pot and add water to cover (about 6 cups). Add 1 teaspoon salt, celery leaves, onion, and bay leaf. Cover and bring to a boil. Reduce heat to medium and simmer until potatoes are fork tender, about 15 minutes.

2. Drain potato mixture in a colander, reserving the cooking liquid. Discard bay leaf. Place potato mixture, heavy cream, and butter in the bowl of a food processor fitted with the metal blade. Pulse until potatoes are smooth and creamy. (Or puree soup in a blender.) Add remaining salt, pepper, thyme, chilies, and milk and pulse to blend. Add some of the reserved potato stock or additional milk to thin soup to desired consistency.

3. To serve, ladle soup into warmed soup bowls and garnish with croutons. Store in a covered container in the refrigerator. Reheat soup on low, adding more milk or potato stock to thin, as needed. Serve hot or cold. Store leftover soup in a covered container in the refrigerator.

TIPS & TOUCHES

• Save the leftover potato stock for gravies or soups.

German Dessert Fruit Soup
(Schnit Suppe)

YIELD: 6 CUPS

{ 1900s }

This is an Americanized version *of the hearty German dessert soup that a community of Germans living in Russia brought with them to Nebraska. Schnit Suppe is delicious hot or cold. It's sweet and spicy and similar to the Jewish dessert, compote. Serve it hot in the cold winter months with a bit of whipped cream and sliced toasted almonds on top. Our thanks to Sue Truax and her mother, Gloria Schleiger Story, who gave us the recipe for this soup.*

1½ cups dried apricots

1½ cups dried pitted prunes

½ cup raisins, tightly packed

1 quart cold water

1 tablespoon flour

½ cup dark corn syrup

⅔ cup heavy cream

⅛ teaspoon salt

¼ teaspoon ground cloves

1. Combine apricots, prunes, and raisins in a large saucepan. Add water to cover. Cover with a lid and bring to a boil. Reduce heat and simmer, stirring occasionally with a wooden spoon, until fruit is tender, 10 to 12 minutes. Combine flour and corn syrup, add to soup, and stir until soup thickens. Remove soup from heat and allow to cool 20 minutes.

2. Stir ½ cup of the soup liquid into heavy cream. Return cream mixture to soup. Add salt and cloves and stir well. Let stand for 5 minutes to let the flavors marry.

3. To serve, warm soup over medium heat (do not boil) and ladle into warmed soup bowls. Store leftover soup in a covered container in the refrigerator.

Tips & Touches

- Fruit soup can be made with different combinations of mixed dried fruit. You can also add canned sweet cherries to the soup.

Pink Depression glass serving pieces, 1930s

Garden Salad Soup

{ Early 1900s }

Sue Truax, from Omaha, Nebraska, *told us about this
simple soup prepared with ingredients picked from the family garden.
Sue stayed with her Uncle Rheinhold and Aunt Grace when her
husband Glenn did his National Guard duty. Uncle Riney and Aunt
Grace were first generation descendents of the Czar's Germans, from
Odessa, Russia. Sue remembers building her own bowl of fresh greens,
warm potatoes, and cold buttermilk, garnished with sweet spring onions.
We made this soup with sour cream, and it was outstanding. This was
a spring luncheon dish when the new potatoes were ready for digging.*

- 1¼ lbs. new potatoes, unpeeled
- 1 fresh head Boston lettuce, romaine, or oak leaf lettuce
- 2 cups buttermilk, or 1 cup sour cream
- 3 green onions or scallions, sliced into ¼-inch rounds
- ⅛ teaspoon kosher salt
- ⅛ teaspoon coarsely ground black pepper

1. Place potatoes in a 4-quart pot, add salted water to cover, and
   bring to a boil over medium heat. Boil 15 to 20 minutes, or until
   potatoes are soft and the tip of a knife penetrates easily. Drain
   and slice ¼-inch thick.
2. Rinse and spin-dry salad greens. Tear into small pieces and divide
   among soup bowls. Mound ¾ cup warm potatoes in each bowl.
   Pour ½ cup buttermilk or spoon ¼ cup sour cream into each
   bowl. Sprinkle with green onions or scallions, salt, and pepper.

Bok Choy and Corn Soup

{ 1 9 8 0 s }

YIELD: 12 CUPS

2 oz. pancetta, diced

5 tablespoons extra-virgin olive oil, divided

2 cups chopped onion

2 cups chopped leeks

½ cup chopped shallots

4 cups chopped bok choy

4 cups corn kernels (3 to 4 ears fresh corn), or 4 cups frozen corn

½ teaspoon salt

½ teaspoon coarsely ground black pepper

¼ cup butter, softened to room temperature

¼ cup flour

2 cups low-sodium chicken stock

¼ cup chili sauce

2 tablespoons chopped fresh parsley

1 cup milk

THIS RECIPE GREW OUT OF OUR INTEREST *in the availability of fresh vegetables and ethnic ingredients such as pancetta and bok choy. The search for healthy food fueled our use of naturally sweet vegetables such as onions, bok choy, and corn when we cooked for family and friends. The crispy pancetta contrasts nicely with the mild flavor of the onions, leeks, and shallots. We suggest that you make this soup when corn is in season.*

1. Sauté pancetta in a large heavy saucepan over medium heat until crisp, about 5 minutes. Remove to a large bowl and set aside. Add 1 tablespoon of the olive oil to pan. Add onion, leeks, and shallots and cook until translucent, 5 to 7 minutes. Remove to bowl with pancetta. Wipe pan with paper towel.

2. Return pan to heat and add 2 tablespoons of the olive oil. Add bok choy and cook until leaves are wilted and stems are soft, about 4 minutes. Remove to bowl with pancetta and onions. Add remaining 2 tablespoons oil to pan, add corn, and cook until softened, about 4 minutes. Remove to bowl. Sprinkle vegetables with salt and pepper and stir.

3. Melt butter in a 4-quart saucepan over low heat. Remove pan from heat. Add flour and stir with wooden spoon to form roux. Return pan to low heat and cook, stirring, for 1 minute. Remove pan from heat. Add stock. Return to heat, increase heat to medium, and cook, stirring until mixture thickens and small bubbles form around edges, 3 to 5 minutes.

4. Fold in pancetta and vegetables. Add chili sauce and parsley. Add milk. Pour in batches into the bowl of a food processor fitted with the metal blade. Pulse until soup is almost smooth but still has some texture. (Or puree soup in a blender.) Serve hot in warmed soup bowls. Store leftover soup in a covered container in the refrigerator. Thin with a little milk when reheating.

TIPS & TOUCHES

- Pancetta is optional, but it gives a nice salty balance to the soup. If you leave out the pancetta, increase salt to ¾ teaspoon.
- Reheat soup slowly on low heat so that milk will not curdle.
- Recipe can be halved.

BAKED BEAN SOUP

YIELD: 10 CUPS   { 1920s }

WE FOUND THIS RECIPE IN A DARLING LITTLE BOOK, *designed and illustrated by Louise Perrett, called* Recipes, My Friends and My Own. *It was created to record handwritten recipes. This soup is very satisfying on a cold winter day. It's also simple to prepare and makes a speedy comforting bowl. The crumbled bacon and sour cream provide a hearty garnish.*

5 cups canned baked beans,
   drained, divided

2 medium onions, sliced (2 cups)

2 stalks celery, sliced (1 cup)

6 cups low-sodium beef stock

1½ cups canned tomato puree

1. Combine 4 cups of the baked beans and onions, celery, and beef stock in heavy-bottomed pot. Bring to a boil, reduce heat, and simmer 30 minutes.

2. Add tomato puree and stir to combine. Pour in batches into the bowl of a food processor fitted with the metal blade. Pulse until completely blended. (Or puree soup in a blender.) Return soup to pot. Add remaining 1 cup beans and cook over low heat, stirring, until warmed through. Serve in warmed soup bowls. Store leftover soup in a covered container in the refrigerator.

TIPS & TOUCHES

- We used pork and beans in tomato sauce for our soup.

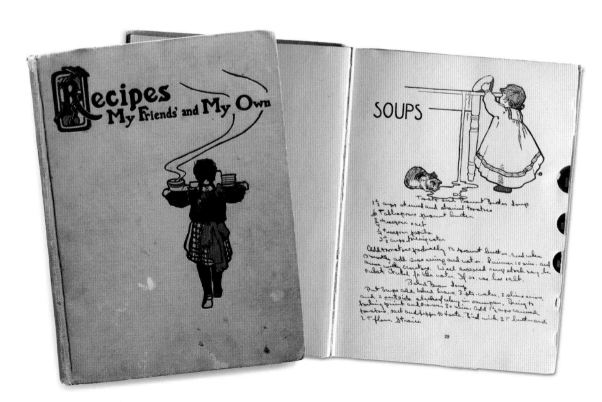

PORTUGUESE RED KIDNEY BEAN SOUP

{ 1920s }

YIELD: 14 CUPS

1 lb. dried kidney beans, rinsed

4 tablespoons extra-virgin olive oil, divided

2 cups coarsely chopped onion

1 cup coarsely chopped celery

2 tablespoons tomato paste

7 cups low-sodium chicken stock

1 teaspoon salt

½ teaspoon coarsely ground black pepper

½ teaspoon paprika

½ cup loosely packed chopped fresh parsley

1½ cups canned tomato puree

8 oz. (1 link) chorizo sausage, peeled and coarsely chopped

1½ cups elbow macaroni

1 tablespoon red wine vinegar

THIS THICK CHUNKY SOUP *is based on the Portuguese red kidney bean soup that David Lima's mother prepared in the kitchen of their home in Providence, Rhode Island. Virginia P. Lima was famous for her Portuguese sweet bread and her wonderful soups and stews. We added the chorizo as seasoning. This is comfort food at its best.*

1. Place beans in bowl, add cold water to cover, and let soak overnight. The next day, drain beans and rinse under cold running water. Set aside.

2. Heat 3 tablespoons of the olive oil in a Dutch oven or heavy-bottomed pot over medium heat. Add onion and celery and sauté until translucent, 5 to 7 minutes. Whisk tomato paste with chicken stock and add to pot. Add salt, pepper, paprika, parsley, tomato puree, and drained beans and stir with wooden spoon to mix. Cover and bring to a boil over medium heat, stirring occasionally. Reduce heat to low and simmer, covered, for 1 hour.

3. Heat remaining tablespoon oil in a frying pan over high heat. Add chopped chorizo and cook about 15 minutes, or until slightly crispy.

4. Add cooked chorizo and browned bits from the bottom of the pan, to soup pot. Cover and continue cooking another 30 minutes. Add macaroni and vinegar. Simmer, covered, another 30 minutes, stirring occasionally, until beans are tender. If beans are still a little firm, continue cooking 15 minutes more. Store leftover soup in a covered container in the refrigerator.

TIPS & TOUCHES

- If you want a stronger sausage flavor, add two links of chorizo.

Mama's Chicken Soup

YIELD: 13 CUPS CHICKEN SOUP, 1½ LBS. BONED CHICKEN

4 whole cloves, or pinch of ground cloves

1 large onion, peeled, cut into quarters

4½- to 5-lb. chicken, cut in pieces with the skin on

5 stalks celery with leaves, coarsely chopped

4 carrots, cut in 1-inch pieces

2 parsnips, cut in 1-inch pieces

2 cloves garlic, peeled, cut in small pieces

3 bay leaves

2 teaspoons kosher salt

½ teaspoon coarsely ground black pepper

16 cups water

THIS IS THE CHICKEN SOUP OUR MOTHER, *Dorothy, made for us when we were growing up. If it was Friday, it was chicken soup. Mama made great pots of it and served some of the chicken in the soup. The remaining chicken she dusted with flour, paprika, and pepper and fried in vegetable oil along with a cut-up onion. We didn't know fried chicken had skin until we were adults. We remember fondly Mama's chicken soup. We make it just the way she did, but we add four whole cloves to the onion. The recipe makes a lot of chicken soup, but it's wonderful to have the extra chicken stock on hand. Cubed or shredded cooked chicken makes a nice salad or stir-fry.*

1. Stick a clove, if using, in each onion quarter and place in a large soup pot (or place ground cloves and onions in pot). Add chicken, celery, carrots, parsnips, garlic, bay leaves, salt, pepper, and water to pot. Cover and bring to a boil. Use a ladle to skim white solids that float to the surface of the soup. Reduce heat, leave cover ajar, and simmer, skimming periodically as more solids rise to surface, until chicken is thoroughly cooked, 2 to 2½ hours.

2. Remove from heat. Uncover, and cool 15 minutes. Remove chicken from soup with slotted spoon; set aside. Strain soup into a large, clean pot. Remove and reserve carrots and parsnips; discard all other solids. Pour soup carefully into containers and let stand until cool. Cover and refrigerate.

3. Remove and discard skin and bones from chicken. Place chicken and reserved carrots and parsnips in two separate covered containers and refrigerate.

4. When the soup has chilled, scrape the fat from the surface with a spoon and reserve in a covered container.

5. To serve, bring soup to a simmer in a saucepan. Add some of the reserved chicken and vegetables and a bit of the reserved chicken fat, if desired. Taste and adjust seasonings. Serve in warmed soup bowls.

Tips & Touches

- Chicken fat is wonderful for making savory pastry, such as Mrs. Yaffee's Pierogi (page 42); store rendered chicken fat in a covered container in the freezer up to three months.
- Heat a bit of chicken fat with the soup for a richer taste and higher cholesterol.

MARGARET'S CREAM OF PARSNIP SOUP

YIELD: 10 CUPS

{ 1970s }

MARGARET YARRANTON WROTE THIS RECIPE *for her English cream of parsnip soup on the back of a discount ticket to an antique show and sale. A good friend and an antique dealer, she often invited us for Thanksgiving dinner at her home in Belmont, Massachusetts. One Thanksgiving, she served this velvety parsnip soup. Margaret came from the Isle of Wight and lived through the rationing of World War II. She has been known to churn her own butter and bake her own Scottish Baps (page 153) for Thanksgiving dinner.*

1. Melt butter in a Dutch oven or heavy-bottomed pot over medium heat. Add parsnips, onion, and celery and cook, stirring with a wooden spoon, until softened, 5 to 10 minutes. Add chicken stock, bay leaf, and nutmeg and simmer 30 minutes.

2. Add lemon juice and stir. Pour soup into a large bowl. Remove and discard bay leaf. Pour 2 cups of soup mixture in the bowl of a food processor fitted with the metal blade. Pulse until smooth. (Or puree soup in a blender.) Return soup to clean pot. Continue working in batches to puree all of the soup.

3. Add half-and-half. Cook over low heat, stirring with wooden spoon, until warmed through. Do not boil. Taste soup and adjust seasonings. Serve in warmed soup bowls. Store in a covered container in the refrigerator.

2 tablespoons butter, softened to room temperature

4 cups chopped parsnips

1 cup chopped onion

1 cup chopped celery

6 cups low-sodium chicken stock

1 bay leaf

¼ teaspoon nutmeg

1 tablespoon lemon juice

1 cup half-and-half

1½ teaspoons salt

½ teaspoon coarsely ground black pepper

TIPS & TOUCHES

- Boiling the soup after adding the half-and-half can cause the soup to curdle.
- This soup is wonderful served with a plate of sliced turkey and a green salad the day after Thanksgiving.

Toy enamelware ladle, early 1900s

SOUP OF THE DAY

Auntie Rose's Vegetable Beef Soup

YIELD: 14 CUPS {1930s}

Rose Levy was our mother Dorothy's best friend *and honorary sister. Auntie Rose's vegetable soup was outstanding, and when our mother made it, the kitchen on Sea Foam Avenue was perfumed with the aroma of simmering legumes and root vegetables. Fishel Zwieg, one of the many kosher butchers on Shirley Street in Winthrop, was known for his generosity in giving loyal customers free soup bones. Our version uses chunks of chuck, or as we liked to call it, "soup meat."*

1 cup green split peas

1 cup yellow split peas

½ cup barley

2 to 3 tablespoons extra-virgin olive oil

1 to 1¼ lbs. beef chuck, cut in 2-inch pieces

1½ cups coarsely chopped onion

4 carrots, cut into 1-inch pieces

3 stalks celery, chopped

2 large cloves garlic, minced

1 teaspoon salt

½ teaspoon coarsely ground black pepper

3 large bay leaves

11 cups low-sodium beef stock, divided

1 cup frozen lima beans

6 oz. dried egg noodles

1. Place green and yellow split peas in a strainer and pick over for gravel or husks. Rinse under cold water. Drain and set aside in a bowl. Do the same for the barley and set aside in separate bowl.

2. Heat olive oil in a large Dutch oven or heavy-bottomed pot over medium-high heat. Add beef chuck, working in batches so as not to crowd pan, and cook until well browned on all sides. Remove meat to a bowl and set aside.

3. Add onions to pot and cook until translucent, about 5 minutes. Return beef to pot. Add green and yellow split peas, carrots, celery, garlic, salt, pepper, bay leaves, and 8 cups of the stock. Stir, cover, and bring to a boil. Reduce heat and simmer 1 hour, stirring occasionally.

4. Add barley and 1 more cup of the stock. Return soup to boil, reduce heat, and simmer, covered, for 15 minutes. Add frozen lima beans and simmer another 15 minutes. Remove beef from soup with slotted spoon, shred, and return to pot.

5. Add remaining 2 cups stock and noodles and cook another 15 minutes, or until dried peas dissolve and barley is soft. Remove from heat and let stand 15 minutes. Soup will thicken on standing. Remove bay leaves. To serve, ladle into warm soup bowls. Store leftover soup in a covered container in the refrigerator.

Tips & Touches

- If the peas and barley are not completely cooked after 1 hour and 45 minutes, soup can be simmered another 15 minutes.

SPLIT PEA SOUP

{ 1 8 9 0 s }

YIELD: 10 CUPS

1 lb. split green peas

1 quart water

1 quart low-sodium chicken stock

1 cup coarsely chopped celery
with leaves

3 bay leaves

1 tablespoon dried parsley

½ teaspoon coarsely ground
black pepper

6 oz. pancetta

1 tablespoon extra-virgin olive oil

2 cups coarsely chopped onion

1 cup coarsely chopped carrot

1 clove garlic, peeled and chopped

THIS IS A VERY OLD RECIPE, *which originally called for a ham bone. Since not everyone has a ham bone in the freezer, we tried it with pancetta, that salty Italian rolled bacon. We found that the nuggets of pancetta lend a rich velvety feel to the soup and provide a sweeter taste than the ham bone. One of our favorite trendy crepe restaurants used to serve a similar soup, Potage St. Germaine, with a small container of cream or sherry. We like this soup just the way it is.*

1. Place split peas in a strainer and pick over for gravel or husks. Rinse under cold water. Place in a Dutch oven or large, heavy-bottomed pot. Add water and chicken stock and stir. Add celery and leaves, bay leaves, parsley, and black pepper and set aside.

2. Cut pancetta into ½-inch cubes. Place in frying pan over medium heat and cook 5 to 7 minutes, or until pancetta is just beginning to release fat but before it begins to brown. Scrape into pot with peas. Add olive oil to frying pan and return to medium heat. Add onion, carrot, and garlic and cook 5 to 8 minutes, stirring with a wooden spoon, until onion is just translucent. Scrape into soup pot.

3. Cover soup, place over medium heat, and bring to a boil. Reduce heat and simmer 1 hour and 15 minutes to 1 hour and 30 minutes, or until peas dissolve and vegetables are tender. Stir every 10 minutes to prevent peas from sticking to bottom of pot.

4. Remove pot from heat and allow soup to cool slightly. Remove bay leaves and discard. Soup will thicken as it stands. Pour 2 cups into the bowl of a food processor fitted with the metal blade. Pulse until blended. (Or puree soup in a blender.) If there are still some pieces of pancetta in soup, leave them. Return soup to clean pot. Continue working in batches to puree all of the soup.

5. To serve, rewarm soup gently over low heat and serve in warmed soup bowls. Store leftover soup in a covered container in the refrigerator.

TIPS & TOUCHES

- Do not fry pancetta until crispy. It should retain enough of its shape to melt into the soup.
- You can use a blender instead of a food processor.

VERMONT CORN CHOWDER

{ *1930s* }

WE FOUND THIS RECIPE IN A MODEST BOX *of handwritten recipes in Concord, Massachusetts. The origin of the recipes was Martha's Vineyard, a small island off the coast of Cape Cod. Mixed in with the recipes for Almond Granola and Cranberry Pudding was this "Vermont" Corn Chowder. This collection of living recipes also contained a genealogy chart for the family of the Vineyard cook. This simple chowder uses one of the staples of the pantry shelf, canned creamed corn.*

2 tablespoons butter, softened to room temperature

1 cup chopped onion

½ cup chopped celery

½ teaspoon salt

½ teaspoon coarsely ground black pepper

¼ teaspoon paprika

1¼ lbs. potatoes, cooked, peeled, and diced

2 cups milk

2 (14¾-oz.) cans cream-style corn

8 oz cheddar cheese, shredded, about 3 cups

2 tablespoons chopped fresh parsley

1. Melt butter in a Dutch oven over low heat. Increase heat to medium, add onion and celery, and cook until tender, 5 to 7 minutes. Add salt, pepper, and paprika and stir with a wooden spoon. Add potatoes, milk, and corn and stir until soup is heated through.

2. Remove Dutch oven from heat and stir in cheese until melted. If necessary, place soup over low heat and cook, stirring, until all of cheese is melted. Do not boil.

3. Ladle soup into bowls and sprinkle with chopped parsley. Store leftover soup in a covered container in the refrigerator.

Toy enamelware cooking pot, American, 1920s

CHAPTER 5

STAFF OF LIFE

This chapter is very close to our hearts because
bread baking so completely defines the
home kitchen. We've always thought of the
women whose manuscript cookbooks
we've discovered and treasured as the bakers of
the bread and the keepers of the hearth because
bread, more than any other food, is what
nourishes us both as individuals and as families.
Bread is sacred. We talk of a companion
as someone with whom we share our bread; we
break bread together. We refer to bread as the
staff of life—the food which supports and
sustains us. • Bread is included in many religious
rituals. In Judaism, a blessing is said over the
Sabbath challah. Christians receive Communion
wafers or Communion bread. In the
Greek Orthodox tradition, the Easter bread,

Lambropsomo, cushions eggs dyed a deep red, symbolizing resurrection and rebirth. These are just a few of the examples of how bread feeds us both spiritually and physically.

During periods of natural disaster or war, the lack of bread can mean the loss of life. When a man supports his family, he is said to put bread on the table. He is referred to as a good provider or a breadwinner. When there was no man in the house, the woman in charge of the family had to find a way to provide bread. She had to secure shelter so she could have a place to bake the bread, and she needed to earn the money to purchase ingredients and fuel. Often women became breadwinners as well as bread bakers. Although many of them brought work home or eventually went out to work, their kitchens were still the center of family life. Nothing changed. The smell of baking bread still means home to most people.

In our search for traditional bread recipes, we found that women and men brought their bread-baking skills and their recipes with them when they emigrated to America. When Margaret Yarranton and her family came to the United States from England more than forty-five years ago, she started the tradition of baking and serving her Scottish Baps at Thanksgiving. Simple raised yeast rolls, they are wonderful with butter and jam, or as a sandwich roll.

Erika Geywitz brought her mother Emma's recipe for Christmas Stollen with her when she came to this country from Germany in the 1960s. A casual conversation with her son, Michael, on a train from Boston to New York, provided us with the recipe for this satisfying yeast bread with its candied fruit and almonds. The recipe for Oma Emma's Stollen can be made any time of the year, but it brings a special cheer to winter holidays. So dedicated is her grandson, Michael, that he even makes his own candied lemon and orange peel for his version of her stollen.

Tin baking pan, American, early 20th century

Although Grandma Gaydos' Gum Boots may not be thought of as bread, they are definitely staff of life material. The story of a fourteen-year-old-girl named Helen Sochko, from Vlahovo, Austria-Hungary, who married John Gaydos, a Greek Orthodox priest, and raised five children in the mining communities of West Virginia, Ohio, and Pennsylvania, is one of courage and faith. With a limited food budget, Helen found ways to feed her children simple delicious food. They called this dish of farmer cheese and farina dumplings rolled in buttered bread crumbs *Gum Boots* because they couldn't pronounce its Czechoslovakian name. Three generations later, the Gaydos family still marvels at the feats of a young girl who washed and pressed the church linen, had the bishop to dinner, and tended to the needs of a large congregation.

One of the most moving stories about bread comes from the Arfa family, whose patriarch left Poland in 1938 as a young baker. He emigrated to America, served in World War II, and started a bakery in Chicago in 1947. For years, the bakery produced outstanding bagels, cakes, and rugelah. The tradition continues because we have adapted the recipe for the Arfa Family's Bagels for your home kitchen. Every time someone takes a pan of these golden bagels from a kitchen stove, the story of a family's search for a new homeland and a better life lives on.

Sally Lunn

YIELD: 16 SLICES

1 (¼-oz.) package dry yeast

½ cup plus 1 teaspoon sugar

¼ cup water, warmed to 115°F

1¼ cups milk

½ cup butter, cut into 8 pieces

1½ teaspoons salt

3 large eggs

3½ cups flour

SALLY LUNN ACTUALLY ORIGINATED *in the eighteenth century, in England, and was brought to America by the colonists. Over the next three centuries, this sweet buttery bread evolved into a quick bread made without yeast. We like the yeast version better because it reminds us of French brioche. There is still some confusion about the origin of the name* Sally Lunn. *Some sources say it was the name of the young girl who sold the bread on the streets of Bath. Others say it found its name from the French* sol et lune, *sun and moon, because it was baked in a round pan.*

1. Dissolve yeast and 1 teaspoon of the sugar in warm water. Set in a warm place for about 10 minutes to proof.
2. Place milk in saucepan and warm over medium heat until bubbles form around edges. Remove from heat, add butter, and stir with a wooden spoon until melted. Add remaining ½ cup sugar and the salt and stir until sugar has dissolved. Remove from heat and allow to cool slightly.
3. Beat eggs in the bowl of a standing mixer fitted with the paddle attachment. Add milk mixture and proofed yeast mixture and beat until combined. Add flour, approximately 1 cup at a time, beating well after each addition. Mix until there are no lumps and dough is smooth, about 2 minutes. Cover bowl with clean dish towel and put in warm place to rise for about 1 hour, or until double in size.
4. Coat a 10-inch by 4¼-inch tube pan with vegetable spray or butter. Lightly dust with flour and tap to remove excess. Stir dough with wooden spoon to deflate. Place dough in prepared pan. Cover with clean dish towel and allow to rise for another hour until double in size.
5. Place the oven rack in the middle position. Preheat the oven to 350°F. Bake Sally Lunn 35 to 40 minutes, or until golden brown. Let cool in pan on a rack for at least 30 minutes. Turn out onto rack and cut into slices. Store wrapped in wax paper at room temperature.

TIPS & TOUCHES

- Sally Lunn can be served toasted with butter and jam or made into French toast or bread pudding.

Ila's Canadian Banana Bread

YIELD: 14 SLICES

{ 1920s }

WE FOUND THIS HANDWRITTEN RECIPE *on a yellowed piece of paper with "From the desk of ILA D. BERRY" printed in red ink on the upper left corner. There was a notation that said "a Canadian receipt." What makes this living recipe remarkable is that the writer was a workingwoman early in the twentieth century who still had time to exchange recipes with coworkers. This banana bread is moist and delicious and perfect with the Banana Nut Salad (page 82).*

1. Place the oven rack in the middle position. Preheat the oven to 350°F. Line the bottom and narrow ends of a 9-inch by 5-inch by 3-inch loaf pan with a single strip of wax paper or parchment paper. Coat the pan and paper liner with vegetable spray.

2. Cut bananas and pear into 1-inch slices, place in a bowl, and mash until blended. Set aside. (There should be about 1½ cups mashed fruit.)

3. Sift flour, salt, baking soda, and pumpkin pie spice into another bowl and set aside.

4. Cream butter, sugar, and honey in the bowl of a standing mixer fitted with the paddle attachment until fluffy. Add mashed fruit mixture and beat to combine. Add dry ingredients in thirds, beating after each addition. Fold in walnuts with a spatula. Pour batter into prepared pan.

5. Bake 50 to 55 minutes, or until a tester inserted into middle of bread comes out clean. Remove from oven and place on cooling rack. Let stand 15 minutes and then turn out onto a rack to cool. Store covered with paper towels and wax paper at room temperature. This bread is even better the next day.

2 large, ripe bananas

4 oz. peeled, cored pear (about ½ large pear)

1½ cups flour

½ teaspoon salt

1 teaspoon baking soda

½ teaspoon pumpkin pie spice

¼ cup butter, softened to room temperature

1 cup sugar

2 tablespoons honey

1 cup toasted walnuts, coarsely chopped

Tips & Touches

- Ila's Canadian Banana Bread is good sliced, buttered and cut into quarters, and served with salads.

Aunt Ruth's Dilly Casserole Bread

{ *1950s* }

YIELD: 1 ROUND LOAF

1 (¼-oz.) packet dry yeast

¼ cup water, warmed to 115°F

1 cup large curd cottage cheese, heated to lukewarm

2 tablespoons sugar

1 tablespoon onion flakes

1 tablespoon butter, softened to room temperature

2 teaspoons dill seed

½ teaspoon salt

¼ teaspoon baking soda

1 large egg

2 to 2½ cups flour

Softened butter, for brushing

Coarse sea salt, for sprinkling

THIS RECIPE CAME FROM OUR AGENT *Karen Johnson's Aunt Ruth, a wonderful midwestern cook and baker. Ruth has been making her Dilly Casserole Bread for many years. This handwritten recipe was part of Karen's kitchen inheritance from her mother, Mary. Recently, at a flea market, Karen happily found a bowl to replace the one she broke that she had been using for baking her Dilly Bread.*

1. Dissolve yeast in water and set aside in a warm place to proof for about 10 minutes. Mixture will bubble when yeast is proofed.
2. Mix cottage cheese, sugar, onion flakes, butter, dill seed, salt, baking soda, egg, and proofed yeast in the bowl of a standing mixer fitted with the paddle attachment. Add flour gradually, beating well after each addition, to make a stiff dough. Cover with a clean dish towel and allow to rise in a warm place until double in size, about 1 hour.
3. Punch down dough, and turn into well-buttered 8-inch round ovenproof casserole. Cover and let rise in a warm place for 1 hour.
4. Set the oven rack in the middle position. Preheat the oven to 350°F.
5. Bake 40 to 50 minutes, or until golden brown. Turn bread out of dish, brush top with soft butter, and sprinkle with salt. Cool bread on rack for at least 10 minutes before serving. Store leftover bread wrapped in wax paper at room temperature.

TIPS & TOUCHES

- Use large curd creamed cottage cheese if you can find it because it has more moisture and gives the bread a richer flavor.

Clara J. Warren's Refrigerator Rolls

FOR YEAST SPONGE

1 (¼-oz.) package dry yeast

¼ cup water warmed to 115°F

1 teaspoon sugar

FOR DOUGH

½ cup butter, cut into 8 pieces

1 cup boiling water

1½ teaspoons salt

¼ cup sugar

2 eggs, beaten

4 cups flour

Melted butter, for brushing

THIS RECIPE WAS TYPED ON A MANUAL TYPEWRITER. *We found it among some recipes from the Midwest, and we are glad that we have the name of the originator. There is even a typed line for Clara's name. We wonder if she typed this herself and signed the recipe. Clara knew how to bake with yeast, and these rolls are wonderful with butter or jam.*

1. For the yeast sponge: Dissolve yeast in warm water. Add sugar. Set in a warm place for 10 minutes to proof.
2. For the dough: Whisk butter into boiling water to melt. Add salt and sugar and mix well. Let cool.
3. Mix cooled butter mixture, eggs, and proofed yeast sponge in the bowl of a standing mixer fitted with the paddle attachment. Add 2 cups of the flour and mix well. Add the remaining 2 cups flour and mix to form a soft dough.
4. Coat a medium bowl with butter or vegetable spray. Place dough in greased bowl. Coat a piece of plastic wrap with vegetable spray (to prevent sticking) and place it loosely over dough. Place in refrigerator and let rise for at least 2 hours or overnight.
5. Coat the cups and top surface of a 12-cup muffin pan with butter or vegetable spray. Turn dough out onto a floured work surface. Pat or gently roll to a 10-inch by 10-inch square. Cut into 12 equal pieces with floured knife. Roll dough pieces into balls, place in prepared muffin pan, and let rise in a warm place for 30 to 60 minutes, or until double in size.
6. Set the oven rack in the middle position. Preheat the oven to 400°F.
7. Brush rolls with melted butter and bake 20 to 25 minutes, or until golden brown. Turn rolls out onto a metal rack to cool. Store rolls wrapped in wax paper at room temperature.

TIPS & TOUCHES

- After brushing the tops with butter, sprinkle kosher salt or poppy seeds on the rolls, if desired.

Arline's Farm House Rye Bread

{ *1940s* }

WE FOUND THIS MIDWESTERN RECIPE *entitled* Farm House Bread *on a handwritten index card. It is not a dark pumpernickel bread, nor is it a Jewish light rye; it is simply an honest loaf, dense and cocoa-colored. It is good spread with butter or jam, and it satisfies when one wants a slice of bread that is both homey and filling. Arline also provided us with the recipe for Swedish meatballs (page 193).*

FOR DOUGH

1 cup scalded milk

2 tablespoons sugar

1¼ teaspoons salt

2 tablespoons butter, softened to room temperature

3¾ cups all-purpose flour

1¾ cups rye flour

¼ cup cocoa

FOR YEAST SPONGE

2 (¼-oz.) packages dry yeast

½ cup water, warmed to 115°F

1 teaspoon sugar

1. To make the dough: In a medium heavy-bottomed pan, heat milk, sugar, and salt over medium heat until small bubbles form around edges. Remove from heat, add butter, and stir until melted. Let cool to room temperature.

2. To make the sponge: Dissolve yeast in warm water. Add sugar. Let stand, uncovered, in a warm place for about 10 minutes to proof.

3. Sift all-purpose flour, rye flour, and cocoa into a medium bowl.

4. Mix proofed yeast and cooled milk mixture in the bowl of a standing mixer fitted with the paddle attachment. Beat in dry ingredients, 1 cup at a time, until well mixed. Change to dough hook and knead for 3 to 4 minutes, or until dough comes together and is smooth and shiny.

5. Coat a medium bowl with vegetable spray or butter. Place dough in greased bowl. Coat a piece of plastic wrap with vegetable spray (to prevent sticking) and place it loosely over dough. Allow dough to rise until double in size, about 1 hour. Punch down dough and divide in half.

6. Coat two 9-inch by 5-inch by 3-inch baking pans with vegetable spray. Shape dough into two loaves on a lightly floured work surface. Place loaves in prepared pans and let rise until double in size, about 1 hour.

7. Place the oven rack in the middle position. Preheat the oven to 375°F.

8. Bake breads until crusty, about 40 minutes. Turn bread out of pans onto a rack and cool to room temperature. Store loosely wrapped in wax paper at room temperature.

Grandma Hails' Buns

{ 1880s }

FOR YEAST SPONGE

2 (¼-oz.) packages quick-rising
   yeast

1½ cups water, warmed to 115°F

1 tablespoon sugar

FOR DOUGH

5 cups flour

3 tablespoons sugar

1½ teaspoons salt

2 teaspoons finely chopped fresh
   rosemary leaves (optional)

½ cup solid shortening

Milk, for brushing

Tips & Touches

- You can split the dough and
  make a dozen rolls and one loaf
  of bread. Bake loaf at 425°F in
  a 9-inch by 5-inch by 3-inch
  loaf pan, coated with vegetable
  spray, for 30 minutes.

YIELD: 2 DOZEN ROLLS, OR
1 DOZEN ROLLS AND 1 LOAF OF BREAD

THIS RECIPE COMES FROM DONNA HENSIL TAUB, *who is the fifth generation of her family to bake these rolls. Donna learned how to make them from her mother Cheryl and her grandmother, Lorraine Paxton. The recipe originated with Donna's great-great grandmother, Sarah Toal Hails, who came to the United States from England. These were the rolls the Paxton-Grigor-Hails Family took on Fourth of July picnics at Ten Mile Creek in Washington County, Pennsylvania. These buns are wonderful for hamburgers, and the dough will also yield a tender loaf.*

1. To make the sponge: Dissolve yeast in warm water. Add sugar and set in a warm place for 10 minutes to proof.
2. To make the dough: Mix flour, sugar, salt, rosemary, if using, and shortening in the bowl of a standing mixer fitted with the paddle attachment. Add proofed yeast sponge and beat to combine. Change to dough hook and knead for 3 to 4 minutes, or until dough comes together and is smooth.
3. Coat a medium bowl with vegetable spray or butter. Place dough in greased bowl. Coat a piece of plastic wrap with vegetable spray (to prevent sticking) and place it loosely over dough. Put dough in warm place to rise until double in size, 30 minutes to 1 hour.
4. Line two 14-inch by 16-inch baking sheets with foil, shiny side up, and coat with vegetable spray, or use silicone liners. Punch down dough and divide into 2 dozen equal pieces. Roll each piece into a ball on a lightly floured surface and place balls on prepared baking pans. Let rolls rise until double in size.
5. Place the oven rack in the middle position. Preheat the oven to 425°F.
6. Brush tops of rolls with milk. Bake 15 to 20 minutes, or until rolls are golden brown. Let cool on metal racks. Store wrapped in wax paper at room temperature.

CHILI CHEESE CORNBREAD

YIELD: NINE 3-INCH SQUARES

{ *1950s* }

Eating this chili cornbread is like *walking through the door of a ranch house, sitting down at a Formica-topped table in the rumpus room, kicking off our loafers, and hitching up our poodle skirts. This is as good as it gets from the 1950s. This is from the manuscript cookbook of the lady from North Carolina.*

1. Set the oven rack in the middle position. Preheat the oven to 375°F. Line the bottom and sides of a 9-inch by 9-inch by 2-inch pan with foil, shiny side up. Coat the foil with butter or vegetable spray.

2. Remove casing from chorizo and coarsely chop. Add chorizo to frying pan, set over medium to high heat, and sauté until lightly browned, 5 to 7 minutes. Remove chorizo from pan with a slotted spoon and place on a platter covered with paper towels. Place a second layer of paper towels on top and press gently to absorb excess fat.

3. Place flour, cornmeal, sugar, baking powder, and salt in a large bowl and set aside. In another bowl, whisk eggs, milk, vegetable oil, and sour cream until smooth. Whisk egg mixture into dry ingredients until combined. Stir in chorizo, cheese, and green chilies. Place batter in prepared pan and bake 35 to 38 minutes, or until top is golden brown and a tester inserted into middle comes out clean. Lift cornbread from pan with foil. Cut into 3-inch squares and serve warm with butter.

½ lb. chorizo sausage

2 cups flour

1½ cups yellow cornmeal

⅓ cup sugar

2 tablespoons baking powder

1½ teaspoons salt

2 large eggs

1 cup milk

½ cup vegetable oil

½ cup sour cream

6 oz. cheddar cheese, shredded (2¼ cups)

1 (4-oz.) can mild green chilies, drained and chopped

TIPS & TOUCHES

- Instead of chorizo, try pepperoni. You will not have to fry it.

Muffin pan, American, 1880s

STAFF OF LIFE

141

OMA GEYWITZ'S STOLLEN

{ 1930s }

WHEN WE MET MIKE RIPLEY ON A TRAIN *and fed him Brown
Sugar Brownies (a recipe from our book* Heirloom Baking)*, we never
thought we'd find a recipe for a true German Christmas stollen. This recipe
is from his grandmother, Oma Emma, who taught her daughter, Erika, to
make her stollen. Mike is the third generation to make the family stollen, and
he is teaching his children to make it, too.*

1. To make the sponge: Dissolve yeast in warm water. Stir in sugar. Set in
   a warm place to proof, about 10 minutes.
2. To make the dough: Mix sugar, butter, egg, salt, lemon juice, milk,
   cinnamon, nutmeg, and vanilla in the bowl of a standing mixer fitted
   with the paddle attachment. Add proofed yeast. Add flour 1 cup at a
   time, beating until smooth after each addition. Change to dough
   hook and knead for 3 to 4 minutes, or until dough comes together
   and is smooth and shiny.
3. Coat a medium bowl with vegetable spray or butter. Place dough in
   greased bowl. Coat a piece of plastic wrap with vegetable spray (to
   prevent sticking) and place it loosely over dough. Allow dough to rise
   until double in size, about 1 hour. Punch down.
4. Coat a 14-inch by 16-inch baking sheet with vegetable spray. Knead
   almonds and dried fruit into dough. On a lightly floured work
   surface, flatten dough with rolling pin or with hands to a 12-inch by
   16-inch rectangle. Arrange dough rectangle with shorter side at
   bottom. Spread butter over the bottom half the dough and fold over.
   Place stollen on prepared baking sheet. Cover with a clean dish towel
   and allow to rise in a warm place about 1 hour, or until double in size.
5. Place the oven rack in the middle position. Preheat the oven to 350°F.
6. Bake stollen 30 minutes , or until golden brown. Remove from
   baking sheet, place on a rack, and immediately brush with butter; the
   butter will melt into the warm stollen. Sprinkle top with 2 tablespoons
   of the confectioners' sugar. Most of the sugar should melt into the
   crust. Let cool to room temperature. Sprinkle with the remaining 2
   tablespoons confectioners' sugar. Slice and enjoy plain or with butter.
   Store loosely wrapped in wax paper at room temperature for about
   1 week. Towards the end of the week, toast the last few slices of stollen.

FOR YEAST SPONGE

1 (¼-oz.) package dry yeast

¼ cup water, warmed to 115°F

1 teaspoon sugar

FOR DOUGH

¾ cup sugar

½ cup butter, softened to room
   temperature

1 large egg

1 teaspoon salt

1 tablespoon lemon juice

¾ cup milk

1 teaspoon cinnamon

¼ teaspoon nutmeg

2 teaspoons vanilla

4½ cups flour

FOR FILLING

1 cup toasted slivered almonds

1½ cups mixed dried fruit,
   chopped, and raisins

2 tablespoons butter, softened

FOR TOPPING

2 tablespoons butter, softened to
   room temperature

¼ cup confectioners' sugar

TIPS & TOUCHES

- We used dried cherries, chopped
  dried apricots, and maraschino
  cherries, as well as golden raisins.
  Candied orange peel, lemon peel,
  and citron are also good in stollen.

Traditional Greek Easter Bread (Lambropsomo)

{ 1 9 4 0 s }

YIELD: 2 ROUND LOAVES OR 1 BRAIDED LOAF

FOR SPONGE

2 (¼-oz.) packages dry yeast

½ cup water, warmed to 115°F

½ cup milk, warmed to 115°F

1 teaspoon sugar

FOR DOUGH

½ cup butter, melted and cooled

3 eggs, beaten

¼ cup sugar

½ teaspoon salt

1½ teaspoons vanilla

¼ teaspoon ground masticha (optional)

4½ cups flour

FOR TOPPING

10 large eggs, hard-cooked, shells dyed red or pastel colors

1 egg, beaten

1 tablespoon sesame seeds

THIS RECIPE COMES FROM THEODORA BENOS GUERAS, *of Winthrop, Massachusetts. Theodora was an accomplished artist as well as an excellent cook. Born in Maine, she learned her heirloom kitchen skills from her mother and grandmother, who were both born in Greece. Theodora was a treasured home cook for more than eighty years, and her family still remembers fondly the traditional loaves of bread she baked at Easter.*

1. To make the sponge: Dissolve yeast in warm water. Stir in warm milk and sugar. Put in a warm place to proof for about 10 minutes. Mixture will bubble when yeast has proofed.

2. To make the dough: Mix melted butter, eggs, sugar, salt, vanilla, and masticha, if using, in the bowl of a standing mixer fitted with the paddle attachment. Add proofed yeast and beat to blend thoroughly. Beat in flour 2 cups at a time. Continue to beat until soft dough forms, 1 to 2 minutes. Change to dough hook and knead for 5 minutes, or until dough is smooth and elastic; or turn dough out onto a lightly floured board and knead 10 minutes.

3. Coat a medium bowl with butter or vegetable spray. Place dough in greased bowl. Coat a piece of plastic wrap with vegetable spray (to prevent sticking) and place it loosely over dough. Put dough in a warm place and allow to rise for about 2 hours, or until double in bulk. Punch down dough and knead again until smooth.

4. For round loaves, coat two 14-inch by 16-inch baking sheets with vegetable spray. For braided loaf, coat one pan with spray.

5. To make two round loaves: Divide dough in half. On a lightly floured surface, shape each piece of dough into a round loaf. Make five depressions in each loaf for the eggs. Place on prepared baking sheets.

6. To make one braided loaf: Divide dough into three equal pieces. On a lightly floured surface, roll each piece into a rope about 18 inches long. Pinch top ends together, braid the ropes tightly, and pinch bottom ends together. Place on prepared baking sheet.

7. Cover loaves or braid with clean dish towels and allow to rise in a warm place 1 to 1½ hours, or until double in size. For the round loaves, place hard-cooked eggs in prepared depressions. For the braid, nestle eggs in between the ropes of the braid. Cover loaves or braid with clean dish towels and allow to rise in a warm place 1 to 1½ hours, or until double in size.

8. Place the oven rack in the middle position. Preheat the oven to 350°F.

9. Brush top of each loaf with beaten egg (do not brush hard-cooked eggs) and sprinkle with sesame seeds. Bake 30 minutes, or until golden brown. (After baking, usually just the tops of the eggs will be visible.) Remove from baking sheet(s) and cool on a rack. Store loosely wrapped in wax paper in the refrigerator.

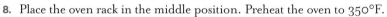

Advertising egg scale, American, 1920s–1930s

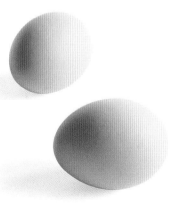

TIPS & TOUCHES

- Eggs are placed three down in the center of the loaf and one egg on each side of the center egg, making a cross. Traditionally, eggs are dyed a deep red, symbolizing the blood of Christ.

- A suitable red dye is available in Greek or Middle-Eastern grocery stores. Conventional red food coloring may fade on the dough as it bakes. Pastel egg dye can be used instead of red dye.

- Masticha is a natural white resin. It is used to flavor breads, cookies, and beverages. It can be found in Middle Eastern grocery stores. Anise extract, vanilla extract, or orange zest can be substituted in Greek pastries.

Grandma Gaydos' Gum Boots
(Farina Dumplings)

YIELD: 20 DUMPLINGS

⅓ cup butter, softened to room temperature

1 cup fine bread crumbs (see How to Make Fine Bread Crumbs on page 178)

1 lb. farmer cheese or pot cheese

½ cup dry farina (Cream of Wheat cereal)

¼ cup flour

1 egg, lightly beaten

TIPS & TOUCHES

- Use homemade fine bread crumbs.
- Sour cream is a nice accompaniment.
- Farina is a milled grain meal, usually made with wheat. It is sold under the brand name Cream of Wheat. It is also used to make Middle Eastern sweets.

HELEN GAYDOS, A YOUNG SLOVAKIAN GIRL *who married a Greek Orthodox priest and raised five children during the Depression, fed her family these delicious hearty dumplings. Her children called them* gum boots *because they couldn't pronounce the Slovakian name. Helen traveled through the Midwest and the South with her husband, serving the needs of several congregations.*

1. Melt butter in a medium frying pan over low heat. Add bread crumbs and cook, stirring with wooden spoon, until bread crumbs absorb butter and turn light brown, about 5 minutes. Set aside on a platter in a warm place.

2. Bring a large pot of water to a boil. Mix cheese, farina, flour, and egg in a large bowl until dough forms. Roll golf ball–size pieces of dough between the palms of your hands to form dumplings. Drop dumplings into boiling water. Cover pot and cook 3 minutes. Remove cover and continue cooking until dumplings bob to top, 5 to 7 minutes total. Remove dumplings from pot with slotted spoon and transfer immediately to the platter with bread crumbs, rolling to coat. Serve immediately. Store leftover dumplings in a covered container in the refrigerator. Reheat gently in a frying pan with a little butter over low heat to warm through.

⇥ DRY CURD, FARMER'S, AND POT CHEESES ⇤

The original *gum boots* recipe called for dry curd cottage cheese, which contains less moisture than regular cottage cheese. It is sold in groceries catering to Eastern European cooks but is not always easy to find. Either farmer's cheese or pot cheese will make a fine substitution. Farmer's cheese is less moist than dry curd cottage cheese, and pot cheese is the least moist of the three.

Margaret's Scottish Baps

{ 1950s }

Margaret Yarranton is a bit of a Renaissance woman. *She is an antiques dealer, an artist, a mother, and a grandmother. She is known to make her own butter and bake her own bread. A native of the Isle of Wight, she often turns the dough for her baps into braided loaves for Thanksgiving.*

1. To make the sponge: Dissolve yeast in warm water in a large bowl. Let stand uncovered in a warm place for 10 minutes to proof.

2. To make the dough: Combine proofed yeast mixture, sugar, salt, butter and 2 cups of the flour in the bowl of a standing mixer fitted with the paddle attachment; mix until smooth. Beat in remaining 2 cups flour. Change to dough hook and knead for 5 minutes at medium speed until dough comes together and is smooth and elastic.

3. Coat a medium bowl with vegetable spray or butter. Place dough in greased bowl. Coat a piece of plastic wrap with vegetable spray (to prevent sticking) and place it loosely over dough. Put in a warm place and allow dough to rise until double in size, 40 minutes to 1 hour.

4. Line two 14-inch by 16-inch baking sheets with foil, shiny side up, and coat with vegetable spray. Dust with cornmeal. Punch down dough and divide into 12 equal pieces. Shape into flat rounds or ovals, ½-inch thick, and place on prepared baking sheets. Cover baps with a clean dish towel and let rise in a warm place 1 hour, or until double in size.

5. Place the oven rack in the middle position. Preheat the oven to 425°F.

6. To make the topping: Mix beaten egg with water. Brush tops of baps with egg wash. Sprinkle with sesame seeds or poppy seeds, if desired. Bake 10 to 15 minutes, or until golden brown. Cool on racks. Store wrapped in wax paper at room temperature.

FOR SPONGE
2 (¼-oz.) packages dry yeast
1½ cups water warmed to 115°F

FOR DOUGH
¼ cup sugar
2 teaspoons salt
¼ cup butter, softened
4 cups flour
Cornmeal, for pan

FOR TOPPING
1 egg, beaten
1 tablespoon water
Sesame seeds (optional)
Poppy seeds (optional)

Tips & Touches

* To make Margaret's Thanksgiving loaves, divide dough in half, then divide each half into three pieces, and braid. Bake at 375°F for 25 minutes until golden in color.

ENORMOUS POPOVERS

YIELD: 8 SERVINGS   { 1940s }

THESE POPOVERS ARE REALLY "ENORMOUS." *They remind us of the popovers served in Boston restaurants in the 1960s and 1970s. They are buttery, crisp, and wonderful. We tried several different ways of making popovers, but we found that this recipe is the best. We also found that we were able to produce the lightest, tallest popovers using ovenproof china custard cups.*

6 large eggs

2 cups milk

6 tablespoons butter, melted and cooled

2 cups flour, sifted

½ teaspoon salt

1. Set the oven rack in the middle position. Preheat the oven to 375°F. Coat eight 8-oz. ovenproof china custard cups with vegetable spray. Place custard cups on a foil-lined jelly roll pan; foil should be shiny side up.

2. Whisk eggs in large bowl until frothy. Add milk and cooled, melted, butter and whisk to combine. Whisk in flour and salt. There will be some lumps. Fill each custard cup with ¾ cup batter.

3. Bake popovers on jelly roll pan about 1 hour, or until tall and buttery brown. Do not open oven door while popovers are cooking.

4. Remove pan from oven; leave oven on. Puncture neck of each popover on four sides to allow steam to escape. Return pan to oven and bake popovers 10 minutes more. Remove popovers from oven and turn out of cups. Serve immediately with butter or jam. Popovers are best eaten the day they are made, but leftovers may be stored in a plastic bag at room temperature and reheated the next day in the oven. They will be neither as light nor as crisp as the day they were fresh, but they will still be tasty.

New England Brown Bread

YIELD: 10-12 SLICES

1 cup raisins

1 cup whole wheat flour

1 cup cornmeal

1 cup graham flour

½ teaspoon salt

1 teaspoon baking soda

¾ cup molasses

2 cups buttermilk

THIS SIMPLE RECIPE IS *more than 130 years old, and it is as delicious today as it was in our great-grandmother's time. The graham flour can be replaced by more whole wheat flour. A more substantial version of this bread is sometimes made with a smaller proportion of rye flour. This is the steamed raisin-filled bread that is traditionally served with New England baked beans.*

1. Coat a 2-quart pudding mold with vegetable spray or butter, dust with flour, and tap out the excess. Prepare a buttered parchment sheet to fit the top of the mold. Select a covered pot large enough to accommodate the mold with a 2-inch clearance around sides. Set a metal rack inside the pot.
2. Toss raisins with 2 tablespoons of the whole wheat flour in a small bowl. Set aside.
3. Mix the remaining ¾ cup plus 2 tablespoons whole wheat flour, cornmeal, graham flour, salt, and baking soda in a large bowl. Add molasses and stir. Add buttermilk and stir to combine. Fold in floured

✈ HOW TO STEAM BREAD ✈

Steaming a bread is very much like steaming a pudding. The cake pan or mold should be no more than two thirds full. Place a buttered parchment round on top of the cake pan or mold, and cover the mold. If the pan or mold does not have a cover, fold two sheets of foil over the buttered parchment and tie securely with white cotton kitchen string.

The bread should be steamed on a rack in a deep, heavy pot in simmering, not boiling, water that comes about one-third up the sides of the mold. To safely prepare the steamer, set the filled mold pan on the rack in the pot. Add enough water to come one-third of the way up the sides of the mold. Remove the mold and bring the water to a boil. Turn off the heat and carefully return the filled mold to the rack. Cover the pot, adjust the heat so that the water simmers, and steam the bread for the suggested time. It's very important to check the water level periodically to make sure it remains stable. *Do not let the water boil out because a tightly covered mold could explode.*

raisins. Spoon into prepared mold, making sure that it is no more than two-thirds full. Place buttered parchment round on top of mold and add cover.

4. Set filled mold on rack in pot. Add water to come about one-third of the way up the side of the mold. Remove mold. Cover pot and bring water to a boil. Turn off heat, lift pot cover, and carefully place filled mold on rack. Cover pot and adjust heat so that water simmers; do not let water boil.

5. Steam pudding approximately 1 hour to 1 hour and 15 minutes, or until a tester inserted into middle comes out clean. Check the water level periodically during the steaming and add water as needed. *Do not let water boil out because a tightly covered mold could explode.*

6. Turn off heat. Remove mold carefully from steamer and place on cooling rack. Carefully remove cover and parchment from top of mold. Let cool for 20 minutes. Invert mold on cooling rack and remove mold from bread. If mold does not release easily, run a small knife around inside of mold, or let stand until bread begins to shrink away from sides of mold. Serve at room temperature with butter. Store loosely wrapped in wax paper in the refrigerator.

 TIPS & TOUCHES

- We found that 1 hour to 1 hour and 15 minutes was usually enough to steam the bread, not the traditional 3 to 4 hours.

CHEESE BREAD

YIELD: 2 LOAVES

FOR DOUGH

1 cup milk

½ cup butter, softened to room temperature

1½ teaspoons salt

¼ cup sugar

2 eggs, beaten

6 oz. extra-sharp cheddar cheese, shredded (2 cups)

4 cups flour

4 oz. extra-sharp cheddar cheese, cut into ½-inch dice (1½ cups or a bit more)

Melted butter, for brushing (optional)

FOR YEAST SPONGE

1 (¼-oz.) package dry yeast

¼ cup water, warmed to 115°F

1 teaspoon sugar

THE CHEDDAR CHEESE, BOTH SHREDDED AND DICED, *in this bread, takes us back to those heavenly days when we ordered our egg salad sandwiches on cheese bread at Schraft's in the 1950s. To think that it was so simple to make this bread at home! The recipe, handwritten on an index card, was tucked into a manuscript cookbook from the Midwest.*

1. To make the dough: Scald milk. Whisk in butter to melt. Add salt and sugar and mix well. Let cool to room temperature.

2. To make the sponge: Dissolve yeast in warm water. Add sugar. Let stand uncovered in a warm place to proof, about 10 minutes.

3. Combine milk-butter mixture, proofed yeast, eggs, and shredded cheese in the bowl of a standing mixer fitted with the paddle attachment. Add 2 cups of the flour and mix well. Add the remaining 2 cups flour and beat to make a soft dough.

4. Coat a medium bowl with butter or vegetable spray. Place dough in greased bowl. Coat a piece of plastic wrap with vegetable spray (to prevent sticking) and place it loosely over dough. Refrigerate for at least 2 hours, or overnight.

5. Coat the bottom and sides of two 9-inch by 5-inch by 3-inch loaf pans with vegetable spray. Turn dough out onto a lightly floured work surface. Divide dough in half. Pat or roll one half gently to an 11-inch by 11-inch square. Scatter half of the diced cheddar cheese over dough square. Fold in thirds to form a loaf. Place seam-side down in prepared pan. Repeat to make the second loaf. Allow to rise in a warm place until double in size, 1 to 1½ hours.

6. Place the oven rack in the middle position. Preheat the oven to 400°F.

7. Brush loaves with melted butter, if using, for a darker crust. Bake 20 to 25 minutes until golden brown. Remove pans from oven. Turn out of pans onto a rack to cool. Store wrapped in wax paper at room temperature.

TIPS & TOUCHES

- Cheese Bread is great toasted in a sandwich with egg salad and bacon.

MIKE'S MOTHER'S SPAETZLE

YIELD: 8 CUPS

4 large eggs

1 cup milk

3 cups flour, sifted

1½ teaspoons salt

⅛ teaspoon nutmeg

Butter, softened to room
  temperature

Buttered bread crumbs (optional)

Grated cheese (optional)

Salt

Coarsely ground black pepper

TIPS & TOUCHES

* It may take a few tries before
  you are satisfied with your
  spaetzle. After making this
  recipe several times, we still like
  to think of our spaetzle as a
  work in progress. Spaetzle can
  be substantial little dumplings,
  when served with butter.

WE MET MIKE RIPLEY TRAVELING ON A TRAIN *to New York City.*
We ended up talking about the recipes his mother, Erika, and his grandmother,
Emma, made in their native Germany. Mike generously shared his family's
recipes for spaetzle and stollen (see Oma Geywitz's Stollen on page 143). Our
interpretation of his mother's spaetzle produces more of a dumpling than a
noodle—good for soaking up gravy.

1. Fill a large heavy-bottomed pot with water and bring to a boil.
2. Place eggs in a large bowl and whisk until combined. Add milk and
   whisk. Add flour, salt, and nutmeg and whisk until blended and
   smooth. Let batter stand for at least 5 minutes.
3. Using a cup measure, fill a spaetzle hopper with batter. Holding
   spaetzle maker over pot of boiling water, slide hopper across base so
   that batter falls through holes and into boiling water. When spaetzle
   rise to surface, cover and boil 5 to 8 minutes, or until spaetzle are
   cooked through, tender, and no longer taste of raw flour. (Scoop out
   a few spaetzle with a slotted spoon and taste them to be sure.) Scoop
   out spaetzle into a colander set in a large bowl of hot water to prevent
   spaetzle from sticking together. Continue to cook remaining spaetzle.
4. Drain spaetzle and place in large bowl. Add butter and either buttered
   bread crumbs or grated cheese. Add salt and pepper to taste. Store
   leftovers in a covered container in the refrigerator.

✈ HOW TO CUT SPAETZLE ✈

Spaetzle are small handmade German noodles served with savory German dishes such as sauerbraten, or
in soup. Although experienced spatzle makers cut spatzle with a knife, from a wooden board into boiling
water, beginners may prefer an inexpensive metal spaetzle maker, available in most kitchen stores. Some
cooks push spaetzle dough through the holes of a metal colander, but this is time-consuming and tricky.
There is an old German saying *Die Spaetzle muessen schwimmen*, which translates, "there should always
be oceans of gravy when serving spaetzle."

Souffléed Common Crackers

{ 1850s }

COMMON CRACKERS ARE A DIRECT DESCENDENT *of hardtack, the seemingly indestructible biscuits carried on sea voyages or by soldiers during the nineteenth and early twentieth centuries. Made of flour, water, and salt, these biscuits were so hard that they usually had to be soaked in liquid before being consumed. Today's common crackers, while substantial, can be enjoyed souffléed or broken into a bowl of soup. Even Fannie Farmer, the head of The Boston Cooking School, suggested preparing them this way to produce crisp puffy crackers.*

1. Set the oven rack in the middle position. Preheat the oven to 400°F. Line a 14-inch by 16-inch baking sheet with foil, shiny side up, and coat with vegetable spray, or use a silicone liner.

2. Split crackers in half and soak in ice water for 7 minutes. Remove crackers from water, place in a single layer on prepared pan, and dot with butter. Bake 40 to 45 minutes, or until crackers are brown and crispy. Check crackers occasionally during baking and turn down heat if they brown too quickly. Serve hot with soup and chowders. Store between sheets of wax paper in a tightly covered tin.

1 (8-oz.) package Vermont Common Crackers

Ice water

½ cup butter, cut into dice

TIPS & TOUCHES

- Broken crackers can be crushed with a rolling pin and used for breading chicken or fish, for stuffing, or for meatloaf.

Sheffield tray, English, early 20th century; Silver napkin rings, American and English, late 19th, early 20th century

THE COUNTRY KITCHEN

SUNDAY NIGHT SUPPERS

The SUNDAY NIGHT SUPPERS Cook Book

COMPLETE SUNDAY MENUS AND RECIPES

RE

36 WAYS to Serve BACON

ARMOUR AND COMPANY
CHICAGO

SEA FOODS
With the tang of the Sea
HOW TO PREPARE AND SERVE THEM
DAVIS CO. (CENTRAL WHARF) GLOUCESTER, MASS.

250 POULTRY Specialties

Bird lore: The "know how" of selecting, preparing, cooking, serving and garnishing—clearly presented for year-round use.

A "HOOK-UP"

CHAPTER 6

HOME PLATES

Some call them main dishes or entrees. We call
them home plates because these are the
recipes that represent what eating at home is all
about. Not all meals come with soup or salad.
Some might not even have dessert, but all meals
have a course that seems to invite us to the table.
Whether the table is set with a lace cloth
and fine silver, or it's just a worn enamel work
surface, the steaming plate of food on top
of it connects us to all that nourishes and
comforts us in the home kitchen. • Of all the
living recipes we've collected, we've never
found one that tells us to start with a five-pound
fillet roast. It's usually the humble piece of
chuck, the brisket, the shoulder of lamb—the less
expensive cuts—that blossom into succulent
home plates when treated to the tender loving

care of the braising, stewing, hashing, or boiling of the home cook. The rib roast, the turkey, or the goose is always saved for special occasions, those holidays or celebrations when family and friends congregate.

When we embark on an heirloom adventure with fish or poultry, the fish might be canned; the poultry might be what's on sale. Thrifty and filling have always been the standards of heirloom cooking. If a home plate was simple to make, that was even better, but it wasn't until women started to work outside the home that they were more willing to use convenience foods such as garlic powder and canned tomato soup, or buy appliances such as blenders, food processors, and electric mixers to replace the meat grinders, raisin seeders, and bean shredders they'd been using to shortcut their time at the stove.

Because so many of the creators of manuscript cookbooks had made the journey from old world to new, they often brought with them the legacy of recipes passed from mother to daughter in the old country. The recipes for Irish Lamb Stew, Sauerbraten, Swedish Meatballs, Stuffed Cabbage, and Welsh Rarebit were transported to new homes, treasured, and

Baster, American, 1920s –1930s; papier maché candy containers, German, 1890s–1920s fish, turkey, and ham

prepared again and again in home kitchens. The Asselin family's *tortière*, Arline Ryan's Swedish Meatballs with Sour Cream Sauce, and Bunny Peluso Slobodzinski's Stuffed Cabbage with Salt Pork Gravy are just a few of these heirloom recipes we re-created in our own home kitchen.

The originators of manuscript cookbooks, always mindful of their household budgets, constructed menus that often featured ground beef, pork, and veal, which once were inexpensive ingredients. Meatloaf was the pizza of the 1930s, and casseroles, with their formulaic composition, were the mainstay of the home kitchen. Following the rules of combining a starch (such as rice, potatoes, or pasta) and a liquid (such as gravy, stock, or milk) with leftover meat, chicken, fish, or beans, the home cook could put together a tasty, satisfying dish in minutes, leave it in the oven for an hour or less, and serve a succulent home plate for supper.

For those who chose not to eat meat, fish, or poultry for philosophical, dietary, or monetary reasons, the casserole was often the answer to the vegetarian's question of what to serve. Clever tricks such as adding homemade bread crumbs to a frittata or combining onions and olives in a savory pie made vegetarian home plates appealing.

We salute the ingenious and loving home cooks whose home plates sustained their families during hard times and helped them to celebrate good times.

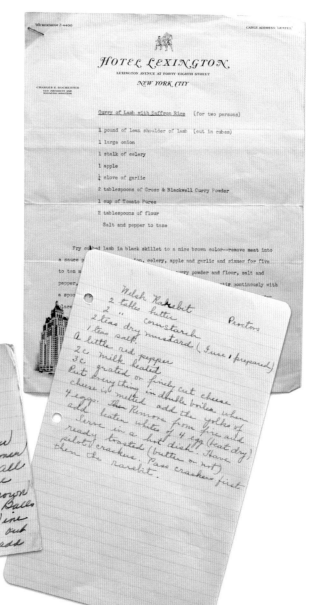

KATHERINE'S SHEPHERD'S PIE

YIELD: 12 SERVINGS

FOR CARAMELIZED ONIONS

2 tablespoons extra-virgin olive oil

2½ cups chopped onion

1 teaspoon salt

5 oz. (⅔ cup) water

FOR FILLING

2 tablespoons extra-virgin olive oil

2 lbs. ground lamb

½ teaspoon dried thyme

1 teaspoon coarsely ground
   black pepper

½ teaspoon Worcestershire sauce

1 teaspoon chopped fresh parsley

¾ cup low-sodium beef stock,
   or as needed

1 tablespoon Wondra quick-mixing
   flour, or as needed

FOR POTATO TOPPING

4 large potatoes, peeled, cut in
   quarters, and cooked in boiling
   water until tender

1 teaspoon salt

2 eggs, beaten

⅛ teaspoon nutmeg

½ cup heavy cream

TIPS & TOUCHES

- Place the mashed potatoes
  in a sturdy plastic bag. Snip
  off a corner diagonally with
  scissors to pipe potatoes.
- Always discard a used pastry
  bag or plastic bag because of
  possible raw egg contamination.

WE FOUND THIS RECIPE IN A MANUSCRIPT COOKBOOK *that contained several hearty "man-pleasing" recipes. Since the recipe book with its categorized sections was inscribed to "Katherine and Fred," this came as no surprise. The recipe for Corned Beef Hash (page 175) was in the same section. Shepherd's Pie has a British heritage, but a similar pie made with ground beef is known as cottage pie in England. You can substitute ground beef for the ground lamb in this recipe, and the resulting pies will both be wonderful!*

1. To make the caramelized onions: Heat olive oil in a large frying pan over medium heat. Add onion and salt and cook, stirring with a wooden spoon, until translucent, 5 to 7 minutes. Reduce heat to low, add water, cover, and cook another 5 minutes, checking occasionally to be sure onions are not catching on bottom of pan. Remove cover, turn heat to medium, and stir with wooden spoon. Continue cooking until water is completely evaporated and onion is golden brown. Remove to a bowl and set aside.

2. Set the oven rack in the middle position. Preheat the oven to 400°F. Coat a 9-inch by 13-inch ovenproof glass baking dish with vegetable spray.

3. To make the filling: Add olive oil to frying pan and heat over medium heat. Add lamb and cook until no longer pink. Add caramelized onions, thyme, pepper, Worcestershire sauce, parsley, and beef stock. Stir with wooden spoon to combine. Add flour, reduce heat to low, and cook, stirring, until flour is absorbed and mixture thickens, approximately 3 to 5 minutes. Adjust consistency of gravy to your taste, adding more stock or flour as needed. Scrape mixture into prepared dish.

4. For the potato topping: Place potatoes in a potato ricer or mash in bowl until smooth. Add salt, eggs, nutmeg, and cream and stir well to combine. Spoon potato mixture into a disposable pastry bag fitted with a rosette tip. Pipe potatoes over top of pie until it is completely covered. Bake 25 minutes, or until potatoes are golden brown. Cover with foil if potatoes brown too quickly. Serve immediately. Cover leftover shepherd's pie with plastic wrap and store in the refrigerator.

EGGPLANT LASAGNA

YIELD: 12 SERVINGS

1¼ to 1½ lbs. eggplant

2 teaspoons salt (or 1½ teaspoons salt if not draining eggplant)

2 large eggs

1 cup flour

6 tablespoons extra-virgin olive oil

¼ teaspoon coarsely ground black pepper

4 to 5 cups of Mary Gualdelli's Tomato Sauce (page 171)

8 oz. provolone cheese, sliced

12 oz. mozzarella cheese, grated

SOMETIME IN THE 1950s, *two women from different cultures met—The Church Lady, from Mansfield, Ohio, and an Italian woman named Mary Gualdelli. The two women shared a common interest in cooking and this recipe passed between them. Eggplant Lasagna was probably a little exotic for the Midwest, but The Church Lady, an accomplished home cook and baker, knew a good thing when she tasted it.*

1. Peel eggplant and cut crosswise into ⅜-inch-thick slices. Sprinkle slices with salt, layer them in a metal colander, and set colander in sink (see Salting Eggplant before Frying on page 169). Set a heavy glass plate on top of eggplant and weight with heavy cans of food. Let drain for 30 minutes to 1 hour. Rinse eggplant slices under cold, running water to wash off excess salt. Pat dry with paper towels.

2. Beat eggs in deep plate or shallow bowl. Place flour on another plate. Dip eggplant slices in egg, dip in flour to coat, and set aside. Heat 2 tablespoons of the olive oil in a large frying pan over medium heat. Add a layer of eggplant slices, sprinkle with pepper (and salt, if you have

Wooden noodle rolling pins, American, 20th century; wooden pie crimpers, American and English, 1890s–1900s

SALTING EGGPLANT BEFORE FRYING

Some recipes suggest that sliced eggplant be salted and drained in a colander to remove excess liquid. Removing this liquid prevents the eggplant from soaking up excess oil when it is fried. When using this method, moderately salt the eggplant slices and place them in colander in the sink or on a deep plate. Set another heavy glass plate on top of eggplant and place cans of food on top to weight the eggplant. Allow the eggplant to drain for 30 minutes to 1 hour. Rinse the slices under running water to wash off excess salt and pat dry with paper towels before frying. Some cooks believe that salting and draining eggplant will remove any bitter juices. The larger varieties of eggplant have more moisture than smaller varieties. Many home cooks do not salt and drain their eggplant.

not drained the eggplant), and cook until nicely browned, 3 to 4 minutes each side. Remove to a platter. Continue to sauté the remaining eggplant slices in batches, adding the remaining olive oil to pan as needed.

3. Set the oven rack in the middle position. Preheat the oven to 350° F. Coat a 9-inch by 13-inch ovenproof glass baking dish with vegetable spray. Line a baking sheet with foil.

4. Spread a layer of tomato sauce over bottom of prepared baking dish. Arrange half of eggplant slices on top. Spread with another layer of tomato sauce. Cover with a layer of Provolone and sprinkle with grated mozzarella. Add remaining eggplant slices in a second layer, spread with tomato sauce, cover with remaining provolone, and sprinkle with remaining mozzarella. Press down gently so that layers adhere.

5. Coat a sheet of foil with vegetable spray and place it, oiled side down, over top of lasagna to cover. Set lasagna on prepared baking sheet to catch any sauce that drips. Bake 40 minutes. Uncover and continue baking until lasagna is bubbling and cheeses are melted. Serve lasagna hot. Allow leftovers to cool, cover with paper towels and then plastic wrap, and store in refrigerator.

MARY GUALDELLI'S TOMATO SAUCE

YIELD: ABOUT 12 CUPS   { 1940s }

WE DON'T KNOW JUST WHO MARY GUALDELLI WAS, *but we know that she and The Church Lady, from Mansfield, Ohio, met in the 1940s and exchanged this recipe for Mary's tomato sauce. This sauce was part of Mary's recipe for Eggplant Lasagna (page 168).*

1. Heat 2 tablespoons of the oil in a frying pan over medium heat. Add onion and cook until translucent, 5 to 7 minutes. Remove onion to a large Dutch oven or heavy-bottomed pot. Add beef, pork, and pancetta, if using, to frying pan, add more oil if needed, and cook until meat is still a little pink. Remove to Dutch oven. Add lamb to frying pan along with a little more oil, if needed, and cook until still slightly pink. Remove to Dutch oven.

2. Add tomato puree, tomato paste, and stock to Dutch oven and stir thoroughly. Add salt, pepper, red pepper flakes, garlic, oregano, thyme, parsley, and brown sugar. Cover and bring to a boil over medium heat. Reduce heat and simmer, stirring occasionally, for 2 hours. Uncover and cook until sauce thickens, about 20 minutes more. Check frequently to make sure sauce doesn't burn. Pour sauce into containers and cool to room temperature. Store in covered containers in the refrigerator or freezer.

4 to 6 tablespoons extra-virgin olive oil

3 cups chopped onion

½ lb. ground beef

½ lb. ground pork

3 oz. pancetta, chopped (optional)

½ lb. ground lamb

2 (28-oz.) cans tomato puree

¼ cup tomato paste

2 cups low-sodium beef stock

1½ teaspoons salt

1 teaspoon coarsely ground black pepper

½ teaspoon red pepper flakes

3 cloves garlic, smashed

1 teaspoon dried oregano

½ teaspoon dried thyme

2 tablespoons chopped fresh parsley

4 teaspoons firmly packed brown sugar

TIPS & TOUCHES

- Beef, pork, and lamb do not have to be completely cooked before adding to sauce. As they continue cooking, they will add more flavor to the sauce.

CURRY OF LAMB WITH SAFFRON RICE

{ 1 9 3 0 s — 1 9 4 0 s }   YIELD: 4 SERVINGS

3 tablespoons extra-virgin olive oil

2 lbs. lean lamb shoulder, cut into
  2-inch cubes

2 tablespoons butter, softened to
  room temperature

2½ cups chopped onions

2 cups chopped celery

2¼ cups peeled and chopped
  Granny Smith apple

2 cloves garlic, minced

¼ cup curry powder

¼ cup flour

1 teaspoon salt

½ teaspoon coarsely ground
  black pepper

2 cups canned tomato puree

1 tablespoon lemon juice

1 teaspoon sugar

Saffron Rice (page 173)

WE FOUND THIS RECIPE NEATLY TYPED *on the letterhead of the Hotel Lexington in New York City. From the executive's name on the letterhead we were able to determine approximately when this recipe was passed on from one of the hotel's employees. An American interpretation of an Indian curry, this recipe uses only the basic curry powder available at the time. There are no exotic spice blends in this dish. The use of saffron in the rice was a very trendy touch.*

1. Place the oven rack in the middle position. Preheat the oven to 350°F.
2. Heat olive oil in Dutch oven or heavy-bottomed pot over medium-high heat. Add lamb and cook until nicely browned. Remove to a bowl. Add butter to Dutch oven and reduce heat to medium. Add onion, celery, apple, and garlic and cook until softened, 5 to 10 minutes. Return lamb to pot, add curry powder, flour, salt, and pepper, and cook 2 minutes more, stirring constantly with wooden spoon.
3. Add tomato puree, lemon juice, and sugar. Add enough water to cover lamb. Cover, set in oven, and bake 1 hour. Uncover and continue baking another 30 minutes, or until lamb is very tender. Serve on a bed of Saffron Rice. Store leftover curry in a covered container in the refrigerator.

✈ CURRY POWDER ✈

Curry powder and Garam Masala are two popular Indian spice blends. In India, there was traditionally no such thing as a "curry" powder. Curries were dishes of meat or vegetables cooked in sauce, and every family had its own mix of spices for each particular dish. British colonials, homesick for the dishes that they had eaten in India, brought back a powdered version of these spice mixtures so they could replicate the curries they had enjoyed abroad. Commercial curry powder, available in most grocery stores, gets its signature yellow color from turmeric. Coriander, cumin, turmeric, fenugreek, cinnamon, clove, cardamom, and nutmeg are just a few of the spices used to prepare curry powder. It is suggested that curry powder be added to a dish at the beginning of cooking so that the raw flavor of the spices is cooked out.

SAFFRON RICE

Similar to the recipe for French Risotto (page 107), this rice dish is prepared with butter instead of olive oil. Saffron gives the rice a distinctive yellow color and an exotic taste.

$\frac{1}{8}$ teaspoon saffron

2 cups low-sodium chicken stock or water, divided

1 tablespoon butter, softened to room temperature

$\frac{1}{2}$ cup chopped onion

1 cup long grain white rice

$\frac{1}{2}$ teaspoon of salt

$\frac{1}{2}$ teaspoon coarsely ground black pepper

1. Combine saffron and $\frac{1}{2}$ cup of the stock or water and set aside.

2. Melt butter in heavy-bottomed saucepan over medium heat. Add chopped onion and cook, stirring with wooden spoon, until translucent, 3 to 4 minutes.

3. Add rice, saffron mixture, salt, and pepper to pan and stir. Add remaining 1$\frac{1}{2}$ cups chicken stock or water, bring to a boil, reduce heat to low, and simmer, covered, until rice is tender, 18 minutes. Remove pan from heat and give rice a stir. Cover and let stand 2 minutes. Stir again before serving. **Yield: 6 servings**

Silver salts and spoons, American, early 1900s

Controversial Irish Lamb Stew

{ *1930s—1960s* }   YIELD: 6 SERVINGS

2 lbs. (3 to 4 large) boiling
  potatoes, peeled

½ teaspoon salt

½ teaspoon coarsely ground
  black pepper

3 tablespoons chopped fresh
  parsley, plus extra for garnish

Leaves from 10 sprigs fresh thyme

2 lbs. shoulder lamb chops,
  trimmed of excess fat

1 cup chopped (¼-inch) leeks,
  white part only

½ cup chopped onion

2½ cups low-sodium beef stock

6 medium carrots, peeled and cut
  into 1-inch chunks

Tips & Touches

- The thin potato slices
  dissolve during cooking to
  thicken the gravy.
- Lamb stew is better served
  the next day. Pour off cooking
  juices and allow to cool in
  refrigerator so that excess fat
  can be skimmed from surface.
  Reheat stew with juices over
  gentle heat.
- You can also use lamb neck
  meat for the stew. It is
  more economical and has
  a good flavor.

WE FOUND THAT THERE ARE AS MANY WAYS *to make an Irish Stew as there are recipes. Some cooks vote for potatoes as a thickener. Some say that the carrots should be prepared separately or not used at all. Some cooks, like Dan Carey, of Belmont, Massachusetts, even use beef instead of lamb, but call it an Irish Stew. Whether you use leeks or thyme or onions, a big bowl of this stew topped with chopped fresh parsley will warm and fortify you.*

1. Cut one of the potatoes into ¼-inch-thick slices. Cut remaining potatoes into large chunks. Layer sliced potatoes over the bottom of a large Dutch oven or a large heavy pot. Sprinkle with some salt, pepper, parsley, and thyme. Add a layer of lamb chops and sprinkle with more salt, pepper, parsley, and thyme. Add a layer of leek and a layer of onion, sprinkling each layer with salt, pepper, parsley and thyme. Repeat layers, using potato chunks instead of slices, and seasoning each layer as before, to use all of the potatoes and lamb chops.

2. Add stock, pouring it down the inside of the pot. Cover pot and bring stew to a boil. Reduce heat and simmer until lamb and vegetables are tender, at least 1½ hours.

3. Steam carrot chunks in a covered steamer basket set over simmering water until tender, about 20 minutes. Add to pot with finished stew and stir gently to combine. Serve stew in heated, deep soup bowls, garnished with chopped fresh parsley.

CORNED BEEF HASH

{ *1 9 2 0 s* }

Hash was another way to use leftovers in a creative way. Home cooks always made extra corned beef so that they could serve their families a hot plate of crispy hash. We found several handwritten recipes for corned beef hash, but this is the one that seemed the best to us, simple and tasty. We didn't go in for the fancy flipping, we just turned the hash in the pan when the bottom got crusty. This recipe is easily doubled for larger portions. It is very nice served with a poached egg and ketchup.

2 cups chopped corned beef

1 cup chopped cooked potato

¼ cup minced onion

½ teaspoon salt

¼ teaspoon coarsely ground
   black pepper

¼ cup low-sodium beef stock,
   heavy cream, or water

1 tablespoon butter, softened
   to room temperature

1 tablespoon extra-virgin olive oil
   or vegetable oil

1 tablespoon chopped fresh parsley

1. Place corned beef, potato, onion, salt, pepper in a bowl. Add beef stock, cream, or water. Mix gently with a wooden spoon to combine and set aside.

2. Heat butter and oil in a 10-inch frying pan over low heat and swirl to coat bottom of pan. Add corned beef mixture and flatten with spatula. Cook until bottom of hash is crispy. Cut hash into sections to make flipping easier. Flip over with a spatula. Press down gently with spatula and cook until bottom is crispy. Turn out hash onto a serving dish and sprinkle with parsley.

TIPS & TOUCHES

* This recipe is just a starting point. You can add more potatoes or different herbs. You can chop the corn beef and vegetables fine or in slightly larger pieces.

Copper saucepan, American, early 1900s

Glazed Corned Beef from Michigan

{ 1930s }

We found this handwritten recipe *on an index card from Michigan. This is the type of dish we could prepare in minutes, stick in a pot, let cook, and serve, while looking as if we spent the afternoon eating bonbons. Although the original called for glazing with white corn syrup, being New Englanders, we decided to use a maple syrup–mustard glaze. No one has complained.*

1. To make the corned beef: Coat an ovenproof baking dish with vegetable spray. Rinse corned beef under cold running water and pat dry with paper towels. Place corned beef in a large heavy pot. Add cold water to cover. Add orange slices, onion, celery, garlic, dill seeds, rosemary, cloves, bay leaf, and cinnamon. Add cold water to cover. Stir until spices are evenly distributed. Cover pot and bring to simmer over medium heat; do not boil. Simmer, covered, stirring occasionally, until a fork penetrates meat easily, approximately 3 to 4 hours (about 1 hour per lb. of meat). Remove corned beef from pot and place, fatty side up, on prepared baking dish. Set aside.

2. To make the glaze: Place maple syrup, mustard, and pepper in a heavy-bottomed saucepan and whisk to combine. Cook over medium heat, stirring with a wooden spoon, until glaze comes to a boil. Reduce heat and continue stirring until glaze reduces and thickens, approximately 3 minutes.

3. Preheat the oven to 375° F. Brush half of glaze over corned beef. Bake 8 minutes. Turn corned beef fatty side down, brush with remaining glaze, and return to oven to bake 8 minutes more. Remove to a serving platter and allow to rest 10 minutes before slicing. Cut against the grain to prevent slices from falling apart. Cover leftovers with plastic wrap and store in the refrigerator.

FOR CORNED BEEF

3 to 4 lbs. corned beef brisket

1 orange, sliced

2 large onions, quartered

3 stalks celery, cut in 1-inch pieces

2 cloves garlic, quartered

1 teaspoon dill seeds

3 sprigs fresh rosemary, or
  ½ teaspoon dried rosemary

6 whole cloves

1 bay leaf

3-inch stick cinnamon, or
  ½ teaspoon cinnamon

FOR GLAZE

¾ cup maple syrup

3 tablespoons prepared mustard

½ teaspoon coarsely ground
  black pepper

EASTER MEATLOAF

{ *1920s–1970s* }   YIELD: 10 SLICES

FOR MEATLOAF

1 medium boiling potato, grated

1 cup fine bread crumbs

2 tablespoons dried parsley

1 teaspoon paprika

1 teaspoon garlic powder

1 teaspoon salt

½ teaspoon coarsely ground
    black pepper

1 cup red wine

1½ lbs. ground beef

½ cup chopped onion

2 eggs, beaten

⅓ cup ketchup

3 tablespoons Dijon mustard

4 large eggs, hard-cooked

FOR TOPPING

2 teaspoon dried parsley

¼ teaspoon garlic powder

ALTHOUGH WE FOUND SEVERAL REFERENCES *to this particular meatloaf while reading our collection of manuscript cookbooks, this recipe has special significance for us. This is the meatloaf Marilynn made for friends at Easter in the early 1970s. Most of the guests were students away from home. Money was tight and kitchen resources were few, but she volunteered to make the holiday dinner which featured slices of this appealing meatloaf. The hard-cooked eggs in each slice make a nice presentation.*

1. To make the meatloaf: Set the oven rack in the middle position. Preheat the oven to 350°F. Line the bottom and narrow ends of a 9-inch by 5-inch by 3-inch loaf pan with a single strip of parchment, allowing a 1- to 2-inch overhang at each end. Coat pan and liner with vegetable spray.

HOW TO MAKE
⤏ FINE BREAD CRUMBS ⤎

There is nothing like the flavor of homemade bread crumbs. They are essential to heirloom recipes for meat loaves, frittatas, and some pastries.

Set oven for 300°F. Place slices of dry white bread or brioche on jelly roll pans and set on middle and lower racks of oven. Bake 1 hour. Turn slices, and bake until bread is very dry, about 1 hour longer. Break bread into pieces and place in the bowl of a food processor fitted with the metal blade. Pulse to form fine crumbs. Put crumbs through a strainer to remove hard pieces. Store bread crumbs in a plastic bag in the refrigerator or freezer. Label and date the contents of the bag. Dry bread crumbs can also be made using a grater or by crumbing in a blender.

2. Squeeze grated potato in clean white dish towel to remove excess liquid. Place grated potato, bread crumbs, parsley, paprika, garlic powder, salt, pepper, and wine in a bowl and stir with a wooden spoon. Add ground beef, onion, eggs, ketchup, and mustard and mix thoroughly with your hands. Do not overmix or meatloaf will be tough.

3. Place half of meatloaf mixture in prepared pan and smooth the top. Arrange shelled hard-cooked eggs in a line on top of meatloaf and gently press down on eggs to anchor them. Place remaining meatloaf mixture on top of eggs. Smooth the top.

4. To make the topping: Mix parsley with garlic powder and sprinkle over meatloaf. Bake about 1 hour and 30 minutes, or until meatloaf pulls away from the sides of pan, bubbles around the edges, and an instant-read thermometer inserted in center of the meatloaf registers 160°F. Grasp both ends of parchment liner and lift meatloaf from pan. Let stand for 5 minutes. Cut into slices and serve.

Wire egg holder, American, 1890s-1900s

Dale's Meatloaf

YIELD: 10 SLICES

1 lb. ground beef

6 oz. loose sausage meat

1¼ cups chopped onion

1 cup fine bread crumbs
(see How to Make Fine Bread
Crumbs on page 178)

1 cup milk

3 large eggs

1 teaspoon salt

½ teaspoon coarsely ground
black pepper

⅛ teaspoon poultry seasoning

1 (10¾-oz.) can tomato soup

2½ strips bacon

4 strips green pepper
(½-inch wide, cut vertically)

TIPS & TOUCHES

- Meatloaf is better the day after it is made. Leftover cold meatloaf makes wonderful sandwiches.
- To tell if a meatloaf is properly seasoned, fry a small patty of raw meatloaf mix to sample. Never taste food containing uncooked egg, poultry, meat, or fish.

WE ASKED A LADY IN MAINE *for her meatloaf recipe after hearing her son reminisce about the meatloaf she made for him when he was growing up in Connecticut. This is a dense meatloaf, more like a paté. It should be cooled before being cut, but in a pinch it can be served hot after it rests for ten minutes. The sausage mixed with the ground beef, and the touch of poultry seasoning, make all the difference.*

1. Set the oven rack in the middle position. Preheat the oven to 400°F. Line the bottom and narrow ends of a 9-inch by 5-inch by 3-inch loaf pan with a single strip of parchment, allowing a 1- to 2-inch overhang at each end. Coat pan and liner with vegetable spray.

2. Combine ground beef and sausage meat in a large bowl. Set aside.

3. In a smaller bowl, combine onion, bread crumbs, milk, eggs, salt, pepper, and poultry seasoning.

4. Working quickly with your hands, add bread crumb mixture to meat and mix to combine. Do not overwork or meatloaf will be tough. Add half of the tomato soup and quickly combine.

5. Place meatloaf in prepared pan. Spread remaining tomato soup over top. Cut strips of bacon in half and arrange alternating strips of bacon and green pepper over top of meatloaf. Bake 1 hour. Turn off oven and let meatloaf stand in oven another 30 minutes, or until an instant-read thermometer inserted in the center of the meatloaf registers 160°F.

6. Remove meatloaf from oven and cool in pan on a rack for 30 minutes. Grasp both ends of parchment liner and lift meatloaf from pan. To serve, cut meatloaf into slices, place in a baking pan, cover with foil, and set in 350°F oven until heated through, 5 to 10 minutes.

SAUERBRATEN

{ 1 9 4 0 s }

YIELD: 8 SERVINGS

FOR BRINING

4- to 5-lb. beef chuck roast

2 cups white vinegar

2 cups water

3 bay leaves

1 onion, cut in quarters

2 carrots, cut in ½-inch rounds

1 cup chopped celery leaves
   or celery

1 large clove garlic, minced

1 teaspoon cinnamon

1 teaspoon whole cloves

1 teaspoon whole allspice, or
   ½ teaspoon ground allspice

1½ teaspoons salt

½ teaspoon coarsely ground
   black pepper

1 lemon, sliced, with pits removed

FOR BRAISING

1 slice bacon

2 tablespoons extra-virgin olive oil,
   or as needed

1 cup chopped celery

Reserved onion and carrot from brine

1½ cups reserved strained brine

1 slice (½-inch) rye or
   pumpernickel bread

FOR GRAVY

7½ cups low-sodium beef stock

¼ cup flour

3 tablespoons firmly packed
   brown sugar

WE FOUND THIS RECIPE HANDWRITTEN *on an index card from Ohio. Making Sauerbraten can seem daunting at first; dividing the recipe into three steps—brining, braising, and making gravy—renders the recipe more doable. We learned from our friend Mike Ripley that his aunt, Ruth Geywitz, who lives in Stuttgart, Germany, has been making sauerbraten for almost sixty years from an almost identical recipe. Ruth adds the bacon when she braises her sauerbraten. This dish is wonderful served on a bed of Mike's Mother's Spaetzle (page 160) to soak up the rich gravy.*

1. To brine the sauerbraten: Rinse beef chuck under cold running water and pat dry with paper towels. Poke holes all over meat with small sharp knife. Place in a nonreactive glass or stainless steel bowl. Combine vinegar and water in a large pot and bring to a boil. Lower heat and add bay leaves, onion, carrots, celery, garlic, cinnamon, cloves, allspice, salt, pepper, and lemon slices and stir to combine. Bring to a boil again and boil an additional 5 minutes. Pour brine over meat. Turn meat once, cover with plastic wrap, and refrigerate for 3 to 4 days, turning at least twice a day.

2. Remove meat from brine, pat dry with paper towels, and set aside. Strain and reserve brine, onion, and carrot. Discard lemon, spices, celery or celery tops, and garlic.

3. To braise the sauerbraten: Fry bacon in a large Dutch oven or heavy-bottomed pot over medium heat until it starts to give off fat. Add olive oil and meat and cook until nicely browned and crusty all over, about 5 minutes each side. Add more oil if necessary. Remove meat to platter. Add celery to Dutch oven and cook, stirring with a wooden spoon, until softened, about 7 minutes.

4. Return meat to Dutch oven, fatty side down. Add reserved onion and carrot from brine. Add water to come about one third of the way up the side of the meat. Add the reserved brine. Break bread slice into pieces and add to Dutch oven.

5. Bring to a boil, reduce heat, and simmer, covered, turning sauerbraten every hour, until tender, 2½ to 3 hours. Remove to a serving platter and allow to cool for at least 20 minutes while you make the gravy.

6. To make the gravy: Strain and reserve braising liquid. Discard vegetables. Bring beef or chicken stock to a simmer in a large saucepan. Measure ½ cup braising liquid into small bowl and refrigerate until chilled. Add flour to cooled braising liquid and whisk to combine. Whisk flour mixture and brown sugar into simmering stock and cook until it thickens to the consistency of gravy.

7. Cut sauerbraten into slices against the grain and serve with gravy and Mike's Mother's Spaetzle (page 160). Sauerbraten is even better the next day. Refrigerate meat and gravy separately. Place plastic wrap directly on the surface of gravy to prevent skin from forming.

TIPS & TOUCHES

- We tried this recipe with top round roast and chuck roast. We prefer using chuck. If you use top round, braise for at least 3 hours and cut slices against the grain.
- Mike's Aunt Ruth uses a mixture of ½ cup sour cream, 3 tablespoons of flour, and ¼ cup water in lieu of our mixture of chilled braising liquid and flour to make her gravy; add the mixture to the simmering stock and cook the gravy exactly the same way.

Sauerbraten

4.- pound round steak
2 cups vinegar
2 cups water
3 bay leaves
1 teasp. whole cloves
1 teasp. whole allspice
1½ teasp. salt
½ teasp. pepper
1 lemon sliced

1 kernal garlic
1 cup. onions, sliced
Celery tops
2 carrots sliced
Crust of rye bread
6 tblsp. butter
1 cup flour
2 teasp. salt
5 cups stock (?)
¼ cup sugar

1- Heat the vinegar & water to the boiling point. Then add the cloves, allspice, the 1½ teasp salt, the ½ teasp.

Romanian Stuffed Cabbage

{ 1930s }

YIELD: 21 PIECES

2½- to 3-lb. cabbage

FOR SAUCE

1½ cups tomato sauce

2 tablespoons ketchup

½ cup lemon juice

¾ cup firmly packed brown sugar

1 cup golden raisins

FOR FILLING

2 large eggs

½ cup fine bread crumbs
(see How to Make Fine Bread
Crumbs on page 178)

1 teaspoon firmly packed
brown sugar

1 teaspoon salt

½ teaspoon coarsely ground
black pepper

½ teaspoon paprika

1½ lbs. ground beef

1 cup finely chopped onion

2 cloves garlic, minced or
1 teaspoon garlic powder

2 tablespoons fresh parsley,
chopped, or 1 tablespoon
dried parsley

¼ cup tomato sauce

¼ cup ketchup

THIS IS THE RECIPE FOR STUFFED CABBAGE *we grew up with. Our mother Dorothy made the true Romanian version, which uses tomatoes, brown sugar, and raisins. Preparation took several hours, but we all felt it was worth it. Because Sheila did not eat raisins then, our mother went into "restaurant mode" and made a separate pot of stuffed cabbage without raisins just for her. The recipe uses one 15-oz. can of tomato sauce, which is divided between the sauce (1½ cup) and the filling (¼ cup).*

1. To prepare the cabbage: Remove 3 or 4 outer leaves from the cabbage head, chop coarsely, and set aside. Cut out the core of cabbage in a cone-shaped section. Bring water to a boil in large heavy pot. Add the head of cabbage until fully immersed and let stand off the heat for 4 minutes. Remove cabbage head to a platter. Using a long-handled fork, carefully remove the leaves from the head, keeping them whole. They should be pliable enough to come off easily. If not, return the cabbage head to the pot and let stand in the hot water until the leaves come away easily.

2. Cut out the hard center spine from each leaf, and discard. Cut any very large leaves in half. Dry leaves on paper towels and set aside. Coarsely chop any leaves that are too small to stuff and set aside with the rest of the chopped cabbage.

3. Set the oven rack in the middle position. Preheat the oven to 350°F. Coat a 9-inch by 13-inch ovenproof glass baking dish with vegetable spray.

4. To make the sauce: Combine tomato sauce, ketchup, lemon juice, brown sugar, and golden raisins in a saucepan. Bring to a boil, reduce heat, and simmer for 15 minutes to blend flavors. Remove from heat and set aside.

5. To make the filling: Beat eggs in a large bowl. Add bread crumbs, brown sugar, salt, pepper, and paprika and stir to combine. Add ground beef, onion, garlic or garlic powder, parsley, tomato sauce, and ketchup and mix well with hands.

6. To stuff the cabbage: Place each cabbage leaf on a flat surface and spoon ¼ cup of filling in the center. Fold edges of cabbage leaf in toward center to enclose meat in a neat package. If a cabbage leaf is too small to contain meat filling, overlap it with another halved leaf or overlap two smaller leaves.

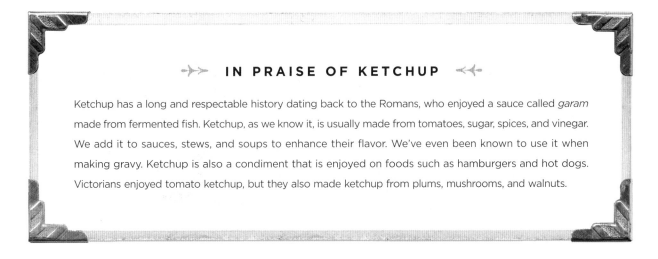

IN PRAISE OF KETCHUP

Ketchup has a long and respectable history dating back to the Romans, who enjoyed a sauce called *garam* made from fermented fish. Ketchup, as we know it, is usually made from tomatoes, sugar, spices, and vinegar. We add it to sauces, stews, and soups to enhance their flavor. We've even been known to use it when making gravy. Ketchup is also a condiment that is enjoyed on foods such as hamburgers and hot dogs. Victorians enjoyed tomato ketchup, but they also made ketchup from plums, mushrooms, and walnuts.

7. Spread about half of the sauce over the bottom of the prepared baking dish. Add stuffed cabbage leaves, seams down, in a single layer. Pour remaining sauce over stuffed leaves. Bake about 1 hour, or until filling is cooked through and sauce is bubbling.

TIPS & TOUCHES

- If you have extra meat mixture, shape into meatballs and place in the pan between stuffed cabbage leaves. Bake as above.

Toy cast iron stove, American, early 1900s; toy tin saucepan, 1890s–1900s

Alice McGinty's London Broil

{ 1960s }

Alice McGinty gave Marilynn her recipe *for a London broil marinade forty years ago when they were both working at a research and development laboratory in Cambridge, Massachusetts. Alice went on to earn a doctorate in history from Tufts University, and she continues to teach well into her eighties. Her London broil marinade uses gin and brown sugar, and there is no doubt this recipe will go down in history. Alice McGinty's London Broil can be either broiled or grilled.*

1. Rinse steak under running water, pat dry with paper towels, and set aside.

2. To make the marinade: Combine olive oil, garlic, brown sugar, wine vinegar, lemon juice, soy sauce, gin, and black pepper in a large nonreactive stainless steel or glass bowl. Place steak in a heavy-duty plastic bag, add marinade, and close securely. Place sealed bag in a nonreactive glass dish in refrigerator for 8 hours or overnight. Shake and turn bag at least three times while steak is marinating.

3. Set the oven rack 6 inches from broiler. Set oven temperature to broil. Line a metal baking pan with foil. If using an outdoor grill, follow the manufacturer's instructions for heating.

4. Remove steak from plastic bag and place on prepared pan or grill. Brush steak on both sides with marinade and discard marinade. Broil or grill for 4 minutes on each side for medium-rare. Remove steak from oven or grill and allow to rest 10 to 15 minutes. Carve against the grain into thin slices and serve. Cover leftovers with plastic wrap and store in the refrigerator.

1½- to 2-lb. flank steak, 1-inch thick

FOR MARINADE

½ cup extra-virgin olive oil

3 cloves garlic, smashed and peeled

¾ cup firmly packed brown sugar

½ cup red wine vinegar

Juice of 2 lemons

⅓ cup soy sauce

3 tablespoons gin

1 teaspoon coarsely ground
  black pepper

Tips & Touches

- London Broil should not be cooked to well-done. It will be too dry.
- Carving against the grain means carving on the diagonal.
- London Broil does not refer to a cut of beef. It refers to a method of cooking beef.

187

BRISKET

YIELD: 8 SERVINGS

4- to 5-lb. brisket

⅓ cup firmly packed brown sugar

2 teaspoons paprika

2 teaspoons kosher salt

1 teaspoon coarsely ground
    black pepper

2 tablespoons extra-virgin olive oil

2½ cups coarsely chopped onion

2 cups chopped carrot

2½ cups low-sodium beef stock

1½ cups red wine or sherry

¾ cup apricot jam

¼ cup ginger jam

½ cup ketchup

3 tablespoons tomato paste

½ teaspoon chopped hot chilies

1 teaspoon prepared mustard

3 to 4 cloves garlic, peeled and
    minced

6 medium boiling potatoes, peeled
    and quartered (optional)

BRISKET HAS ALWAYS BEEN A FAVORITE CHOICE *for holiday meals. It pretty much cooks itself in its braising liquid, and it's better the next day, so we recommend preparing it ahead and reheating it. Brisket used to be an inexpensive cut that served several people and provided a respectable amount of leftovers. There are as many brisket recipes as there are home cooks. We've reviewed multiple brisket recipes and found the common denominator to be a mix of sweet and sour ingredients, the aromatics—onions, carrots, and garlic— and a tomato-based braising liquid.*

1. Set the oven rack in the middle position. Preheat the oven to 375°F. Line a large roasting pan with foil and coat with vegetable spray.

2. Rinse brisket under cold, running water and pat dry with paper towels. Place brisket in prepared pan, lean side up.

3. Combine brown sugar, paprika, salt, and pepper in a small bowl. Rub half of seasoning mixture over top of brisket. Bake, uncovered, for 15 minutes. Remove pan from oven and turn brisket fatty side up. Carefully spread remaining seasoning mixture over brisket with the back of a tablespoon. Return to oven and bake, uncovered, for another 15 minutes.

4. Meanwhile, heat oil in a large frying pan over medium heat. Add onion and carrot and cook until slightly limp, about 5 minutes. Remove from heat, cover, and set aside.

5. Whisk beef stock, wine or sherry, apricot jam, ginger jam, ketchup, tomato paste, chilies, and mustard in a large bowl until blended.

6. Remove roasting pan from oven. Pour stock mixture into pan. Lift brisket with tongs to allow liquid to flow underneath. Scatter some of the cooked onion and carrot on bottom of pan and set brisket on top. Sprinkle brisket with half of garlic and remaining onion and carrot. Add the rest of the garlic to pan. Cover pan tightly with foil. Reduce oven temperature to 325°F, return brisket to oven, and bake until fork tender, about 4 hours. Add potatoes, if using, 3 hours into the cooking, lifting foil carefully.

➤➤ ALL ABOUT BRISKET ◄◄

Brisket is a cut that comes from the breast section of the cow. It is usually cut into two sections: the flat cut, which is leaner, and the point cut, which contains more fat. The additional fat gives the point cut more flavor than the flat cut. Brisket responds well to long, hot, moist braising, which causes tough fibers to disintegrate into meltingly delicious meat. There seem to be as many ways to prepare brisket as there are cooks. Some recipes suggest a dry rub and a sear before braising. Others add carrots, potatoes, and onions. Some add tomato or chili sauce, coupled with a packet of instant onion soup, while others use prepared cranberry sauce or kosher wine. Some home cooks even marinate and baste their brisket with Coca-Cola. Brisket at its best is a succulent cut of beef with glorious gravy.

7. Remove pan from oven. Transfer brisket to a platter, set platter on a rack, and cool to room temperature, about 25 minutes. Remove potatoes, if used, to another platter.

8. Strain braising liquid into a clean bowl, reserving carrot and onion. Place carrot and onion in the bowl of a food processor fitted with the metal blade. Pulse to puree. Add pureed vegetables to braising liquid and whisk to blend; pureed vegetables will thicken gravy. Store cooled gravy in a covered container in the refrigerator. When brisket is completely cooled, cut into slices against the grain and cover with plastic wrap and then with foil. Cover potatoes with plastic wrap. Refrigerate gravy, brisket, and potatoes overnight.

9. The next day, place gravy, brisket slices, and potatoes in a large frying pan, cover, and cook over low heat until heated through, 5 to 7 minutes.

Tips & Touches

- For the best flavor, always cook a brisket the day before you plan to serve it.
- Remove any fat that rises to top of gravy after refrigerating it.

CREOLE VEAL CHOPS

YIELD: 4 TO 6 SERVINGS

6 tablespoons extra-virgin olive oil

1½ cups coarsely chopped onion

3 pounds shoulder veal chops

1 cup flour

½ teaspoon paprika

¼ teaspoon salt

¼ teaspoon coarsely ground
   black pepper

3 large eggs

2 cups ketchup

2 cups water

3 tablespoons lemon juice

2 teaspoons sugar

¼ cup tomato paste, optional

TIPS & TOUCHES

- If using Dutch oven, you might have to add a little chicken stock to cover chops.
- For a more pronounced tomato flavor, add ¼ cup tomato paste to sauce.

BOTH GRANDMA KATZIFF AND OUR MOTHER *used this recipe for Creole Veal Chops. Since Mama and Grandma Katziff shared a kitchen for five years, the recipe went back and forth between them, with each one adding her own touch. In our family, "Creole" meant using tomato ketchup as a sauce. No one ever traveled to Louisiana, as far as we knew, so we invented our own version of "Creole" cooking. You will have to use two frying pans or a large Dutch oven for this recipe.*

1. Heat 2 tablespoons of the olive oil in a 10-inch frying pan over medium heat. Add onion and cook until brown around the edges, 3 to 5 minutes. Remove onion to a bowl, reserving frying pan.

2. Rinse veal chops under cold, running water and pat dry with paper towels. Place flour, paprika, salt, pepper, and veal chops in large plastic bag, seal, and shake until veal is evenly coated with flour. Remove veal from bag and shake in strainer over the sink to remove excess flour.

3. Beat eggs with a fork on deep plate or shallow bowl. Heat 2 tablespoons olive oil in reserved frying pan over medium heat. Dip chops in beaten egg to coat, add to pan, and cook until crispy, about 5 minutes on each side. Do not crowd veal chops. Heat remaining olive oil in another frying pan of the same size and fry remaining veal chops in same way.

4. Add reserved onions to pans. Whisk together ketchup and water in a large glass measuring cup until smooth. Add lemon juice and sugar and whisk to blend. Divide sauce between both pans and simmer, uncovered 15 minutes. Cover pans, reduce heat to low, and simmer very gently for another 30 minutes. Pieces of egg crust will break off from chops and thicken sauce. Serve with rice or noodles. Store leftover veal chops in a covered container in the refrigerator.

ARLINE RYAN'S SWEDISH MEATBALLS WITH SOUR CREAM SAUCE

{ 1920s }

This heirloom recipe was found handwritten on an index card from Indiana. These delicate meatballs in a sour cream sauce are a wonderful home plate served with wide noodles or rice to make the most of the gravy. This lady knew how to cook one of the best examples of midwestern heirloom cooking. Serve this dish with a salad of torn greens dressed with oil and vinegar.

1. Place veal and pork in the bowl of a food processor fitted with the metal blade. Process until smooth. Add onion, cream or half-and-half, flour, cracker crumbs, nutmeg, salt, pepper, and summer savory. Pulse until texture is almost as smooth as a paste. Remove mixture from food processor and shape into balls, using about 2 tablespoons of meat mixture for each meatball.

2. Heat 1 tablespoon of the butter and 1 tablespoon of the oil in each of two large frying pans over medium heat. Add meatballs and cook, turning with tongs, until evenly browned, 5 to 7 minutes. Add ¼ cup white wine and ½ can of chicken stock to each pan and simmer 5 minutes.

3. Remove pans from heat. Remove meatballs to a platter and set aside. Consolidate all of the cooking juices in one pan. Whisk ¼ cup of the warm pan juices with the flour in a small bowl, return to pan, and whisk to blend. Set pan over low heat and bring to a bare simmer; do not allow sauce to boil. Whisk in sour cream a few tablespoons at a time. Return meatballs to pan and turn in sauce until completely heated through. Place on a serving dish and garnish with chopped fresh parsley.

1½ lbs. ground veal

¾ lb. ground pork

1 cup finely chopped onion

¾ cup light cream or half-and-half

2 tablespoons flour

¾ cups soda cracker crumbs

¾ teaspoon nutmeg

½ teaspoon salt

½ teaspoon coarsely ground black pepper

Pinch of summer savory (optional)

2 tablespoons butter, softened to room temperature

2 tablespoons vegetable oil

½ cup white wine

1 (14½-oz.) can low-sodium chicken stock

2 tablespoons flour

1 pint sour cream

2 tablespoons chopped fresh parsley, for garnish

TIPS & TOUCHES

- Veal and pork should be ground twice if not using a food processor.
- Check sauce for lumps before adding sour cream and strain if necessary.

WISCONSIN BEER-BAKED BEANS WITH SHORT RIBS

{ 1950s }

YIELD: 8 CUPS

2 cups dried navy beans

¾ cup firmly packed brown sugar

1 cup ketchup

1 tablespoon salt

½ teaspoon coarsely ground black pepper

2½ cups chopped onion

1 lb. pork short ribs with bones, sliced between bone to separate

6 oz. beer

TIPS & TOUCHES

- We found that 4 hours, including the boiling time, produced succulent beans with a rich sweet tomato sauce. These beans keep their shape. For a softer texture, bake the beans one hour longer.
- We suggest that you count the ribs before cooking and retrieve the same number of bones before serving.
- To make this recipe in a slow cooker, follow the manufacturer's instructions and adjust the cooking time.

THIS RECIPE COMES FROM OUR AGENT *Karen Johnson's grandmother, Eva Viola Johnson. The dish is a hearty mass of beans, sweeter than the New England recipe, but spicy and rich. Pork short ribs make it more of a main dish than a side. Onions and beer intensify the flavor of the sauce. This recipe is just as appealing as its no-nonsense New England cousin, Boston baked beans.*

1. Place beans in a strainer and pick over for gravel or husks. Rinse under cold water. Place beans in a large nonreactive bowl, add cold water to cover, and let soak overnight. The next day, drain beans and discard soaking water. Rinse beans under cold, running water.

2. Transfer beans to a Dutch oven or heavy-bottomed pot. Add fresh water to cover by about 2 inches. Cover and bring to a boil. Reduce heat slightly so that water continues to boil and cook, stirring occasionally, for 1 hour. Drain beans, reserving 1½ cups of the cooking liquid. Return beans to clean pot and set aside.

3. Set the oven rack in the middle position. Preheat the oven to 350°F.

4. Place bean cooking liquid in a small saucepan. Add brown sugar, ketchup, salt, and pepper. Whisk to combine. Bring mixture to a boil, reduce heat, and simmer 5 minutes. Add sauce to pot with beans and stir. Add onion. Add short ribs, burying them below the surface of the beans and distributing them evenly throughout.

5. Cover pot, place beans in oven, and bake for 2 hours, stirring once every hour. Add beer to beans, mix gently, and bake 1 hour more, or until beans are tender and succulent and sauce is sweet and reduced. Remove pot from oven carefully. Remove ribs from beans with tongs. Remove meat from ribs and return meat to pot. Serve immediately. Store leftover beans in a covered glass or plastic container in the refrigerator.

Bunny Slobodzinski's Stuffed Cabbage with Salt Pork Gravy

{ *1960s* }

YIELD: APPROXIMATELY 20 STUFFED CABBAGE ROLLS

2½- to 3-lb. cabbage

1 (4-inch square) piece salt pork, or 5 oz. piece pancetta (optional)

4 tablespoons extra-virgin olive oil, divided

2 lbs. "fresh cut" or uncured boneless pork butt, trimmed of fat and cut into ½-inch pieces, or 2 lbs. ground pork

1 cup coarsely chopped onion

2 cups cooked long grain rice

2 tablespoons dried parsley

½ teaspoon coarsely ground black pepper

2 cups low-sodium chicken stock

BUNNY PELUSO SLOBODZINSKI MARRIED HER HUSBAND, *Edwin, when she was just twenty-one. Bunny had been brought up in a Neapolitan-American household, but with advice from her mother-in-law, Rosalie, and armed with a copy of a Polish cookbook and a lot of ingenuity, she learned to prepare traditional Polish meals, relying on her new husband to critique the dishes she placed before him. This recipe is based on one Bunny makes. The use of rendered salt pork fat or pancetta for the gravy is optional.*

1. To prepare the cabbage: Remove 3 or 4 outer leaves from the cabbage head, chop coarsely, and set aside. Cut out the core of cabbage in a cone-shaped section. Bring water to a boil in another large heavy pot. Add the head of cabbage until fully immersed and let stand off the heat for 4 minutes. Remove cabbage head to a platter. Using a long-handled fork, carefully remove the leaves from the head, keeping them whole. They should be pliable enough to come off easily. If not, return the cabbage head to the pot and let stand in the hot water until the leaves come away easily.

2. Cut out the hard center spine from each leaf, and discard. Cut any very large leaves in half. Dry leaves on paper towels and set aside. Coarsely chop any leaves that are too small to stuff. Sprinkle all chopped cabbage over bottom of a large Dutch oven or large pot and set aside.

3. If using salt pork, cut off the thick skin and discard. Cut salt pork (or pancetta) into strips or cubes and place in a saucepan. Cook over low heat until fat is rendered, 8 to 10 minutes. Pour off fat carefully into bowl, leaving salt that has collected at the bottom of pan, and set aside.

4. To make the filling: Heat 2 tablespoons of the olive oil in a large, heavy frying pan over medium heat. Add half of the pork and cook until no longer pink. Remove to a large bowl. Add the remaining 2 tablespoons oil and onion and cook over medium heat until onion is brown around the edges, 5 to 7 minutes. Add the rest of the pork and cook until no longer pink. Remove to bowl with the rest of the cooked pork. Add cooked rice, parsley, and pepper and combine.

5. To stuff the cabbage: Place each cabbage leaf on a flat surface and spoon ¼ cup of filling in the center. Fold edges of cabbage leaf in toward center to enclose meat in a neat package. If a cabbage leaf is too small to contain meat filling, overlap it with another halved leaf or overlap two smaller leaves.

6. Place stuffed cabbage, seams down, on top of chopped cabbage leaves in Dutch oven or large heavy-bottomed pot. Pour chicken stock into pot and add enough water to just cover stuffed cabbage. Bring to a simmer, cover, and cook over medium heat for 1½ hours.

7. Remove stuffed cabbage to a platter. Cut 2 slits in each stuffed leaf. Drizzle a bit of rendered fat from salt pork (or pancetta) over stuffed leaves. Serve stuffed cabbage hot. Place leftovers seam-side down in a container, cover with plastic wrap, and refrigerate. Stuffed cabbage can be frozen for up to 6 months. Thoroughly defrost in the refrigerator overnight before serving. Then reheat in frying pan with olive oil or butter.

Tips & Touches

- We substituted the pancetta for the salt pork because it's a little less salty.
- Add ½ teaspoon of salt to the filling if you do not use the salt pork or pancetta.

Silver napkin rings, American, early 20th century

GERMAIN ASSELIN'S STUFFING PIE
(Tourtière)

YIELD: 6 TO 8 SERVINGS

{ 1930s }

THIS RECIPE CAME FROM THE FAMILY OF *Germain Asselin, who passed it on to his daughter Bonnie. Germain Asselin's Stuffing Pie is very similar to the French-Canadian tourtière, or meat pie. His version used more beef to pork, but we changed the proportions to make a heartier version. The Asselins use poultry seasoning, while other versions use a touch of thyme and savory. Bonnie grinds her crackers, but we found that pulsing them in a food processor is as good. French-Canadians serve tourtière at Reveillon celebrations on Christmas Eve and New Year's Eve, but this savory meat pie is especially comforting on cold wintry days.*

1. To prepare the crust: For detailed instructions, see Sheila's Savory Pie Crust on page 248. Coat a 9-inch ovenproof glass pie plate with vegetable spray. Roll out pastry dough. Fit half of the dough into bottom of pie plate and trim off excess. Chill pastry for top and bottom crust in the refrigerator while you make the filling.

2. Heat olive oil in a large frying pan over medium heat. Add onion and shallot and cook, stirring with a wooden spoon, until translucent, 5 to 7 minutes. Do not brown. Add ground pork and beef and sauté, breaking up clumps of meat with wooden spoon, until meat is no longer pink. Remove mixture to a large bowl. Add poultry seasoning, salt, pepper, and cloves. Add cracker flakes and combine. Set mixture aside until cool.

3. Set the oven rack in the middle position. Preheat the oven to 450°F. Line a 14-inch by 16-inch baking sheet with foil, shiny side up, and coat with vegetable spray, or use a silicone liner.

4. Add cooled filling to pie shell. Brush edges of pastry shell with beaten egg. Add top crust and seal and crimp edges. Make 2 slits in center of pie to allow steam to escape. Brush top crust and edges with beaten egg.

5. Place pie on foil-lined baking sheet and bake 30 minutes, or until top is golden brown. Check for browning after 20 minutes. If crust is browning too quickly, cover loosely with foil. Remove pie to a rack and cool slightly. Serve while still hot. Cover cooled leftover pie with a paper towel and plastic wrap and store in the refrigerator.

Pastry for double-crust pie, divided in half and chilled (see Sheila's Savory Pie Crust on page 248)

2 tablespoons extra-virgin olive oil

¼ cup chopped onion

2 tablespoons chopped shallot

1 lb. ground pork

½ lb. ground beef

1 teaspoon poultry seasoning

1 teaspoon salt

½ teaspoon coarsely ground black pepper

¼ teaspoon ground cloves

1 cup crushed soda crackers, pulsed to large flakes in the bowl of a food processor fitted with the metal blade

1 egg, beaten

TIPS & TOUCHES

- Reheat leftover tourtière uncovered in 300°F oven for 20 minutes, or until warmed through.
- Serve slices of tourtière with Dijon mustard or horseradish sauce.
- Reveillon means waking. In French-speaking countries, guests stay up most of the night celebrating Christmas or the New Year.

Deviled Ham and Cheese Strata

{ 1 9 3 0 s }

YIELD: 12 SERVINGS

FOR DEVILED HAM

1 lb. cooked ham

1 cup minced sweet gherkins

½ cup minced onion

½ cup mayonnaise

1 tablespoon dried parsley

1 teaspoon paprika

½ teaspoon chopped, brined hot peppers

1 teaspoon salt

1 teaspoon coarsely ground black pepper

3 cups whole milk ricotta cheese

FOR BREAD LAYERS

15 to 16 (½-inch-thick) slices white bread

½ cup butter, melted

FOR CUSTARD

1½ cups milk

1½ cups half-and-half

8 eggs, beaten

8 oz. provolone or cheddar cheese, sliced and cut in strips

FOR TOPPING

2 tablespoons butter, melted

1 cup Ritz cracker crumbs

1 cup grated Parmesan cheese

THIS IS A LARGE STRATA WITH SEVERAL LAYERS, *but it's worth the effort. The sour-sweet flavor of the gherkins and the salty ham are tamed by the addition of creamy ricotta cheese. We found the recipe for this old-fashioned dish handwritten on an index card. This is really just a savory bread pudding, but it can become the star of breakfast, lunch, or brunch. We serve it with a green salad to balance the richness.*

1. To make the deviled ham: Place ham in the bowl of a food processor fitted with the metal blade. Pulse until finely chopped. Remove ham to a bowl. Add gherkins, onion, mayonnaise, parsley, paprika, peppers, salt, and black pepper, and combine. Fold in ricotta and set aside.

2. To prepare the bread: Trim off and discard crusts. Cut bread slices in half. Brush each piece on both sides with melted butter and set aside.

3. To make the custard: Coat a 9-inch by 13-inch ovenproof glass baking dish with vegetable spray. Combine milk and half-and-half in a large bowl. Add eggs and whisk to combine. Pour a small amount of custard in bottom of baking dish. Tilt and swirl dish until bottom is covered.

4. Spread deviled ham generously on a piece of bread and place it, ham side up, on the bottom of the baking dish. Continue with several more pieces of bread, spreading with ham and cutting them as needed to fit, until the bottom of dish is completely covered. Cover ham with a second layer of bread. Pour over half of the custard and layer half of the cheese on top. (The bread will start to absorb custard.) Use a spatula to spread the remaining deviled ham generously cover the top. Layer the remaining cheese on top of the ham and pour over the remaining custard. If there isn't room for all of the custard, refrigerate it; you'll be able to add the rest of it later as the custard in the baking dish is absorbed by the bread.

5. Use a knife to cut 8 slits through the layers of the strata to allow the custard to soak through. Place baking dish on tray to catch drips. Cover the top of the strata with plastic wrap and press down firmly with your palm all over until the custard rises to the top. Let stand 10 minutes, pushing down gently on top of pudding two more times.

6. Refrigerate strata on the tray overnight. Add any leftover custard to strata as it becomes possible. The next day, remove strata from refrigerator and allow to sit at room temperature for at least 1 hour.

7. To add the topping: Toss melted butter with crumbs and cheese. Spread topping over top of strata.

8. Set the oven rack in the middle position. Preheat the oven to 350°F. Place baking dish with strata on a rack in a large metal pan. Pour hot water from a glass measuring cup into the pan until the water comes halfway up the sides of the baking dish. Place carefully in oven. Bake approximately 1 hour, or until topping is golden brown, strata bubbles along sides, and a tester inserted into middle comes out clean. *Do not let the water evaporate from the water bath.* Check strata periodically during baking to be sure topping is not burning; cover loosely with foil if topping seems to be drying out.

9. Remove baking dish carefully from oven and water bath. Allow to cool on a rack slightly before serving to prevent strata from falling apart. Store leftover strata covered with plastic wrap in the refrigerator.

Tips & Touches

- It's going to take some time for the bread to absorb the custard, but when you take this puffy strata out of the oven, your patience will be rewarded.
- Use soft white bread for the strata because it absorbs the custard faster than a firmer bread.

Graters, American, early 20th century

Ham Loaf

YIELD: 10 SLICES

FOR HAM LOAF

1 (20-oz.) can sliced pineapple

1 cup milk

1 cup fine bread crumbs (see How to Make Fine Bread Crumbs on page 178)

¾ lb. baked or boiled ham, cut into chunks

1 medium onion, quartered

¾ lb. ground pork

3 eggs, beaten

¼ teaspoon coarsely ground black pepper

¼ teaspoon ground cloves

1 tablespoon firmly packed brown sugar

FOR SAUCE

Reserved pineapple juice (see step 2)

1 tablespoon sherry (optional)

1 tablespoon prepared mustard

¼ cup firmly packed brown sugar

Tips & Touches

- Place a foil-lined pan on an oven rack below the ham loaf to catch any drips.

THIS SAVORY LOAF IS MADE WITH *both ground ham and ground pork. A touch of cloves along with pineapple and brown sugar makes it a festive dish for Sunday night suppers. We found this recipe in the manuscript cookbook of a woman who loved entertaining but who also clearly understood the words* economical *and* delicious. *Served cold with a dab of sharp mustard, this ham loaf tastes like pâté.*

1. Place the oven rack in the middle position. Preheat the oven to 350°F. Coat a 9-inch by 5-inch by 3-inch loaf pan with vegetable spray.
2. To make the ham loaf: Drain pineapple, reserving fruit and juice separately. Combine milk and bread crumbs in a large bowl and stir. Set aside for 5 minutes.
3. Place ham in the bowl of a food processor fitted with the metal blade. Pulse until ham is the texture of ground pork. Remove to bowl with bread crumbs. Add onion to bowl of food processor and pulse until finely chopped. Scrape into bowl with ham. Add pork to bowl and mix to combine. Add eggs, pepper, and cloves. Mix all ham loaf ingredients with your hands (wear disposable gloves if desired) until just combined. Place in prepared loaf pan.
4. To make the sauce: Combine reserved pineapple juice, sherry, if using, mustard, and ¼ cup brown sugar in a small bowl and whisk to combine.
5. Pour half of the sauce over ham loaf, place in oven, and bake for 1 hour. Remove ham loaf from oven and arrange about half of pineapple rings on top. Pour as much of remaining sauce as will fit on top of loaf, sprinkle with 1 tablespoon brown sugar, and return to oven for 30 minutes, or until an instant-read thermometer inserted into the middle of the loaf reads 160°F. Cool in pan on a rack for 15 minutes. Turn out loaf onto a serving platter and surround with remaining pineapple slices.

Salmon Squares

{ 1920s }

This is one of those universal *handwritten recipes that we find frequently in our collection of manuscript cookbooks. It seems that canned salmon was one of those standbys that every home cook relied on. However, canned salmon was never an inexpensive staple. It was just convenient. We've updated our version of Salmon Squares by using canned wild salmon, fresh parsley, fresh dill, and more cream. Using regular canned salmon is also fine.*

1. Set the oven rack in the middle position. Preheat the oven to 350°F. Coat a 2-quart, 8-inch by 11-inch rectangular ovenproof glass baking dish with vegetable spray or butter. Make a water bath: Set a rack in a metal pan large enough to hold the glass baking dish.

2. To make the salmon squares: Place bread crumbs in a bowl. Heat milk in a saucepan until small bubbles form around the edges; do not boil. Pour hot milk over bread crumbs. Add egg yolks, mix to combine, and set aside.

3. In another bowl, combine rice, cream, salmon, onion, 4 tablespoons of the melted butter, the dill, parsley, salt, pepper, and paprika. Add bread crumb mixture and stir to combine.

4. Beat egg whites in the bowl of a standing mixer fitted with the whisk attachment until soft peaks form. Fold egg whites into salmon mixture and transfer to prepared baking dish. Smooth the top. Mix remaining 2 tablespoons melted butter with cracker crumbs and sprinkle over top.

5. Bring water to a boil for the water bath. Place dish in water bath. Use a glass measuring cup to pour hot water into pan to come about halfway up the sides of glass dish. Cover water bath with foil. Place carefully in oven and bake 30 minutes, checking water level periodically and replenishing as needed. *Do not let the water evaporate.* Remove foil and bake another 30 minutes, or until a tester inserted into the salmon comes out clean.

6. Carefully remove salmon from oven. Cool salmon in baking dish on rack for about 10 minutes. Cut into squares and serve with dill mayonnaise. Store leftover squares wrapped in wax paper in the refrigerator.

7. To make the dill mayonnaise: Stir together mayonnaise, dill, lemon juice, sugar, and salt in a small bowl and refrigerate.

FOR SALMON SQUARES

2 cups fine bread crumbs (see How to Make Fine Bread Crumbs on page 178)

1 cup milk

2 eggs, separated

1 cup cooked rice

1 cup heavy cream

1 (14.75-oz.) can wild salmon, skin and bones removed

1/4 cup finely chopped onion

6 tablespoons butter, melted

1 1/2 tablespoons finely chopped fresh dill

1 tablespoon finely chopped fresh parsley

1 teaspoon kosher salt

1/2 teaspoon coarsely ground black pepper

1/4 teaspoon paprika

20 Ritz crackers, crushed (about 1 cup)

FOR DILL MAYONNAISE

1 cup mayonnaise

3 tablespoons finely chopped fresh dill

2 teaspoons lemon juice

1/2 teaspoon sugar

Pinch of salt

Daddy's Fried Lox

YIELD: 4 SMALL SERVINGS

½ lb. lox bits

¼ cup flour

2 tablespoons solid vegetable shortening

1½ cups sliced onion

THIS IS ONE OF THE WONDERFUL BREAKFAST DISHES *our father Harry made for our Sunday breakfasts when we were growing up. We bought our lox and white fish at Revere Smoked Fish, which was located in Chelsea, Massachusetts. We suggest that you use the less expensive lox bits, rather than the fancy cuts of lox. We always ate Daddy's Fried Lox with scrambled eggs and a salad of lettuce, tomato, and cucumber.*

1. Rinse lox bits under cold running water. Place in a glass bowl and add cold water to cover. Cover with plastic wrap and refrigerate for at least 8 hours or overnight. Change the water at least twice during soaking to remove extra salt.

2. Rinse lox again and pat dry with paper towels. Toss with flour. Place in strainer and shake to remove excess flour. Set aside.

3. Melt shortening in a frying pan over medium heat. Add onion slices and sauté until they are just browned around edges. Remove onion or push to one side of frying pan. Add lox to pan and fry until coating is a pale brown. Turn and fry the other side until crust is browned and crispy. Serve lox with onions and a salad. Store leftovers wrapped in wax paper in the refrigerator. Fried lox is also good served cold the next day.

Tips & Touches

- Lox is salt-cured salmon. Do not use smoked salmon.
- Purple onion looks nice with fried lox.

ELINOR'S SHRIMP CREOLE

{ 1940s }

YIELD: 4 SERVINGS

2 tablespoons extra-virgin olive oil

1½ cups chopped onion

1½ cups chopped green bell pepper

1½ cups chopped celery

⅓ cup chopped pimentos

3 cloves chopped garlic

1 teaspoon salt

½ teaspoon coarsely ground black pepper

1 teaspoon dried thyme

2 bay leaves

¼ teaspoon chopped, brined hot peppers

1 (28-oz.) can whole plum tomatoes in juice

1 (15½-oz.) can tomato sauce

1 tablespoon firmly packed brown sugar

1 lb. cooked shrimp

2 cups cooked rice

THIS IS ANOTHER RECIPE FROM ELINOR JENNINGS, *with whom Marilynn worked in the late 1960s. A true Southern lady, Elinor loved the flavor of the shrimp and spices in this dish. She recommended simmering the sauce for at least forty-five minutes to enjoy the true flavor of this dish. Elinor was proud of the fact that she timed her dishes to the minute. Once again, this is a home cook's interpretation of a popular restaurant dish.*

1. Heat olive oil in a large heavy-bottomed pot over medium heat. Add onion, bell pepper, and celery and cook until onions just begin to brown. Add pimentos, garlic, salt, black pepper, thyme, bay leaves, and hot peppers and stir to combine.

2. Add tomatoes with juice and break up with wooden spoon. Add tomato sauce and brown sugar and stir to combine. Bring to a boil, reduce heat, and simmer, covered, for 15 minutes, stirring occasionally. Uncover pot and continue cooking another 45 minutes, or until sauce thickens. Stir occasionally to prevent sauce from catching on bottom of pot. Remove from heat.

3. Add shrimp and let stand in sauce 10 minutes to absorb flavor. Reheat gently. Serve shrimp on a bed of rice. Store leftovers in a covered container in the refrigerator.

TIPS & TOUCHES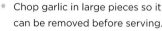

- Chop garlic in large pieces so it can be removed before serving.
- Mounding rice in custard cups and unmolding on plates makes a festive presentation.

CURRIED SHRIMP

YIELD: 6-8 SERVINGS

{ 1960s }

THIS IS A RECIPE FOR CURRIED SHRIMP *that an American home cook would have prepared in her kitchen in the 1960s. It carries the rather contradictory notation "for sudden planned party." It's an easy recipe presenting a westernized version of an exotic dish. Curry powder and canned coconut milk can usually be found on the shelf of your local grocery store. The sweetened coconut balances the flavor of the curry.*

1. Heat oil in a large frying pan over medium heat. Add onions and sauté until translucent stirring with a wooden spoon, about 5–7 minutes. Remove to a large bowl and set aside.

2. In another bowl, combine curry powder, salt, cayenne pepper, flour, and coconut milk. Whisk to a paste. Add milk and Worcestershire sauce and whisk until smooth. Add to bowl with onions and stir to mix well. Add shrimp and shredded coconut.

3. Place curry mixture in large heavy-bottomed pot over low heat. Simmer very gently 10 to 15 minutes. Do not overcook or shrimp will be tough. Do not allow curry to boil. Serve on a bed of hot cooked rice. Store leftovers in a covered container in the refrigerator.

3 tablespoons extra-virgin olive oil

5 cups coarsely chopped onion

2 teaspoons curry powder

1 teaspoon salt

⅛ teaspoon cayenne pepper

3 tablespoons flour

½ cup coconut milk

½ cup milk

1 tablespoon Worcestershire sauce

3 cups cooked shrimp

⅓ cup shredded sweetened coconut

Cooked rice

Silver salt and spoon, American, early 20th century

Dot's Tuna Crescents

{ 1950s }

YIELD: 4-6 SERVINGS

FOR DOUGH

3 cups flour

2 teaspoons baking powder

1 teaspoon salt

½ cup vegetable oil

⅔ cup milk

1 egg, beaten (for egg wash)

FOR FILLING

2 6-oz cans tuna, drained and flaked

1 cup finely chopped celery

¼ cup mayonnaise

1 egg, beaten

THIS RECIPE GAVE US AN ALTERNATIVE TO *eating tuna in sandwiches or salads. Our mother usually made these on winter nights when a hot meal was welcome. The celery and tuna unite to form an almost Asian flavor, and the crescents are very good with the Lime-Ginger Mayonnaise. Smaller versions are nice as appetizers.*

1. To make the dough: Combine flour, baking powder, and salt in the bowl of a food processor fitted with the metal blade. Pulse for 3 seconds. Pour in oil and milk. Process until dough comes away from the sides of bowl. Process another 20 seconds. Remove dough from bowl of processor and divide in half.

2. To make the filling: Mix tuna, celery, mayonnaise, and egg in a small bowl.

3. Set the oven rack in the middle position. Preheat the oven to 450°F. Line a 14-inch by 16-inch baking sheet with foil, shiny side up, and coat with vegetable spray, or use a silicone liner.

4. Place half of the dough between two 12-inch squares of wax paper. Roll out dough until it reaches edges of wax paper. Remove top sheet of paper. Cut dough into 6 rectangles, 6 inches by 4 inches.

Toy saucepans, French, 1920s–1930s

GINGER-LIME MAYONNAISE

This is a quick mayonnaise based on several of the recipes we found. It's wonderful with Tuna Crescents or as a salad dressing. Freshly grated ginger brings out the flavor of the mayonnaise. If you don't have ginger jam on your pantry shelf, apricot jam is a good substitute for adding a bit of sweetness.

1 cup mayonnaise

2 tablespoons grated fresh ginger

5 tablespoons fresh lime juice

2 teaspoons grated lime zest

2 tablespoons ginger jam

Scrape the skin from ginger with edge of spoon. If the skin is tough, use a vegetable peeler. Grate ginger on a Microplane zester/grater. Whisk mayonnaise, ginger, and lime juice and zest in small bowl. Add ginger jam and whisk to combine. **Yield: 1¼ cups**

5. Divide half of the filling evenly among dough squares, placing it horizontally in the center third of each square. Flour your hands and fold the top third of the dough squares over the filling, then roll towards you to make cylinders. Roll cylinders two or three times toward you with the palm of your hand until they look very neat and even (like a mini egg roll). Press dough together at both ends and seal using the tines of a salad fork. Bend both ends in towards the center to form crescents. Place crescents on prepared pan and brush with beaten egg. Bake 10 to 15 minutes, or until crust is golden brown. Repeat with remaining dough and filling to make six more crescents; bake one pan at a time unless you have a double-oven. Serve immediately. Store leftover crescents wrapped in wax paper in the refrigerator. Reheat in a low oven.

TIPS & TOUCHES

- Tuna Crescents are wonderful with Lime-Ginger Mayonnaise.

DANISH ROAST GOOSE STUFFED WITH APPLES AND PRUNES (*Stegt Gås*)

{ 1 9 6 0 s }

YIELD: 6 SERVINGS

2 cups pitted prunes

4 cups boiling water

Young goose, about 10 lbs.

1 lemon, cut in half

1½ teaspoons salt, divided

1 teaspoon coarsely ground
black pepper

2 cups peeled, cored, and
chopped apples

1 large onion, peeled and quartered

Gravy (see How to Make Gravy for
Your Goose on page 213)

GOOSE WITH ITS MOIST DARK MEAT *and glistening skin is the traditional heart of the Danish Christmas feast. This recipe is from Ed Steenberg, of Minneapolis, Minnesota. Ed helped his mother, Erma, raise geese and ducks in Minnesota during the 1940s, and he has been cooking geese for Christmas for almost fifty years. His recipe is one of the most challenging in* Heirloom Cooking with the Brass Sisters, *but if you follow the instructions, you will be rewarded with a picture—perfect roast goose. Ed suggests serving roast goose with Red Cabbage (Rødkål) (page 104) and Caramelized Potatoes (Brunede Kartofler) (page 89). The slightly sour, pungent taste of the red cabbage and the crispy texture of the potatoes balance the rich flavor of the goose. This recipe does not boil the goose before roasting.*

1. Place prunes in a saucepan and pour boiling water over them. Let stand 20 to 30 minutes, or until prunes absorb water and become plump and soft. Drain prunes and let cool until easy to handle.

2. Wash goose under cold running water and pat dry with paper towels. Remove any loose fat from around the cavities. Cut off wing tips. Rub goose, inside and out, with lemon halves. Sprinkle inside and out with 1 teaspoon of the salt and the pepper. Stuff the body cavity with

 THE VALUABLE GOOSE

The goose has always been prized by heirloom cooks for its dark flavorful meat and crispy skin. Its fine down and feathers were used for stuffing coverlets and pillows, and its quills were formed into pens. Goose fat was doubly valuable; it was an excellent choice for frying potatoes and other foods and was thought to have medicinal benefits when rubbed on the chests of those suffering from congestive colds. We don't recommend the latter.

⇢⇢ HOW TO ROAST A GOOSE ⇠⇠

Roasting a goose should be done cautiously because you are working with hot fat and boiling water. If you follow these steps, they will enable you to have a safer, easier experience with your goose.

1. Read the recipe through at least twice.
2. Clear off the counter and have utensils and ingredients within easy reach.
3. Place the goose on a roasting rack in pan.
4. Stuff the cavity with prunes, apples, and onions. Be careful when placing your hand in the cavity because sharp bones can scratch.
5. Use *metal* skewers and *wet* cotton kitchen string to truss the goose. Do not use string made from plastic. It will melt.
6. Use heavy pot to boil water for basting.
7. Have another heavy pot at hand when draining fat from the goose. Empty this pot periodically to another container so that fat will not remain on stove while goose is roasting.
8. Be careful when turning the goose in the pan. Any fat that spills in the oven can cause a fire. The safe way is to remove the roasting pan from the oven, place it on a flat surface, and then turn the goose.
9. Be sure that goose reaches the correct temperature before serving.

prunes, apples, and onion. Close the body cavity with metal skewers and lace with *wet* cotton kitchen string. Close the neck cavity with a skewer. Truss the bird securely with wet cotton kitchen string. Prick the skin around the thighs, back and lower breast with a fork so the fat will drain during roasting.

3. Place oven rack in middle position. Preheat the oven to 425°F. Line a large roasting pan with foil, shiny side up. Set a rack over the foil.
4. Place the goose, breast side up, on rack in prepared pan. Roast 15 minutes, to brown lightly. Reduce oven temperature to 350°F. Turn the goose on one side and roast 1 hour, basting every 15 to 20 minutes with boiling water to help dissolve the fat. Carefully remove fat from pan periodically with a bulb baster. The bulb may be hot to handle.

5. Turn goose onto its other side. Continue roasting until juices run clear when the thigh is pierced with a small knife and an instant-read thermometer inserted into thigh registers 165°F, about 2 hours and 45 minutes total. If the juice is rosy-colored, roast another 5 minutes or so, or until the juice runs clear yellow. Continue to drain fat and baste goose every 15 minutes. After the bird has roasted 2 hours and 30 minutes, salt the goose with remaining ½ teaspoon salt and turn breast side up. Salting will help to crisp the skin.

6. When the goose is fully cooked, remove from oven. Remove goose to a platter. Scoop out and discard apples, prunes, and onions. Strain pan juices into a medium saucepan. Skim the fat. Reserve fat and pan juices separately to make gravy.

7. Let the goose rest in a warm place for 15 minutes. Carve and serve with gravy. Wrap leftover goose in wax paper and store in the refrigerator.

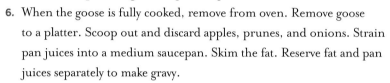

TIPS & TOUCHES

- Geese are long and narrow. Be sure you have proper size pan so that a goose will fit easily without crowding.
- Skim fat from drippings, strain, and thicken for gravy.
- The apples, prunes, and onions accumulate excess fat from the goose while adding flavor to the meat. Discard the stuffing after goose is cooked.

➺➺ HOW TO MAKE GRAVY FOR YOUR GOOSE ⤙⤙

2 tablespoons goose fat
2 tablespoons Wondra quick-mixing flour
2 cups strained goose pan juices or low-sodium chicken stock
Salt and coarsely ground black pepper

Melt goose fat in a heavy-bottomed frying pan over low heat. Add flour and whisk until combined. Cook for about 1 minute, stirring with a wooden spoon. Gravy is usually made with a roux (a mixture of flour and fat) and is thicker than a pan sauce. For thicker gravy, use 3 tablespoons flour rather than 2 tablespoons. Gradually pour in pan juices or chicken stock, stirring constantly, and cook until gravy begins to thicken. Chicken stock can be added to the juices from the goose or substituted for them. Increase the heat to medium and continue cooking until gravy reaches desired consistency. If there are any lumps or bits, put gravy through strainer. Adjust seasonings. Store leftover gravy in a covered container in the refrigerator. **Yield: 2 cups gravy**

Libby's Curried Turkey Pie

YIELD: 6 SERVINGS

FOR CRUST

2½ to 3 cups soft bread crumbs (see How to Make Soft Bread Crumbs on page 215)

¼ cup butter, melted

2 to 4 tablespoons water

¼ cup finely chopped onion

¼ cup finely chopped celery

¼ cup finely chopped fresh parsley, or 2 teaspoons dried

2 teaspoons poultry seasoning

½ teaspoon coarsely ground black pepper

¼ teaspoon salt

FOR FILLING

¼ cup raisins

1½ cups boiling water

2 tablespoons butter, softened to room temperature

¼ cup chopped white mushrooms

1 (10½-oz.) can cream of mushroom soup, or 1 recipe Homemade "Canned" Cream of Mushroom Soup (page 233)

½ cup milk

2 cups chopped (¾-inch) cooked turkey

½ cup frozen peas, thawed

1 tablespoon finely chopped onion

2 teaspoons curry powder

¼ teaspoon salt

THIS IS A GREAT WAY TO SERVE LEFTOVER TURKEY. *It's quick and easy and was a little exotic in the 1950s because of the curry powder. The homemade bread crumbs make a big difference in this dish. We treasure Libby's living recipes, which were found at a yard sale in her hometown of Groton, Massachusetts.*

1. Set the oven rack in the middle position. Preheat the oven to 375°F. Coat a 9-inch ovenproof glass pie plate with vegetable spray. Line a 14-inch by 16-inch baking sheet with foil, shiny side up, and coat with vegetable spray, or use a silicone liner.

2. To make the crust: Place bread crumbs and melted butter in a large bowl and mix thoroughly. Add 2 tablespoons water and stir. Add up to 2 more tablespoons water, as needed, until bread crumbs are completely moistened. Add onion, celery, parsley, poultry seasoning,

BRINGING AN ORIGINAL ✈ INTO THE ✈ TWENTY-FIRST CENTURY

The original recipe for Libby's Curried Turkey Pie called for cream of mushroom soup. But we've provided a substitute white sauce and butter fried mushrooms (see Basic White Sauce on page 233). Frozen peas and fresh mushrooms replace canned ones, while a mixture made from fresh bread crumbs is used for the pie's crust.

HOW TO MAKE SOFT BREAD CRUMBS

Heirloom recipes for breading and for pastries often require soft bread crumbs. Making your own soft bread crumbs insures that they are flavorful and fresh. Remove and discard the crusts from slightly dry bread. Tear the bread into pieces and place in the bowl of a food processor fitted with the meal blade. Pulse a few times. Crumbs should be larger and softer than fine bread crumbs. Commercially prepared Japanese bread crumbs (called *panko*) are a good substitute for homemade soft bread crumbs. Panko can be found in most grocery stores as well as those specializing in international foods.

pepper, and salt and combine with hands. Reserve one third of the mixture. Press remaining mixture over bottom and up sides of prepared pie plate to form crust. Place pie plate on prepared baking sheet, and set aside.

3. To make the filling: Place raisins in small bowl and pour boiling water over. Let stand 5 minutes. Drain and set aside.

4. Melt butter in a saucepan over medium heat. Add mushrooms and cook until softened and lightly browned, 5 to 7 minutes. Set aside.

5. Place canned mushroom soup in a large bowl. Add milk and whisk. Add raisins, mushrooms, turkey, peas, onion, curry powder, and salt. Stir with a wooden spoon until combined.

6. Pour mixture into prepared crust. Sprinkle reserved crust mixture over the top. Bake, uncovered, 30 to 35 minutes, or until pie starts to bubble and topping is crunchy. Cover pie with foil if crust browns too quickly. Serve immediately. Cover cooled leftover pie with a paper towel and plastic wrap and store in the refrigerator.

Tips & Touches

- Chicken can be substituted for turkey.
- Add a little more butter if the crust mixture seems dry.
- Packaged herbed stuffing mix can also be used.
- Do not add milk when using homemade Mushroom Soup.

Turkey Divan

YIELD: 4 SERVINGS

FOR TURKEY CASSEROLE

1 lb. frozen broccoli

3 cups thinly sliced cooked turkey

3 tablespoons butter, softened to room temperature

3 tablespoons flour

¾ teaspoon salt

⅛ teaspoon coarsely ground black pepper

⅛ teaspoon paprika

1 cup milk

½ cup half-and-half

1 cup grated cheddar cheese

FOR TOPPING

2 cups soft bread crumbs (see How to Make Soft Bread Crumbs on page 215)

3 tablespoons butter, melted

Tips & Touches

- You can use fresh broccoli instead of frozen.

THIS RECIPE IS AN OLD ONE *and came from our friend Elinor Jennings. When we mentioned this delicious recipe to a young woman we met in a spice shop, her eyes misted with memories of long-ago servings of chicken divan. This is another imaginative way to serve leftover turkey. The combination of broccoli and cheese turns simple ingredients into a party dish. As our friend Nellie Carey would say, "You could serve this!"*

1. Set the oven rack in the middle position. Preheat the oven to 350°F. Coat a 9-inch by 13-inch ovenproof glass baking dish with vegetable spray.

2. To make the casserole: Cook broccoli in boiling water according to package directions until just tender, still bright green, and firm. Drain well. Cut stalks in half length-wise. Arrange broccoli over bottom of prepared baking dish. Cover with turkey slices and set aside.

3. Melt butter in a saucepan over low heat. Add flour, salt, pepper, and paprika and stir with a wooden spoon to combine. Gradually add milk and half-and-half, raise heat to medium, and cook, stirring, until sauce is thickened and smooth, about 5 minutes. Add cheese and stir to melt. Pour cheese sauce over turkey and cooked broccoli.

4. To make the topping: Mix bread crumbs with melted butter. Sprinkle topping over casserole. Bake about 40 minutes, or until sauce bubbles around edges. Cover casserole with foil if topping browns too quickly. Store leftovers in a covered container in the refrigerator.

Miniature tin roasting pans, American, early 20th century

Hot Chicken Salad

{ 1930s }

THIS DISH ISN'T WHAT IT SOUNDS LIKE. *It's more of a chicken casserole than a salad. It's very colorful with its chopped green pepper and pimento and is very representative of a dish that a home cook would serve to her family in the 1950s, the Golden Age of the Casserole. This is a treasured Southern recipe from a manuscript cookbook from North Carolina.*

1. Set the oven rack in the middle position. Preheat the oven to 450° F. Coat a 9-inch by 13-inch ovenproof glass baking dish with vegetable spray.

2. To make the casserole: Heat butter and olive oil in a large frying pan over medium heat. Add celery, onion, mushrooms, pimentos, and green bell pepper and cook until vegetables are softened but only partially cooked, 5 to 7 minutes. Add almonds and stir to coat with butter and oil. Stir in salt and black pepper. Remove to a large bowl. Add chicken and mayonnaise and stir to coat ingredients with mayonnaise. Spoon into prepared baking dish and smooth the top. Set aside.

3. To make the topping: Heat butter and oil in a frying pan over medium heat. Add bread crumbs and cook, stirring, until they turn a light brown color, being careful not to burn them. Remove from heat and stir in cream.

4. Spread topping over casserole and bake about 15 minutes, or until top is golden brown and bubbly. Serve hot. Store leftovers covered with wax paper in the refrigerator.

FOR CASSEROLE

2 tablespoons butter, softened to room temperature

2 tablespoon extra-virgin olive oil

1 cup chopped celery

½ cup chopped onion

1 cup sliced white mushrooms

½ cup chopped pimento

⅔ cup chopped green bell pepper

1 cup slivered almonds

1 teaspoon salt

½ teaspoon coarsely ground black pepper

4 cups chopped cooked chicken

1 cup mayonnaise

FOR TOPPING

1 tablespoon butter, softened to room temperature

1 tablespoon extra-virgin olive oil

1 cup fine bread crumbs (see How to Make Fine Bread Crumbs on page 178) or panko

½ cup heavy cream

Miniature *au gratin* dish, American, 1920s–1930s

TIPS & TOUCHES

- It might be necessary to brown bread crumbs in two batches.
- Bread crumbs should be fried to a light brown, not dark brown.
- Use a combination of butter and olive oil to sauté vegetables and brown bread crumbs because it prevents the butter from burning or turning black.
- Wild mushrooms can be substituted.

Chicken Pot Pie

YIELD: 6 SERVINGS

Pastry for 9-inch single-crust pie, chilled (see Sheila's Savory Pie Crust on page 248)

FOR FILLING

¼ cup butter, softened to room temperature

¼ cup flour

1 cup low-sodium chicken stock

½ cup half-and-half

½ teaspoon salt

½ teaspoon paprika

⅛ teaspoon coarsely ground black pepper

1 tablespoon grated onion

1 tablespoon extra-virgin olive oil

1 cup sliced white mushrooms

1 cup sliced (¼-inch thick) carrots

2 cups diced (½-inch) cooked chicken

1 cup fresh or frozen peas

THIS RECIPE CAME FROM THE MANUSCRIPT COOKBOOK *of The Pie Lady from North Carolina. An expert on making cakes and sweet pies, she also excelled in making this old-fashioned savory Chicken Pot Pie. She wrote this recipe on an invoice for Remco Supply, located on Wendover Avenue in Greensboro, North Carolina. Remco sold fasteners, tools, shelving, shop equipment, and storage racks.*

1. To make the pastry for the top of the pie: For detailed instructions, see Sheila's Savory Pie Crust on page 248.

2. To make the filling: Melt butter over low heat in a 2-quart saucepan. Add flour and whisk to blend. Turn heat to medium and cook, stirring with a wooden spoon, for 1 minute. Add stock and half-and-half and continue cooking, stirring constantly, until sauce begins to thicken, 4 to 6 minutes. Remove sauce from heat, and stir in salt, paprika, black pepper, and grated onion. Pour into large bowl and cool to room temperature.

3. Heat olive oil in frying pan over medium heat. Add mushrooms and cook until softened and lightly browned, 5 to 7 minutes. Cook carrots in boiling water about 10 minutes, or until tender; drain. For filling, fold chicken, mushrooms, carrots, and peas into reserved sauce.

4. Place the oven rack in the middle position. Preheat the oven to 400°F.

5. Add filling to 9-inch ovenproof glass pie pan. Add crust on top and crimp edges. Cut 6 decorative slits. Brush crust and edges with beaten egg.

6. Place pie on foil-lined baking sheet and bake 30 minutes , or until crust is golden brown and filling is bubbling. Cover pie with foil if crust browns too quickly. Cut into wedges and serve immediately. Cover leftovers with wax paper and store in the refrigerator.

Anna Morse's Lemon Chicken

{ 1 9 6 0 s }

Anna Morse was a member of a group *of women who commuted daily from their Marblehead and Swampscott homes to Boston during the 1950s and 1960s. The friends enjoyed chatting and exchanging recipes during their train rides and referred to themselves as The Railroad Club. Eventually they formed an investment club. Most of the members have passed on, so we are grateful to Anne Kemelman, one of the club's members, who gave us the background for this recipe. Anne was married to mystery writer Harry Kemelman. A talented artist, Anne still paints at the age of 98.*

6 to 8 pieces chicken, or
    4 large boneless, skinless
    chicken breasts

5 tablespoons lemon juice

1/3 cup flour

1 1/2 teaspoons salt

1/2 teaspoon paprika

3 tablespoons extra-virgin
    olive oil

2 tablespoons butter, softened
    to room temperature

2 lemons, sliced 1/8- to
    1/4-inch thick

3 tablespoons firmly packed
    brown sugar

1 cup low-sodium chicken stock

1. Coat the bottom and sides of a 9-inch by 13-inch ovenproof glass baking pan with vegetable spray. If using a metal baking pan, line it with foil, shiny side up, and coat with vegetable spray. Rinse chicken under cold, running water and pat dry with paper towels. Place lemon juice in a shallow bowl. Dip chicken in lemon juice, place on a platter, and set aside. Pour leftover lemon juice into prepared pan.

2. Place flour, salt and paprika in a plastic bag. Add chicken, seal, and shake to coat with flour. Place chicken in a strainer and tap over sink to remove excess flour. Set aside.

3. Set the oven rack in the middle position. Preheat the oven to 375°F.

4. Melt olive oil and butter in large, heavy frying pan over medium heat. Add chicken and cook until both sides are golden brown. Remove chicken to prepared baking pan and scatter lemon slices over. Sprinkle with brown sugar.

5. Pour chicken stock into frying pan set over medium heat, and simmer, scraping with a wooden spoon to retrieve all of the browned bits clinging to bottom of the pan. Cook until slightly thickened. Pour sauce into a corner of the baking pan, being careful not to disrupt the lemon slices and the brown sugar topping. Gently shake pan to distribute sauce over bottom. Cover pan with foil and bake until chicken is cooked through, about 30 minutes for boneless, skinless chicken breasts, 40 to 45 minutes for bone-in pieces of chicken. Baste with pan juices at least once during cooking. Serve Lemon Chicken on a bed of Saffron Rice (page 173) with pine nuts and golden raisins.

Reta Corbett's Wild Rice and Chicken Casserole

{ *1940s* }

YIELD: 4 SERVINGS

1 cup wild rice

3 cups cubed cooked chicken,
cut in ½-inch cubes

1 teaspoon salt

½ teaspoon coarsely ground
black pepper

½ cup butter, softened to room
temperature

½ cup flour

2 cups milk

2 cups low-sodium chicken stock

1¼ cups toasted slivered almonds

ELINOR JENNINGS GAVE US RETA'S RECIPE For *Wild Rice and Chicken Casserole nearly forty years ago. It is a very fancy-sounding dish that's easy to make and looks as if you've been in the kitchen all afternoon. Wild rice is now more available than it used to be, and it's a nice ingredient to have on your pantry shelf.*

1. Cook wild rice in boiling water according to package directions, undercooking it slightly.
2. Season chicken with salt and pepper.
3. Melt butter in a saucepan over low heat. Add flour and whisk until blended. Cook, stirring, for 1 minute. Add milk and chicken stock. Increase heat to medium and cook, stirring constantly, until sauce starts to thicken and small bubbles form around the edges, 4 to 6 minutes. Season to taste with salt and pepper.
4. Set the oven rack in the middle position. Preheat the oven to 400°F. Coat a 9-inch by 13-inch ovenproof glass baking dish with vegetable spray.
5. To assemble the casserole: Spread one third of wild rice over bottom of prepared baking dish. Cover with one third of chicken and one third of sauce. Repeat twice more to use all of the rice, chicken, and sauce. Sprinkle with almonds. Bake, uncovered, 30 to 35 minutes, or until bubbling. Cover with foil if almonds brown too quickly. Serve immediately. Store leftovers in a covered container in the refrigerator.

Miniature enamelware bucket and bowl, German, late 19th century

ROSE HOWARD'S CHEESE FRITTATA

YIELD: 4 SERVINGS

{ 1950s }

THIS RECIPE WAS ORIGINALLY CALLED *Cheese Fondue, but we found we couldn't dip anything in it. Not light enough to be a soufflé, it was almost a crustless quiche. This is actually a substantial baked luncheon dish, similar to an omelet, closer to a frittata, and great served with a touch of sour cream and some chopped fresh tarragon. You'll need your whisk for this recipe. Another suggestion from the file of The Church Lady from Mansfield, Ohio.*

1. Set the oven rack in the middle position. Preheat the oven to 350°F. Butter a 1½-quart ovenproof glass or ceramic baking dish or coat with vegetable spray.

2. Scald milk in a heavy saucepan over medium heat, stirring with a wooden spoon, until small bubbles form around edges. Remove saucepan from heat, add cheese and butter, and whisk until smooth. Place over low heat and whisk in bread crumbs. Remove pan from heat.

3. Whisk egg yolks in a small bowl. Pour a small amount of cheese mixture into bowl with yolks and whisk quickly to temper. Return yolks to pan with cheese mixture and whisk until thoroughly combined. Add salt and remove from heat.

4. Beat egg whites in the bowl of a standing mixer fitted with the whisk attachment until soft peaks form. Do not overbeat. Add about one fourth of beaten whites to cheese mixture and stir gently to combine. Fold in remaining whites. Pour batter into prepared pan and bake 40 minutes, or until a tester inserted in middle comes out clean. Serve immediately. Store leftovers wrapped in wax paper in the refrigerator. Reheat in a low oven.

1 cup milk

4 oz. sharp cheddar cheese, grated

1 tablespoon butter, softened to room temperature

1 cup soft bread crumbs (see How to Make Soft Bread Crumbs on page 215)

3 eggs, separated

½ teaspoon salt

TIPS & TOUCHES

- Mixing a small amount of the egg whites into the batter and then folding in the rest of the egg whites makes the combining easier.

Miniature enamelware pot, American, early 1900s

Mama's Pie Crust Pizza with Mushroom Tomato Sauce

{ 1 9 5 0 s }

YIELD: 4 SERVINGS

FOR MUSHROOM TOMATO SAUCE

3 tablespoons extra-virgin olive oil, divided

1 cup thinly sliced onion

1½ cups diced green bell pepper

2 cloves garlic, minced

1 tablespoon butter, softened to room temperature

12 oz. white mushrooms

1 (29-oz.) can tomato puree

2 tablespoons tomato paste

½ cup water

2 tablespoons red wine vinegar

¼ cup firmly packed brown sugar

¼ teaspoon coarsely ground black pepper

¼ teaspoon dried oregano

¼ teaspoon dried thyme

½ teaspoon salt

FOR CRUST

2½ cups flour

½ teaspoon salt

½ teaspoon dried oregano

½ cup butter, softened to room temperature

½ cup solid vegetable shortening, chilled

¼ cup ice water

FOR TOPPING

Mushroom Tomato Sauce

6 oz. American or cheddar cheese, shredded

1 teaspoon dried oregano

BECAUSE WE KEPT A KOSHER HOME, *our mother tried to reproduce commercial pizza without using any meat. Her dough was the one she used for her delectable pie crust and required no yeast. The topping was simply canned tomato soup, shredded American cheese, and a dusting of dried Italian seasoning. We've added a quick Mushroom Tomato Sauce.*

1. To make the sauce: Heat 2 tablespoons of the olive oil in a Dutch oven or large heavy-bottomed pot over medium heat. Add onion and bell peppers and cook 5 to 7 minutes. Then add garlic and cook 1 minute. Remove vegetables from pot and set aside. Add remaining tablespoon of oil and butter to pot and sauté mushrooms over medium heat until softened, 5 to 7 minutes. Drain and discard liquid from mushrooms; add mushrooms to bowl with other vegetables.

2. Add tomato purée, tomato paste, and water to pot and stir with a wooden spoon over medium heat to combine. Stir in vinegar, brown sugar, pepper, oregano, thyme, and salt. Add vegetables, and cook, stirring, until sauce starts to boil around the edges. Reduce heat to low and simmer until sauce thickens, at least 15 minutes. Let sauce cool before using.

3. To make the crust: Place flour, salt, and oregano in the bowl of a food processor fitted with the metal blade. Pulse three times to mix. Add butter and shortening and pulse until crumbly. Add ice water. Pulse until mixture comes together. Remove dough from food processor and divide into quarters. This will make it easier to pat into the pan. Unless your kitchen is very warm, you don't have to chill the dough before using.

4. Set the oven rack in the middle position. Heat the oven to 400°F. Line bottom and sides of a 14-inch by 17-inch baking sheet or an 11-inch by 17-inch jelly roll pan with foil, shiny side up, and coat with vegetable spray.

5. Working with one quarter at a time, pat dough into pan making sure dough reaches into edges and corners. Crimp edges of dough with the tines of a salad fork.

6. To add topping: Spoon sauce, a few tablespoons at a time, onto dough, and spread evenly with spatula. A small amount of sauce may be left over. Distribute cheese evenly over top. Sprinkle with oregano. Bake 25 to 30 minutes, or until edges of the crust are light brown and cheese is bubbling.

ONION AND OLIVE TART

{ 1950s }

THIS RECIPE MADE US REWRITE *that old saying to "Good things come in big packages." The original recipe made enough Onion and Olive Tart for an army, so we reduced the ingredients until we came up with a delightful little tart, just enough for a small gathering of family and very good friends. Smaller slices are wonderful for appetizers, and large slices make a good main course for lunch with a salad of crisp greens. Manuscript cookbooks of the 1950s often contained recipes suitable for quantity cooking.*

1. To prepare the crust: Coat an 8-inch round tart pan with vegetable spray. Roll out pastry dough. Fit dough into bottom of tart pan and trim, leaving a ¾-inch overhang. Chill in refrigerator while you make the filling.

2. To make the filling: Heat butter and oil in a frying pan over medium heat. Add onion and cook, stirring with wooden spoon, until translucent, 5 to 7 minutes. Remove pan from heat. Add garlic, salt, pepper, ½ teaspoon of the thyme leaves, flour, olives, and Parmesan cheese and stir to combine.

3. In a separate bowl, beat 2 of the eggs. Add a small amount of onion mixture and stir quickly to temper eggs. Add remaining onion mixture and stir to combine. Allow filling to cool.

4. Set the oven rack in the middle position. Preheat the oven to 350°F.

5. Add cooled filling to tart pan. Beat remaining egg and brush onto edges of pastry shell. Place tart on a foil-lined baking sheet and bake 35 to 40 minutes, or until top is set. Sprinkle with remaining ½ teaspoon fresh thyme leaves, cut into wedges, and serve immediately. Store leftovers covered with wax paper in the refrigerator. Reheat in a low oven.

Pastry for single-crust pie, chilled (see Sheila's Savory Pie Crust on page 248)

FOR FILLING

2 tablespoons butter, softened to room temperature

2 tablespoons extra-virgin olive oil

2 cups finely chopped onion

1 clove garlic, minced

¼ teaspoon salt

¼ teaspoon coarsely ground black pepper

1 teaspoon fresh thyme leaves, divided

2 tablespoons flour

½ cup black, brined calamata olives, pitted, or pimento-stuffed green olives, chopped

¾ cup grated Parmesan cheese

3 eggs, divided

TIPS & TOUCHES

- You might want to choose a square or rectangular tart pan for a different presentation.

227

SUSANNE SIMPSON'S APPLE PUFF-PANCAKE

{ 1960s }

YIELD: 6 SERVINGS

6 large eggs

1½ cups milk

1 cup flour

¼ cup sugar

1 teaspoon vanilla

¾ teaspoon salt

½ teaspoon cinnamon

½ cup butter, softened to room temperature

2 Granny Smith apples, peeled, cored, and sliced

3 tablespoons firmly packed brown sugar

TIPS & TOUCHES

- Any firm baking apple can be used.
- Do not overbeat batter.
- Try serving with a little sour cream on the side.

THIS LIVING RECIPE PRODUCES AN INTRIGUING DISH *suitable for brunch or lunch. Although the puffy edges are very much like a popover, the center tastes like an omelet filled with cinnamon and baked apples. This recipe came to Massachusetts via Susanne's friends in Michigan and Pennsylvania. We used a 12-inch quiche dish, and we got wonderful results.*

1. Set the oven rack in the middle position. Preheat the oven to 425°F. Coat a 12-inch ovenproof fluted quiche dish with butter or vegetable spray.

2. Mix eggs, milk, flour, sugar, vanilla, salt, and cinnamon in a large bowl with a wooden spoon. Batter will be slightly lumpy. Set aside.

3. Melt butter in prepared quiche dish in oven. This should take about 3 minutes. Remove dish from oven and tilt pan to coat bottom with butter. Arrange apple slices over bottom of dish in spiral fashion. Return to oven and heat about 5 minutes, or until butter sizzles. (Do not let butter or apples brown.) Remove dish from oven and immediately pour in batter. Sprinkle with brown sugar. Bake 20 to 25 minutes, or until pancake is puffed and lightly browned. Serve immediately. Apple pancake is best served the day it is made. Store leftovers loosely covered with wax paper in the refrigerator.

Toy kitchen utensils, American, early 20th century

Aunt Ida's Apple Cranberry Noodle Pudding

YIELD: 8 TO 10 SERVINGS   { 1940s }

THIS RECIPE CAME FROM AUNT IDA *Katziff's recipe file. It is actually a kugel, one of those Eastern European dishes that contains layers of noodles, fruit, and butter. There's no cheese in this pudding, which can be eaten as a main dish, a snack, or a dessert. The recipe is brief and to the point and was probably taken down over the telephone from one of Ida's four sisters, or from her good friend, Dorothy Lerman, who was a magnificent home cook into her nineties.*

1. Set the oven rack in the middle position. Preheat the oven to 350°F. Coat a 9-inch by 13-inch ovenproof glass baking dish with vegetable spray.

2. To make the pudding: Cook noodles in a large pot of boiling water for 7 to 10 minutes, or until just tender. Drain noodles and rinse under cold water. Place noodles in a large bowl. Add melted butter, ¼ cup of the sugar, and 1 teaspoon of the cinnamon. Whisk eggs with pineapple juice to blend, add to noodles, and stir to combine. Set aside.

3. Mix remaining teaspoon of cinnamon with remaining ¼ cup sugar and toss with apples in another bowl.

4. Spread half of noodles in prepared baking dish. Add all of the apples in an even layer. Spread cranberry sauce over apples. Sprinkle evenly with walnuts. Layer remaining noodles on top.

5. To make the topping: Toss melted butter with walnuts to coat and scatter over top of pudding. Sprinkle with brown sugar. Bake 35 to 45 minutes, or until pudding is bubbling and top is golden brown. Serve warm or at room temperature. Store leftovers in a clean dish covered with wax paper in the refrigerator.

FOR PUDDING

1 (12-oz.) package egg noodles

¾ cup butter, melted

½ cup sugar, divided

2 teaspoons cinnamon, divided

4 large eggs

1½ cups pineapple juice

3 apples (about 1½ lbs. total), peeled, cored, and sliced ¼-inch thick

1 (16-oz.) can whole cranberry sauce

¾ cup toasted walnuts, chopped

FOR TOPPING

2 tablespoons butter, melted

½ cup toasted walnuts, finely chopped

¼ cup firmly packed brown sugar

Billionaire's Macaroni and Cheese

YIELD: 6-8 SERVINGS

1 lb. elbow macaroni

¼ cup butter, softened to
    room temperature

¼ cup flour

2 cups milk

8 oz. extra-sharp cheddar cheese,
    grated (2¼ cups)

1 teaspoon salt

1 teaspoon coarsely ground
    black pepper

1 teaspoon paprika

2 tablespoons grated onion

3 eggs, beaten

1 cup whole milk ricotta

1 cup half-and-half

8 oz. provolone cheese, cut
    in strips

FOR TOPPING

¼ cup butter, melted

1½ cups soft bread crumbs
    (see How to Make Soft Bread
    Crumbs on page 215)

5 oz. Parmesan cheese, grated
    (1¾ cups)

THIS RECIPE CAME FROM THE MOTHER OF *one of "The Girls,"
our first customers when we started buying and selling antiques more than
thirty years ago. The Girls shared an apartment in a large ornate building
in Cambridge, called The Lowell. They invited us to lunch and served us
Millionaire's Macaroni and Cheese on unmatched plates at a card table.
We had a wonderful time eating this rich, savory dish, but we've changed
its name because of inflation.*

1. Cook macaroni in a large pot of boiling water for 5 to 7 minutes, or
    until still slightly firm. Drain and rinse under cold water. Transfer
    to a large bowl.

2. Melt butter in a heavy-bottomed saucepan over low heat. Remove pan
    from heat, add flour, and stir with a wooden spoon until completely
    combined to make a roux. Set pan over medium heat and cook roux until
    little bubbles form around the edges, 1 to 2 minutes. Remove pan from
    heat and add milk, stirring to blend. Return pan to heat and cook,
    stirring constantly, until thickened. Off the heat, add cheddar cheese, salt,
    pepper, paprika, and onion. Stir until cheese melts and sauce is smooth.
    If cheese doesn't melt completely, stir gently over low heat until melted.

3. Fold cheese sauce into cooled macaroni with a spatula. Whisk eggs
    with ricotta and add to bowl with macaroni. Add half-and-half and
    stir until combined.

4. Set the oven rack in the middle position. Preheat the oven to 350°F. Coat
    a 9-inch by 13-inch ovenproof glass baking dish with vegetable spray.

5. Place half of macaroni mixture in prepared baking dish and smooth
    the top. Cover with strips of provolone. Top with remaining macaroni
    and smooth.

6. To make the topping: Mix melted butter, bread crumbs, and Parmesan
    cheese. Sprinkle topping evenly over macaroni. Cover dish with foil
    and bake 30 minutes. Remove foil and continue baking another 10 to
    15 minutes, or until macaroni is bubbling and top is nicely browned.
    Serve at once. Store leftovers in a covered container in the refrigerator.

TIPS & TOUCHES

- This dish can be made one day
  ahead and kept refrigerated
  before baking.
- This is a great buffet dish.

Welsh Rarebit

YIELD: 4 CUPS

2 tablespoons butter, softened to room temperature

2 tablespoon flour

2 cups milk

2 teaspoons dry mustard

¾ teaspoon salt

¼ teaspoon coarsely ground black pepper

⅛ teaspoon cayenne pepper

3 cups grated American or cheddar cheese

2 eggs, beaten

¼ teaspoon chopped, brined hot peppers (optional)

THIS IS ONE OF THE FIRST RECIPES *Marilynn learned to prepare in cooking class at Winthrop Jr. High. This version of Welsh Rarebit came from the manuscript cookbook of a lady who liked to entertain and who served roast lamb and blueberry pie to the Minister. Welsh Rarebit (or Rabbit) is a tangy cheese sauce served over toast or crackers, perfect for a luncheon dish for the ladies or a snack for the gentlemen. Some rarebits call for beer or ale, but this one is made with milk. The only clue to the origin of our recipe is the word* Proctors, *which might be the name of the hostess who served it to the lady who transcribed it.*

1. Melt butter in a heavy-bottomed 2-quart saucepan over low heat. Whisk flour into butter to combine. Turn heat to medium and cook mixture for 1 minute, stirring with a wooden spoon, to make a roux. Add milk and cook, stirring constantly, until sauce begins to thicken and small bubbles form around the edges, 4 to 6 minutes. Do not overcook.

2. Add mustard, salt, pepper, cayenne pepper, and cheese and stir briskly. Cook over low heat until cheese is completely melted. Remove from heat.

3. Whisk about ¼ cup of the sauce into beaten eggs to temper them. Return egg mixture to rarebit and whisk to combine. Set pan over low heat and continue cooking, whisking constantly, until eggs are cooked and rarebit is heated through, about 2 minutes. Do not boil. Add peppers if desired. Serve Welsh Rarebit on toast or Pilot crackers, a crunchy "down-east" favorite in New England.

TIPS & TOUCHES

• You can substitute 1 teaspoon of prepared mustard for the dry mustard.

• Adjust seasonings to taste.

BASIC WHITE SAUCE

YIELD: APPROXIMATELY 1¼ CUPS SAUCE

{ 1950s }

White sauce is the first sauce students were taught how to make in the cooking classes of the 1950s. It is the base for several other sauces; in Heirloom Cooking, we use a variation on it to prepare a cheese sauce, Welsh Rarebit, and our version of the ever-popular casserole standby, Mushroom Soup. Be sure to try this recipe if you prefer not to use canned mushroom soup in your cooking.

2 tablespoons butter, softened to room temperature

2 tablespoons flour

1 cup milk

Salt and coarsely ground black pepper to taste

1. Melt butter in a heavy-bottomed 2-quart saucepan over low heat. Whisk flour into butter to combine. Turn heat to medium and cook mixture for 1 minute, stirring with a wooden spoon or whisk.

2. Add milk and stir to combine. Add salt and pepper and cook, stirring constantly, until sauce starts to thicken and small bubbles form around the edges, 4 to 6 minutes. Do not overcook.

TIPS & TOUCHES

- Add a little more milk at the end for a thinner sauce.

➤➤ HOMEMADE "CANNED" ◄◄
CREAM OF MUSHROOM SOUP

2 tablespoons butter, softened to room temperature

3 tablespoons flour

1 cup milk

⅛ teaspoon salt

¼ teaspoon freshly ground white pepper

¼ teaspoon onion powder

½ cup white mushrooms, sliced and fried in butter

1. Melt butter in a heavy-bottomed 2-quart saucepan over low heat. Whisk flour into butter to combine. Turn heat to medium and cook mixture for 1 minute, stirring with a wooden spoon.

2. Add milk and stir to combine. Add salt, white pepper, and onion powder and cook, stirring constantly, until sauce starts to thicken and small bubbles form around the edges, 4 to 6 minutes. Do not overcook. Add a little more milk at the end for a thinner sauce.

3. Remove pan from heat and fold in mushrooms. **Yield: Approximately 1¾ cups sauce**

CHAPTER 7

SWEET FINALES

We have to admit that we are partial to dessert. If we could have it three times a day that would not be too often for us. We even confess to eating dessert for breakfast, especially after a party the night before. We relish tales of a restaurant in Pennsylvania that prides itself on serving dessert at the beginning of the meal, and we fondly remember a venerable chain of department stores that allowed male customers two desserts when they ate at its in-store tearoom. • Dessert can be as simple as a plate of cookies or as elaborate as a Red Velvet Cake decorated with mounds of vanilla frosting and toasted pecans. It is the sweet conclusion to a meal—that sublime time when the table is cleared, the coffee is put on to perk, and another pitcher of sweet iced tea is passed around.

Sometimes dessert is served as a buffet, and guests circle the sweet spread, carefully considering each offering, or defying custom, as our Uncle Julius did, and sitting down at the buffet table to enjoy all that it displayed.

Baking has always been more precise than cooking when it comes to measurements, oven temperatures, and times, so it is no surprise that dessert is often more of a challenge than any other part of the meal. It also offers the opportunity for the home cook to express her creativity with that extra swirl of frosting, a rosette of whipped cream, or a sprinkle of toasted coconut. It does not surprise us that heirloom recipes are often referred to as "rules" because of the necessity to abide by the regulations of ingredients and instructions.

Dessert knows its place. It is an important part of the ritual of friends and family coming together for the comfort of a meal and spirited conversation, especially at the holidays. It is defined by the Coconut Pie with the flakey fluted crust, the tender crumb of a Milk Chocolate Pound Cake, or the soft and comforting layers of a Sweet Potato Pudding. The appetizer may stimulate; the soup may warm; the main dish may satisfy; but the dessert is what sweetly completes the meal.

As we made our culinary journey through our collection of manuscript cookbooks, we were not surprised to find that the appeal of dessert is universal. Many of the same desserts appear in these handwritten recipes, but they are personally interpreted by home cooks. Some women have transcribed a whole catalog of desserts that are part of their repertoire. A woman from North Carolina showed herself to be an outstanding dessert maker with her recipes for Green Tomato Pie, Buttermilk Cake, and Shoofly Pie. Two well-loved women in service generously share their recipes for Chocolate Angel Pie and Lemon Angel Pie with the family and friends of their employers.

Silverplate tea caddy, English, early 1900s; tea strainer, nut cup, and sugar tongs, American early 20th century

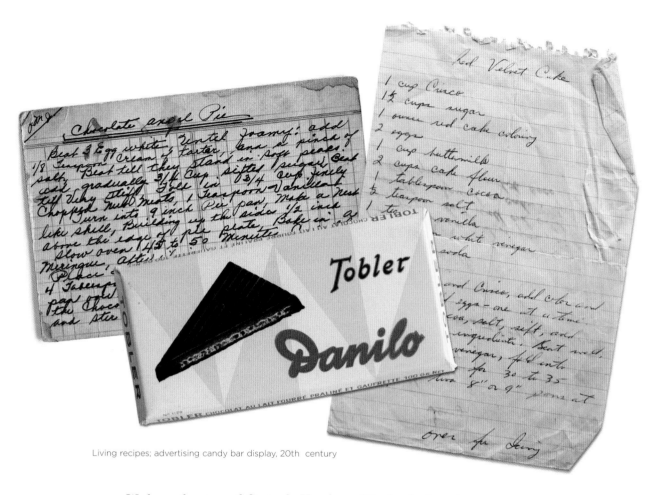

Living recipes; advertising candy bar display, 20th century

We learn the story of Gertrude Huerkamp Woods, the ingenious young woman who raised her five children on the family farm, sketched lady's hats for her father's dry goods store, went to the St. Louis World's Fair on her honeymoon, and baked a wonderful steamed pecan cake, treasured for its abundance of nuts and raisins and its generous ration of bourbon. Mrs. Woods stored her cake in a black cast-iron pot, wrapped in a whiskey-soaked tea towel to mellow.

In this chapter, we salute those who bring forth the birthday cake glowing with candles, the creators of that architecturally faulty but delicious dessert, the Blueberry Buckle, and two enterprising women from Marblehead, Massachusetts, who capture forever the symbol of the maritime heritage of their Northeastern home with a captivating spicy molasses cookie in the shape of a whale.

Often, at the end of a gathering, guests who are comfortable with one another's company linger to relate stories that have been told many times before. As the remnants of dessert are quietly removed, there are some who stealthily palm a cookie, nibble a leftover morsel of cake, or munch a forgotten piece of crust. For them, the company and dessert are both sweet.

We encourage you to add some sweetness to your own lives by baking these desserts in your own kitchen.

Red Velvet Cake

{ 1930s }

YIELD: 8 SLICES

FOR CAKE

2 cups cake flour

½ teaspoon salt

1 tablespoon cocoa

1 cup solid vegetable shortening

1½ cups sugar

2 large eggs

1 (1-oz.) bottle red food coloring

1 teaspoon vanilla

1 cup buttermilk

1 teaspoon baking soda

1 tablespoon vinegar

FOR ICING

1 cup milk

¼ cup cake flour

¼ teaspoon salt

1 cup butter, softened to room temperature

1 cup sugar

1 teaspoon vanilla

1½ cups toasted pecans, coarsely chopped (optional)

TIPS & TOUCHES

- Divide batter equally among or between prepared pans. Using a kitchen scale to weigh pans of batter is helpful.
- Wearing disposable gloves when adding red food coloring will keep hands clean.

THIS IS *the* SOUTHERN DESSERT. *Versions of this cake have made their appearance in the boutique bakeries and cafés of New York and Boston. We use vegetable shortening and the bottle of red food coloring that were originally called for. You will not taste the red food coloring. We have heard that some bakers have turned to beets to color Red Velvet Cake. If you don't have time to travel down South, just bake this iconic cake, which comes from The lady from North Carolina.*

1. Set the oven rack in the middle position. Preheat the oven to 350°F. Line the bottoms of three 7-inch cake pans or two 9-inch cake pans with parchment paper and coat with vegetable spray. Dust with flour and tap out the excess.
2. To make the cake: Sift together flour, salt, and cocoa and set aside.
3. Cream shortening and sugar in the bowl of a standing mixer fitted with the paddle attachment until soft and fluffy. Add eggs one at a time. Add red food coloring. Add vanilla to buttermilk. Add sifted dry ingredients to batter alternately with buttermilk, beating after each addition. Add baking soda to vinegar and fold into batter.
4. Place batter in prepared pans and bake for 30 to 35 minutes, or until a tester inserted into middle comes out clean. Place on a rack and allow to cool 20 minutes. Run a butter knife gently around edges and invert cakes onto a second rack. Let cool completely.
5. To make the icing: Whisk milk, flour, and salt in a heavy-bottomed saucepan until combined. Stir constantly with a wooden spoon over medium heat until thickened, about 2 minutes. Transfer to a bowl and allow to cool.
6. Cream butter and sugar in the bowl of a standing mixer fitted with the paddle attachment until fluffy. Add vanilla. Add cooled milk and flour mixture and beat on highest speed for 5 minutes until thick and creamy.
7. Place bottom layer of cake on a cake round, lined with four small pieces of wax paper, and spread frosting over top of this cake layer with offset spatula. Set top cake layer in position and frost the top and sides. (If using three 7-inch layers, ice top of bottom and middle layer only, add third layer, and frost top and sides.) Immediately cover sides of cake with chopped pecans, if using. Store under cake dome or loosely wrapped in wax paper at room temperature.

Buttermilk Cake

YIELD: 16 SLICES

FOR CAKE

3 cups cake flour

½ teaspoon salt

½ teaspoon baking powder

½ teaspoon baking soda

1 cup butter, softened to room temperature

2 cups sugar

3 large eggs

1 cup buttermilk

1½ teaspoons vanilla

FOR VANILLA ICING

1 cup confectioners' sugar, sifted

Pinch of salt

2 teaspoons vanilla

5 teaspoons water

Tips & Touches

- Buttermilk Cake can be baked in three 8-inch round pans for 40 to 45 minutes. It can be iced with your favorite frosting.

THIS ALL-OCCASION CAKE FROM NORTH CAROLINA *is easy to make and delicious. It's equally good dusted with confectioners' sugar or drizzled with Vanilla Icing. It can be baked in a tube pan or in multiple cake pans, lending itself to layers sandwiched with generous amounts of frosting. A salutation piped on top makes this an ideal birthday cake.*

1. Set the oven rack in the middle position. Preheat the oven to 350°F. Coat bottom and sides of 10-inch by 4¼-inch tube pan with vegetable spray. Cut a parchment paper liner to fit the bottom of the pan. Add the liner and coat with vegetable spray. Dust pan with flour and tap out excess.

2. To make the cake: Sift flour, salt, baking powder, and baking soda and set aside.

3. Cream butter and sugar in the bowl of a standing mixer fitted with the paddle attachment. Add eggs one at a time. Add vanilla to buttermilk. Add dry ingredients alternately with buttermilk, beginning and ending with dry ingredients.

4. Place batter in prepared pan and bake for 60 minutes, or until a tester inserted into cake comes out dry. Cool in pan on a rack for 15 minutes before removing from pan.

5. To make the icing: Sift confectioners' sugar and salt into a bowl. Add vanilla and whisk to combine. Add water 1 teaspoon at a time and whisk until smooth. Drizzle icing over cake. Store leftover cake wrapped in wax paper at room temperature.

DORSET APPLE CAKE

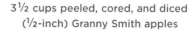

{ *1940s* }

THIS RECIPE WAS CAREFULLY TYPED *with a manual typewriter on a small scrap of paper. We've interpreted this traditional English recipe from Dorset, where Jane Austin and Thomas Hardy were born. Almost a scone, but a little lighter, the flavors of the apples, spices, and lemon zest come together in this English cake. It's wonderful with a cup of India tea or black coffee, or for the more adventuresome, a glass of port.*

1. Set the oven rack in the middle position. Heat the oven to 350°F. Cover bottom and sides of a 9-inch by 9-inch by 2-inch metal pan with foil, shiny side up. Coat the foil with butter or vegetable spray.

2. Toss apples, sugar, raisins, and lemon zest in a bowl and set aside.

3. Sift flour, baking soda, salt, cinnamon, and nutmeg into a large bowl. Work in butter with your fingers. Add vanilla to cream; add to batter and mix in with a wooden spoon. Add beaten eggs, one half at a time. Fold in apple-raisin mixture with a spatula.

4. Place dough in prepared pan and smooth top with an offset spatula. Sprinkle sanding sugar over top and bake 40 minutes, or until a tester inserted into cake comes out clean. Place cake on rack in pan to cool. Cut into squares and serve warm or at room temperature. Store leftovers covered with wax paper in the refrigerator.

3½ cups peeled, cored, and diced (½-inch) Granny Smith apples

½ cup sugar

½ cup golden raisins

Grated zest of 1 lemon

2 cups flour

2 teaspoons baking soda

½ teaspoon salt

¼ teaspoon cinnamon

¼ teaspoon nutmeg

½ cup cold butter, cut into dice

1 teaspoon vanilla

⅓ cup heavy cream

2 eggs, beaten

2 tablespoons coarse sanding sugar

TIPS & TOUCHES

- Use any firm cooking apple.
- Treat this dough like a scone dough—do not overwork.
- This cake is wonderful with a little whipped cream on the side.

Cast iron apple peeler, American, early 1900s

Milk Chocolate Pound Cake

YIELD: 8 SLICES

FOR CAKE

2½ cups flour

⅛ teaspoon salt

1 cup butter, softened to room temperature

1½ cups sugar

4 large eggs

8 oz. milk chocolate, chopped and melted

½ cup plus 1 tablespoon chocolate syrup

2 teaspoons rum

1 cup buttermilk

1 cup toasted pecans, chopped

FOR FROSTING

4 cups confectioners' sugar, sifted

Pinch of salt

½ cup butter, softened to room temperature

½ cup solid vegetable shortening

2 teaspoons rum

2 tablespoons water or milk

8 oz. milk chocolate, chopped and melted

TIPS & TOUCHES

- Melt chocolate in a microwave at 10-second intervals or in a double boiler.
- Cake can also be baked in a 10-inch by 4¼-inch tube pan for 60 minutes and dusted with confectioners' sugar.

THIS IS ANOTHER RECIPE FROM THE MANUSCRIPT COOKBOOK *of the lady from North Carolina. We substituted rum for the vanilla extract because we found this milky chocolate cake reminded us of the particular milk chocolate rum–flavored candy served at our mother's bridge parties. These candies came in star shapes, and we always managed to sneak a few before the ladies came to play bridge. Use 8-oz. milk chocolate candy bars for the cake and for the frosting.*

1. Set the oven rack in the middle position. Heat the oven to 325° F. Line the bottoms of three 7-inch cake pans with parchment paper and coat with vegetable spray. Dust with flour and tap out the excess.

2. To make the cake: Sift together flour and salt and set aside. Cream butter and sugar in the bowl of a standing mixer fitted with the paddle attachment until fluffy. Add eggs one at a time, blending well after each addition. Add melted chocolate, chocolate syrup, and rum and beat to combine. Add dry ingredients alternately with buttermilk. Fold in pecans. Place batter in prepared pans and bake for 45 minutes, or until a tester inserted into cake comes out dry. Cool in pans on a rack for 15 minutes before turning out of pans.

3. To make the frosting: Place confectioners' sugar and salt in the bowl of a standing mixer fitted with the paddle attachment. Add butter and shortening and cream until fluffy. Add rum and water or milk and beat until combined. Add melted chocolate and beat until fluffy. Thin with a little milk if necessary to achieve a better spreading consistency.

4. Place bottom layer of cake on a cake round lined with four small pieces of wax paper to catch drips. Spread frosting over top of cake layer with offset spatula. Set middle cake layer in position and frost top. Top with top layer and frost top and sides. Store under a cake dome or loosely wrapped in wax paper in the refrigerator.

Edinburgh Tea Squares

YIELD: 48 SQUARES

FOR FILLING

1 cup dried apricots

1 cup sugar

1 tablespoon lemon juice

FOR SQUARES

2 cups sifted flour

1 teaspoon salt

2 cups rolled oats

1 cup fine bread crumbs (see How to Make Fine Bread Crumbs on page 178)

1½ cups butter, softened to room temperature

2 cups firmly packed brown sugar

1 cup toasted pecans, coarsely chopped

THIS IS ANOTHER ONE OF THOSE FOUND TREASURES, *a living recipe handwritten in pencil on a sheet of paper like the ones we used for our arithmetic homework. The original called for dates. We tried it with both dates and apricots, and the slightly sour taste of the apricots won because it balanced the sweetness of the squares. This is a simple recipe that looks inviting when served in frilled white paper cups.*

1. Place the oven rack in the middle position. Heat the oven to 350°F. Line bottom and sides of a 9-inch by 13-inch by 2-inch metal pan with foil, shiny side up. Coat with butter or vegetable spray.
2. Place apricots and sugar in a large saucepan. Cover with water and bring to a boil. Reduce heat and simmer until apricots are soft, about 15 minutes. Drain and place in a bowl to cool. Place apricots in the bowl of a food processor fitted with the metal blade. Add sugar and lemon juice. Pulse until a soft paste forms. Set aside.
3. Combine flour, salt, oats, and bread crumbs in a large mixing bowl and set aside.
4. Cream butter and brown sugar in the bowl of a standing mixer fitted with the paddle attachment. Add dry ingredients and combine. Fold in pecans with a spatula.
5. Spread half of mixture over bottom of prepared pan, smoothing with an offset spatula. Add filling in an even layer and smooth the top.

➔ HOW TO TOAST NUTS ◀

Preheat oven to 350°F. Spread nuts on a foil-lined baking sheet, with the foil shiny side up. Toast nuts for 5 minutes. Remove baking sheet from oven. Shake nuts to promote even toasting and return to oven for another 5 minutes. Cool on rack. Store cooled toasted nuts in sealed plastic bags labeled with name of nut, quantity, and date toasted.

Cover with remaining oat and nut mixture and smooth with spatula. Bake about 45 minutes, or until top is a light golden brown. Cool in pan on a rack to room temperature and then refrigerate for 3 hours. Cake will firm up as it cools. Cut into squares with a wide-blade knife and serve. Store between sheets of wax paper in a covered tin.

TIPS & TOUCHES

* Do not use instant oatmeal for dough.

Traveling tea set, English, early 20th century

Coconut Pie from North Carolina

{ 1950s }

YIELD: 8 SERVINGS

Unbaked 9-inch pie shell
(see Sheila's Sweet Pie Crust
on page 248)

¼ cup butter, softened to room
temperature

1 cup sugar

⅓ cup buttermilk

2 large eggs

¼ teaspoon salt

1 teaspoon vanilla

½ package (3½- to 4-oz.)
shredded, sweetened coconut

THIS RECIPE CAME FROM THE PIE LADY *from North Carolina who was active in her church and who specialized in truly Southern cakes and pies. This is one of the simplest recipes for a delicious dessert we've tried. We will not judge you if you use a premade pie crust, but you may find you have a bit of filling leftover.*

1. Place the oven rack in the middle position. Preheat the oven to 350°F.

2. Cream butter and sugar in the bowl of a standing mixer fitted with the paddle attachment. Add buttermilk. Add eggs one at a time. Add salt and vanilla. Fold in coconut. Pour filling into pie shell. Bake about 40 minutes, or until top is firm and crust is golden brown. Cool completely on a rack. Store loosely wrapped in wax paper in the refrigerator.

Tips & Touches

• Whipped cream can be piped in a crisscross pattern on top of pie just before serving. This is a very sweet pie, and a little goes a long way.

Miniature enamelware funnel and flour holder, German, late 19th–early 20th century

SHEILA'S SWEET OR SAVORY PIE CRUST

{ 1 9 5 0 }

MAKES DOUGH FOR 1 DOUBLE-CRUST 9-INCH PIE,
2 SINGLE-CRUST 9-INCH PIES, OR
TWO 8-INCH OR 9-INCH TARTS

SWEET PIE CRUST

2½ cups flour

⅓ cup sugar

¼ teaspoon salt

1 cup cold butter, cut into 16 slices

¼ cup ice water

1 egg, beaten (optional; for double-crust pie)

SAVORY PIE CRUST

2½ cups flour

¼ teaspoon salt

½ teaspoon chopped fresh herbs or ⅛ teaspoon dried herbs (optional)

½ cup cold butter, cut into 8 slices

½ cup chilled vegetable shortening

¼ cup ice water

1 egg, beaten (optional; for double-crust pie)

WE'VE USED THIS EASY-TO-MAKE CRUST *for 45 years. It is like the ones we've found in our manuscript cookbooks. We've provided both a sweet and a savory version. The sweet version is like the one used by heirloom cook, Bertha Bohlman, whom we mentioned in* Heirloom Baking.

TO MAKE PASTRY

1. Place dry ingredients in the bowl of a food processor fitted with the metal blade. Pulse three times to mix. Add butter (or butter and shortening) and pulse until crumbly. Add ice water. Pulse until mixture comes together.

2. Remove dough from bowl of processor, divide in half, and shape each half into a disk. Unless your kitchen is very warm, you don't have to chill dough before rolling out.

TO MAKE A DOUBLE-CRUST PIE

1. Coat a 9-inch ovenproof glass pie plate with vegetable spray.

2. Roll out each disk of dough between 2 sheets of floured wax paper or parchment paper until 2 inches wider than diameter across top of pie plate.

3. Fold one rolled disk in half and then in quarters. Place folded dough into bottom quarter of pie plate. Carefully unfold dough and let it relax into pie plate. Trim excess dough from rim. Chill bottom crust while preparing filling.

4. Brush edges of bottom crust with beaten egg. Fill pie and flip second crust over top of pie. Trim excess dough around rim, leaving just enough dough to make a crimped edge. Press edges of dough together gently with your fingers. Crimp edges with tines of a salad fork or pie crimper. Cut six 1-inch decorative slits in center of top crust to allow steam to escape. Brush top crust and edges with beaten egg. Bake as directed in recipe.

TO MAKE A SINGLE-CRUST PIE

1. Coat a 9-inch ovenproof glass pie plate with vegetable spray.

2. Roll out one disk of dough between 2 sheets of floured wax paper or parchment paper until 2 inches wider than diameter across top of pie plate.

3. Fold rolled disk in half and then in quarters. Place folded dough into bottom quarter of pie plate. Carefully unfold dough and let it relax into pie plate. Trim excess dough around rim, leaving enough to form a decorative edge. Flute the edge or shape as desired.

4. Chill crust while preparing filling. Fill and bake pie as directed in recipe.

To prebake a pie shell

1. Place the oven rack in the middle position. Preheat the oven to 400°F.

2. Prick the pie shell pastry with a fork. Cut a piece of foil slightly larger than the pie shell and coat it with vegetable spray. Place the foil, greased side down, in the pie shell, fitting it loosely into bottom and sides. Fill the foil with uncooked rice or beans to prevent the crust from bubbling during baking. Bake 18 minutes.

3. Remove the foil and rice or bean filling carefully. Prick any existing bubbles in the dough. Return the shell to the oven and continue baking, checking every 5 minutes for browning. If the edge of the crust appears to be browning too quickly, cover loosely with foil. Remove the pie shell from the oven when it is golden brown. Cool on a rack before adding the pie filling, unless otherwise directed. The rice or beans can be cooled, sealed in a plastic bag, and reused several times to prebake pie shells.

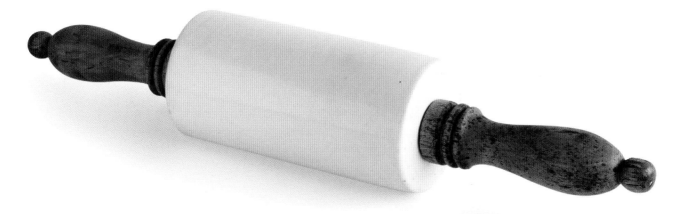

Wood and china rolling pin, English, late 19th century–early 20th century

MARY MELLY'S CHOCOLATE ANGEL PIE

YIELD: 8 SLICES

1 lb. semisweet or bittersweet chocolate, chopped

¼ cup milk

2 tablespoons sugar

⅛ teaspoon salt

4 egg yolks, at room temperature

1 cup heavy cream

1 teaspoon vanilla

9-inch Meringue Pie Shell, baked and cooled (page 251)

Whipped cream, for garnish

Chocolate shavings, for garnish

MARY MELLY WAS THE BELOVED HOUSEKEEPER *of Bob and Ethel Wise, of Brookline, Massachusetts. Bob and his brother Jack owned Supertaste Ice Cream. Mary was always considered one of the family, and she generously gave her recipes to members of the Wise family and their friends. Angel Pie is a first cousin to the Australian Pavlova—a meringue shell filled with fruit and topped with whipped cream.*

1. Place chocolate, milk, sugar, and salt in the top of a double boiler over simmering water. Heat, stirring occasionally with wooden spoon, until chocolate is melted. Remove top of double boiler and let mixture cool for about 5 minutes. Whisk in egg yolks, one at a time. Return mixture to simmering water and heat, stirring, until mixture registers

Metal candy shop scoops, English, early 1900s

MERINGUE PIE SHELL

4 egg whites

1/2 teaspoon cream of tartar

1 cup sugar

1 teaspoon vanilla

1. Place the oven rack in the middle position. Preheat the oven to 300°F. Coat a 9-inch ovenproof glass pie plate with vegetable spray or butter, making sure to coat the rim, and set aside.

2. Place egg whites in the bowl of a standing mixer fitted with the whisk attachment. Whip on low speed. With motor running, add cream of tartar. Gradually increase speed to medium until soft peaks form. Gradually add sugar. Add vanilla. Increase speed to high and beat to form glossy, firm peaks. Sugar should be completely absorbed into meringue.

3. Gently spoon egg whites into prepared pan. Use the back of a tablespoon to even the bottom and build up sides of pie shell. Bake 50 minutes. Turn off oven and leave pie shell in oven for 1 hour to dry out. Remove from oven, place on a rack, and allow to cool completely. Store at room temperature, tightly wrapped in wax paper or in a covered tin, until ready to fill. Make sure prepared filling is completely cool before mounding in pie shell.

160°F on a thermometer. Remove from heat and transfer to bowl. Let cool to room temperature. To speed cooling, place bowl with chocolate mixture into a larger bowl of ice water.

2. Whip cream in the bowl of a standing mixer fitted with the whisk attachment to form soft peaks. Add vanilla and beat until stiff. Add cooled chocolate mixture in two batches, beating after each addition. Spoon into prepared meringue shell. Place toothpicks at intervals in topping and cover pie gently with tent of plastic wrap. Refrigerate for at least 3 hours to set. Remove toothpicks and decorate with swirls of whipped cream and shaved chocolate and serve. Store leftover pie loosely covered with plastic wrap in the refrigerator.

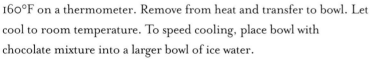

Tips & Touches

- Filling can also be spooned into custard cups and served as chocolate mousse.

Mrs. Naka's Lemon Angel Pie

YIELD: 8 SLICES   { 1950s }

We learned about this living recipe *from Holly Tarson,
whose husband's grandparents, the Peppers, lived in Berkeley, California.
A Japanese couple named Mr. and Mrs. Naka worked for the Peppers
as gardeners, and Mrs. Naka used the Meyer lemons from the Peppers' yard
to make a creamy lemon pie in a meringue crust. Years later, after Dr. and
Mrs. Pepper had passed away, Holly's husband, Geoff, and his parents
continued to visit the Nakas, who served them cashews and 7-Up and
their favorite lemon pie. The generous Mrs. Naka always kept an extra pie
in her freezer for them to take home.*

4 egg yolks

½ cup sugar

3 tablespoons lemon juice

1 teaspoon grated lemon zest

Pinch of salt

1 cup heavy cream

9-inch Meringue Pie Shell, baked
and cooled (page 251)

1. Place egg yolks, sugar, lemon juice, lemon zest, and salt in a heavy-
   bottomed saucepan. Whisk until combined. Cook over medium heat,
   stirring continuously, until the mixture thickens and looks like
   custard, 5 to 7 minutes. Remove from heat, transfer to a 1-quart bowl,
   and place plastic wrap directly on the surface of the custard to keep a
   skin from forming. Let cool completely.

2. Whip cream until soft peaks form. Break up cooled lemon custard
   with whisk. Stir in a small amount of whipped cream. Fold custard
   into whipped cream. Add mixture to pie shell and gently smooth the
   top. Stick several toothpicks into filling, cover loosely with wax paper,
   and refrigerate for at least 24 hours before serving. Decorate pie
   with additional swirls of whipped cream. Store leftover pie loosely
   wrapped in wax paper in refrigerator. Mrs. Naka's pie tastes best on
   the day it is made. It can also be frozen.

Tips & Touches

- Meyer lemons are slightly
  sweeter than conventional
  lemons. They are available for a
  short season in grocery stores.
  Substituting a conventional
  lime for part of the zest and
  juice brings the flavor of this pie
  closer to that of the original.

Green Tomato Pie

{ 1940s }

YIELD: 8 SLICES

Pastry for double-crust pie, divided in half and chilled (see Sheila's Savory Pie Crust on page 248). Leave out optional herbs.

4 cups peeled, cored, and sliced green tomatoes (5 to 6 tomatoes) (see Tips & Touches)

1 tablespoon apple cider vinegar

Grated zest of ½ lemon

1¼ cups sugar

6 tablespoons flour

½ teaspoon salt

½ teaspoon allspice

¼ teaspoon cinnamon

¼ teaspoon ginger

2 tablespoons cold butter, cut into ¼-inch dice

1 egg, beaten

TOMATOES ARE ACTUALLY A FRUIT, *even though we think of them as a vegetable, so it's not unusual to use tomatoes in the filling for this fruit pie, with its subtle flavor of allspice. This recipe comes from The Pie Lady, in North Carolina. This is a seasonal pie best made when summer slides into fall and there are green tomatoes on the vine, a week away from turning ripe. Choose medium-size green tomatoes. The larger ones will be tough and reedy.*

1. To make the crust: For detailed instructions, see Sheila's Savory Pie Crust on page 248. Coat a 9-inch ovenproof glass pie pan with vegetable spray. Roll out pastry dough. Fit half of dough into bottom of pie plate and trim off excess. Chill in refrigerator.
2. Place tomato slices in a large bowl. Sprinkle with vinegar and lemon zest. Mix sugar, flour, salt, allspice, cinnamon, and ginger in another bowl. Add to tomatoes and mix thoroughly to coat.
3. Place the oven rack in the middle position. Preheat the oven to 450°F.
4. Place tomato filling in prepared pie shell and dot with butter. Brush edges of shell with beaten egg. Add top crust, seal and crimp edges, and cut decorative slits. Brush top crust and edges with beaten egg. Place pie on pan covered with foil, shiny side up, to catch drips.
5. Bake 20 minutes and check crust for browning. If crust browns too quickly, cover pie loosely with foil. Reduce oven temperature to 350°F and bake another 25 minutes, or until crust is golden brown and filling is bubbling. Remove foil, if using, for last 5 minutes.
6. Cool pie on a rack. Serve slightly warm or at room temperature. Store pie loosely covered with paper towel and wax paper in the refrigerator. Let pie come to room temperature before serving.

TIPS & TOUCHES

- Green tomatoes do not react in the same way as ripe tomatoes to a hot and then a cold water bath for removing skins. We had to peel the green tomatoes with a vegetable peeler.
- Place a piece of wax paper under pie plate when brushing crust with egg wash.
- Wipe any egg wash that drips under the rim of pie plate with paper towel.

SHOOFLY PIE

{ *1950s* }

THIS IS A VERY TRADITIONAL *Pennsylvania Dutch or German pie.
We found it in the manuscript cookbook of The Pie Lady, from North
Carolina, another example of how heirloom recipes can cross state borders.
Dark corn syrup can be substituted for the molasses. We suggest serving
small pieces of this very rich pie.*

1. To make the streusel: Place sugar in a medium bowl. Sift together
   flour, salt, cinnamon, nutmeg, and ginger on a sheet of wax paper
   and add to sugar. Work in butter with fingers (wear disposable gloves if
   desired) until the texture resembles coarse sand.
2. To make the crust: For detailed instructions, see Sheila's Sweet Pie
   Crust on page 248. Coat a 9-inch ovenproof glass pie pan with
   vegetable spray. Roll out pastry dough. Fit into bottom of pie plate
   and trim off excess. Chill in refrigerator.
3. Set the oven rack in the middle position. Preheat the oven to 400°F.
4. Place molasses in a bowl. Dissolve baking soda in water and add to
   molasses, stirring with a wooden spoon. Pour into prepared pie shell.
   Sprinkle streusel over surface of pie and bake 15 minutes. Reduce
   oven temperature to 350°F and bake another 25 minutes, or until a
   tester inserted into pie comes out clean.
   Place pie on rack and cool completely
   before cutting. Store leftover pie
   loosely wrapped in wax paper
   in the refrigerator.

FOR STREUSEL

¼ cup sugar

1 cup flour

⅛ teaspoon salt

⅛ teaspoon cinnamon

⅛ teaspoon nutmeg

⅛ teaspoon ginger

¼ cup cold butter, cut into
½-inch dice

Pastry for single-crust pie, chilled
(see Sheila's Sweet Pie Crust
on page 248)

½ cup molasses

½ teaspoon baking soda

½ cup water, heated to just under
a boil

TIPS & TOUCHES

* Do not use hot tap water, which
  might contain mineral deposits.

Sugar bag, English, early 20th century

Blueberry Buckle

{ *1870s* }

YIELD: 16 SQUARES

FOR STREUSEL

½ cup firmly packed brown sugar

2 tablespoons sifted flour

⅛ teaspoon salt

½ teaspoon cinnamon

⅛ teaspoon nutmeg

3 tablespoons cold butter,
   cut into ½-inch dice

½ cup toasted pecans, coarsely
   chopped

FOR BUCKLE

1¾ cups plus 2 tablespoons
   sifted flour

2 cups fresh blueberries

2 teaspoons baking powder

½ teaspoon salt

¼ teaspoon cinnamon

¼ teaspoon nutmeg

½ cup butter, softened to room
   temperature

¾ cup sugar

1 large egg

1 teaspoon vanilla

½ cup milk

Tips & Touches

- Warm leftover buckle slightly
  in a low oven for few minutes
  before serving.

BUCKLES ARE FRUIT DESSERTS *covered with a sweet crumb topping that buckles in the middle after baking. We make our buckles during spring and summer to enjoy the best of seasonal fruit. Buckles are a little like coffee cakes with a crunchy praline topping. We like to cut our buckles while they're still in the pan. We used several similar heirloom recipes to come up with this delicious treat.*

1. Set the oven rack in the middle position. Preheat the oven to 375°F. Line the bottom and sides of an 8-inch by 8-inch by 2-inch pan with foil, shiny side up. Coat the foil with butter or vegetable spray.

2. To make the streusel: Place sugar, flour, salt, cinnamon, and nutmeg in a bowl. Work in butter with fingers (wear disposable gloves if desired) until mixture looks like irregular crumbs. Add pecans to mixture and combine. Set aside.

3. To make the buckle: Sift flour in a bowl. In another bowl, mix 2 tablespoons of sifted flour with blueberries and set aside. Sift baking powder, salt, cinnamon, and nutmeg into remaining flour.

4. Cream butter and sugar in the bowl of a standing mixer fitted with the paddle attachment until fluffy. Add egg and beat to combine. In a glass measuring cup, stir vanilla into milk. Add dry ingredients and milk alternately to batter in thirds. Fold in blueberries. Pour batter into prepared pan. Sprinkle streusel over top. Bake 45 to 50 minutes, or until a tester inserted in the middle comes out clean. After 30 minutes, cover buckle loosely with foil to prevent the crumbs from browning too quickly.

5. Remove buckle from oven and cool on a rack until still slightly warm. Cut into squares and serve with whipped cream or vanilla ice cream. Buckle is good served warm or at room temperature. Store loosely covered with wax paper in the refrigerator.

SWEET POTATO PUDDING

YIELD: 12 SERVINGS   { 1930s }

WE FOUND SEVERAL RECIPES FOR THIS PUDDING *in our collection of manuscript cookbooks, but this is the version we decided to try. Our friend Yvette Gooding was mentored by her late grandmother, Lannie Waters Edmondson, a magnificent home cook. Yvette makes this pudding frequently for her two sons, Patrick and Andrew. This pudding calls for grated raw sweet potatoes, so it has a bit of texture to it. This is a very good choice for a holiday dessert.*

4 large sweet potatoes (about 11 cups grated and chopped)

½ cup butter, softened to room temperature

1 cup firmly packed brown sugar, divided

½ cup granulated sugar

3 large eggs

2 teaspoons vanilla

½ teaspoon cinnamon

½ teaspoon nutmeg

¼ teaspoon salt

¾ cup milk

¼ cup heavy cream

1. Set the oven rack in the middle position. Preheat the oven to 350°F. Coat a 9-inch by 13-inch ovenproof glass baking dish with vegetable spray.

2. Peel and quarter sweet potatoes. Grate in a food processor fitted with the metal grating blade or by hand. Process grated sweet potato in the bowl of a food processor fitted with the metal blade or chop hand-grated potatoes with a knife. Sweet potatoes should be smooth.

3. Cream butter, ½ cup of the brown sugar, and the granulated sugar in the bowl of a standing mixer fitted with the paddle attachment. Add eggs and vanilla. Add cinnamon, nutmeg, salt, milk, and cream and combine. Fold in grated, chopped sweet potato. Place in prepared dish. Sprinkle remaining ½ cup brown sugar over top of pudding.

4. Bake 1 hour, or until top of pudding is caramelized and a tester inserted into middle comes out clean. Cover with foil if pudding browns too quickly. Serve pudding hot or cold with whipped cream. Store leftover pudding in a dish covered with wax paper in the refrigerator.

China custard cups; wire holder, American, 1930s

THE SAMELS-CARBARNES FAMILY ADVENTURES

YIELD: 72 COOKIES

1 cup butter, softened to room temperature

1½ cups sugar

2 cups chopped, pitted dates

2 tablespoons milk

2 eggs, beaten

½ teaspoon salt

1 teaspoon vanilla

1 cup toasted walnuts, chopped

4 cups crispy rice cereal

7-oz. package shredded, sweetened coconut

DEBRA SAMELS FIRST TASTED THESE COOKIES *when her mother, Mary Bohen Carbarnes, made them for the Platteville Free Methodist Church Christmas Bazaar in Wisconsin. Mrs. Carbarnes, who was the chairman of the bazaar, grew up near an Amish community and was a talented home baker. She put together a family cookbook for her five daughters. Zoe and Jack Samels, her grandchildren, both love to make Adventures.*

1. Line a baking sheet with parchment paper.
2. Place butter and sugar in a heavy-bottomed 2-quart saucepan and whisk to combine. Add dates and place pan over medium heat. Bring to a boil, stirring with a wooden spoon, and remove from heat.
3. Combine milk and eggs in a small bowl. Add ⅓ cup of hot date mixture and whisk quickly to temper eggs. Return egg mixture to saucepan and stir briskly. Bring to a boil over medium heat, stirring with a wooden spoon. Boil 2 minutes. Remove mixture from heat. Add salt and vanilla.
4. Place walnuts and crispy rice cereal in a large bowl. Add date mixture and stir to combine. Allow to cool. When cool enough to handle, scoop dough by the tablespoonful and roll into balls. Roll balls in coconut and place on prepared baking sheet. Adventures will firm up while standing. Place in fluted paper cups and serve. Store between sheets of wax paper in a covered tin.

Toasted Almond Butter Cookies

YIELD: 72 COOKIES

FOR COOKIES

3⅓ cups flour

1⅔ cups confectioners' sugar

½ teaspoon salt

2 teaspoons grated lemon zest

2 cups cold butter, cut into 16 slices

3 egg yolks, lightly beaten

FOR TOPPING

2 egg whites

1 cup toasted slivered almonds

WE FOUND THIS RECIPE FOR A RICH *and nutty butter cookie in a manuscript cookbook containing recipes with an Austrian flavor. The recipes were typed on a manual typewriter and appeared to be from the 1930s. We believe that someone went over a collection of handwritten scraps and transcribed them so that they would be handed down in the family. This book was lovingly compiled.*

1. To make the cookies: Place flour, confectioners' sugar, salt, and lemon zest in the bowl of a food processor fitted with the metal blade. Pulse three times to mix. Add butter and pulse until crumbly. Add egg yolks and pulse until mixture comes together.

2. Remove dough from bowl of processor, divide in half, and shape each half into a disk. Wrap in plastic wrap or wax paper and chill for at least 2 hours, or until firm enough to form into balls.

3. Set the oven rack in the middle position. Preheat the oven to 350°F. Line a 14-inch by 16-inch baking sheet with foil, shiny side up, and coat with vegetable spray, or use a silicone liner.

4. Roll heaping teaspoons of dough into balls the size of marbles. Place 12 to 15 balls on each baking sheet.

5. To add the topping: In a small bowl, whisk egg whites to break them up. Cut out a 4-inch by 4-inch square of wax paper. Place the wax paper on top of a ball. Using the bottom of a drinking glass, gently press the ball flat. Continue to do this with each ball. (This method eliminates using any excess flour, but if you prefer, you can flatten cookies with the bottom of a glass dipped in flour.) Brush tops of cookies with egg white and sprinkle with slivered almonds. With your fingers, gently press the almonds into the dough. Bake 10 to 12 minutes, or until edges of cookies turn golden brown. Place baking sheet on rack and cool for 3 minutes. Remove cookies from baking sheet with a metal spatula and place on rack to cool completely. Store between sheets of waxed paper in a covered tin

TIPS & TOUCHES

- If dough becomes too soft to handle, return it to the refrigerator and chill until firm enough to handle.
- Do not press balls paper-thin.

The Five Isabelles' Orange Drop Cakes

{ *1920s* }

WE RECEIVED THIS RECIPE FOR *buttery Orange Drop Cakes from Mandy Timney Finizio. She found it handwritten on the inside back cover of her Grandmother Porter's 1922 copy of* Good Housekeeping's Book of Menus, Recipes, and Household Discoveries. *When Mandy's mother, also an Isabelle, was a child, Mrs. Porter taught her how to bake these legendary treats. There has been an Isabelle in each of the last five generations of Mandy's family, and all of them know how to make these cookies.*

1. For the drop cakes: Set the oven rack in the middle position. Preheat the oven to 375°F. Line a 14-inch by 16-inch baking sheet with foil, shiny side up, and coat with vegetable spray, or use a silicone liner. Prepare two trays, if desired.

2. Sift flour, baking powder, baking soda, and salt in a large bowl and set aside. Cream butter and sugar in the bowl of a standing mixer fitted with the paddle attachment until fluffy. Add eggs one at a time, beating after each addition. Add orange zest. Add one third of the dry ingredients and the orange juice and beat to combine. Add the remaining dry ingredients, one third at a time, alternating with the buttermilk. Beat until smooth.

3. Drop dough by tablespoon on prepared baking sheet or use a disposable plastic piping bag for more uniform results. Do not pipe or drop more than 25 cookies per baking sheet (five rows of five cookies). Flatten any peaks on cookies with a finger dipped in cold water. Sprinkle with sanding sugar, if using. Bake 12 to 13 minutes, or until cookies are golden, with lightly browned edges. Place baking sheet on a rack and let cool 2 minutes. Transfer cookies to rack with metal spatula and cool completely.

4. To make the icing, if using: Sift confectioners' sugar into a large bowl. Add orange zest, orange juice, and salt and whisk briskly to combine. Icing should be soft enough to drizzle over cakes; thicken with confectioners' sugar or thin with orange juice, as needed. Drizzle icing over cakes and let stand on racks until icing is completely dry. Store between sheets of wax paper in a covered tin.

FOR DROP CAKES

4½ cups flour

3 teaspoons baking powder

1 teaspoon baking soda

½ teaspoon salt

1 cup butter, softened to room temperature

2 cups sugar

2 large eggs

3 tablespoons grated orange zest

½ cup orange juice

1 cup buttermilk

Coarse sanding sugar (optional)

FOR ICING (OPTIONAL)

1 lb. confectioners' sugar

2 tablespoon grated orange zest

3 tablespoons orange juice

Pinch of salt

Tips & Touches

- Cookies can be finished with either sanding sugar or icing, not both.

NATHALIE'S GINGER WHALE COOKIES

{ 1950s—1960s } YIELD: APPROXIMATELY 7 DOZEN 3½-INCH COOKIES

4 cups flour

½ teaspoon salt

1 teaspoon cinnamon

½ teaspoon nutmeg

½ teaspoon ginger

⅛ teaspoon cloves

½ cup butter, softened to
room temperature

¼ cup sugar

1 large egg

1 cup molasses

2 teaspoons baking soda

2 tablespoons hot water

¼ cup small raisins or
chocolate dots

WE'VE HAD THIS RECIPE FOR ALMOST FIFTY YEARS. *Printed on a small piece of light blue paper, it came with a handmade cookie cutter in the shape of a whale. Designed and sold by Nathalie Woods, from Marblehead, Massachusetts, this crisp ginger cookie sports a raisin for an eye and its tail can be placed at any angle. Sheila bought the cookie cutter while visiting her friend, Ruth Hadley, in Marblehead. This recipe is also similar to one we found in a manuscript cookbook, credited to "Edna."*

1. Sift flour, salt, cinnamon, nutmeg, ginger, and cloves into a large mixing bowl and set aside.
2. Cream butter and sugar in the bowl of a standing mixer fitted with the paddle attachment until fluffy. Add egg. Add molasses and combine. Dissolve baking soda in hot water and add to creamed ingredients. Add sifted dry ingredients in thirds and mix thoroughly. Scoop cookie dough onto sheet of wax paper or plastic wrap, form into disk, and chill in refrigerator for at least 2 hours or overnight.
3. Set the oven rack in the middle position. Preheat the oven to 375 °F. Line a 14-inch by 16-inch baking sheet with foil, shiny side up, and coat with vegetable spray, or use a silicone liner. Prepare two trays, if desired.
4. Divide chilled dough in four parts. On a floured piece of wax paper, roll dough ¼-inch thick. Cut out cookies with fish or whale-shaped cutters. Place 2 inches apart on prepared baking sheet, putting no more than 16 cookies on sheet. Add a raisin to each cookie for an eye. Bake 10 to 12 minutes. Cool on a rack until firm. Store between sheets of wax paper in a covered tin.

TIPS & TOUCHES

- Scraps of dough can be put together and rerolled. These cookies may be a little crisper.
- Various cookie cutters can be used, but a pod of whales is very nice.

GERTRUDE WOODS' STEAMED PECAN CAKE

{ 1915 }

2 tablespoons Wondra

¾ cup raisins

1 cup toasted pecans, coarsely chopped

1½ cups flour, divided

¾ teaspoon baking powder

¼ teaspoon salt

¾ teaspoon nutmeg

½ cup butter, softened to room temperature

½ cup firmly packed brown sugar

2 eggs, separated

¼ cup molasses

½ cup whiskey or grape juice

WE BELIEVE THAT THIS STEAMED PECAN CAKE should come with a warning because of its high alcohol content. It makes a wonderful confection for the holiday season or any time you feel like a sophisticated treat. This recipe was handed down through the Woods–Drain families and comes from Cynthiana, Kentucky. During Prohibition, Mrs. Woods replaced the whiskey with grape juice. You can do the same or compromise with half grape juice and half whiskey. We also like this cake when it's mellowed for at least two weeks in the refrigerator.

1. Liberally butter a 6-cup mold or coat with vegetable spray; dust with Wondra and tap out excess. Prepare a buttered parchment sheet to fit the top of the mold. Select a covered pot large enough to accommodate the mold with a 2-inch clearance around the sides. Set a metal rack inside the pot.

2. Place raisins and pecans in a small bowl. Add 1 tablespoon of the flour and toss to coat. Set aside.

3. Sift remaining flour, baking powder, salt, and nutmeg into a large bowl and set aside. Cream butter and sugar in the bowl of a standing mixer fitted with the paddle attachment until fluffy. Add egg yolks and then molasses.

4. Add dry ingredients in three parts, alternating with whiskey or grape juice. With mixer running, add raisins and pecans and beat 30 seconds, or until they are evenly distributed throughout batter. (Or fold them in.) Beat egg whites until they form soft peaks and fold into batter.

5. Pour batter into prepared mold until no more than two thirds full. Place buttered parchment round on top of mold. Fold two sheets of foil over open top and tie securely with kitchen string.

6. Set filled mold on rack in pot. Add water to come one third of the way up the sides of the mold. Remove mold. Cover pot and bring water to a boil. Turn off heat, lift pot cover, and carefully place filled mold on rack. Cover pot. Adjust heat so that water simmers; do not let water

TIPS & TOUCHES

- Use Wondra for dusting mold.
- This is a very substantial cake, best enjoyed in thin slices.
- The aroma of the whiskey is very prevalent when the cake is removed from the steamer. Some of the whiskey will evaporate on cooling, but this is a very potent cake.

come to a boil. Steam pudding for 40 minutes, or until a tester inserted in the middle comes out clean. Check the water level periodically during the steaming and add water as needed. *Do not let water boil out because a tightly covered mold could explode.*

7. Turn off heat. Remove mold carefully from steamer and place on a cooling rack. Carefully remove foil and parchment from top of mold. Allow to cool on rack for 20 minutes. Cake should release easily when mold is inverted. If mold does not release cake easily, run a butter knife around edges or let sit until cake begins to shrink away from sides of mold. Store loosely wrapped in wax paper, or wrapped in cheesecloth soaked in whisky, in the refrigerator.

➤➤ FEEDING A FRUITCAKE ◄◄

Every heirloom cook had a favorite recipe for a substantial cake laden with raisins, nuts, and candied peels. But some fruitcakes assumed a more adventuresome role when they became a secret avenue for consuming spirits. Not only did the batters for fruitcake call for outrageous amounts of whiskey or brandy; the finished cake, when cool, was often wrapped in brandy-soaked cheesecloth and squirreled away in a cold dark place to season. Some home cooks even poured brandy or whiskey into holes they'd poked into their fruitcakes. The cakes were inspected periodically and the cheesecloth refreshed with more whiskey. This was called "feeding the cake." Faced with the restrictions of Prohibition, resourceful heirloom cooks resorted to using a less potent means of flavoring their cakes— grape juice. It was never the same, because they couldn't mellow them with alcohol, but with the repeal of Prohibition, home cooks once again fed their fruitcakes with spirits. It must be said that these well-fed fruitcakes were served in very thin slices.

Contributors

An employee, Hotel Lexington

Dina Arfa

Leon Arfa

Arthur

Germain Asselin

Sara Baser

Ila D. Berry

Bertha Bohlman

Mary Bradshaw

Dorothy Katziff Brass

Harry Brass

Mrs. E. R. Brown

Jane Bullard

Mary Bohen Carbarnes

Barbara Carey

Marion Carter

M. E. Carter

Reta Corbett

Elizabeth Corkery

Helaine Davis

Jean Downey

Lannie Edmondson

Edna

Constance Etz Ferdon

Mandy Timney Finizio

Erika Fitzpatrick

Mrs. Fredman

Marion Freeman

Helen Sochko Gaydos

Emma Geywitz

Ruth Geywitz

Lizzie Goldberg

Frieda Goldman

Yvette Gooding

Mary Gualdelli

Theodora Gueras

Sarah Toal Hails

Helen

Harriette C. Hodges

Rose Howard

Dale Irving

Elinor Inman Jennings

Eva Viola Johnson

Mary Johnson

Mrs. Julian

Katherine and Fred

Katy

Celia M. Katziff

Ida Tucker Katziff

Rose Levy

Virginia P. Lima

Dot Luke

Louella MacPherson

Nick Malgieri

A Lady from Martha's Vineyard

Alice McGinty

Mary Melly

Anna Morse

Mrs. Naka

A Lady From North Carolina

Geneva Bellevue O'Brien

Natalie Pangaro

Lorraine Paxton

Paxton-Grigor-Hails Family

Isabelle Porter

Uncle and Aunt Grace Rheinhold

Michael Ripley

Aunt Ruth

Arline Ryan

Debra Samels

Barbara Silberstein

Susanne Simpson

Rose "Bunny" Slobodzinski

Ed Steenberg

Gloria Schleiger Story

Ione Sutton

Mary C. Talbot

The Church Lady

The Pie Lady

The Lady from Martha's Vineyard

Suzanne Truax

Clara J. Warren

Gertrude Woods

Nathalie Woods

Mrs. Yaffee

Margaret Yarranton

SOURCES

INGREDIENTS AND EQUIPMENT

The Baker's Catalogue
Tel: 800-827-6836
www.bakerscatalogue.com
Grains, ingredients, equipment

Bob's Red Mill Natural Foods
Tel: 800-349-2173
Fax: 503-653-1339
www.bobsredmill.com
Flours, grains

**Christina's Homemade Ice Cream,
Spice & Specialty Foods**
1255 Cambridge Street
Cambridge, MA 02139
Tel: 617-492-7021
Fax: 617-576-0922
Spices, extracts, flours, chocolate

Dairy Fresh Candies
57 Salem Street
Boston, MA 02113
Tel: 800-336-5536
Fax: 617-742-9828
sales@dairyfreshcandies.com
Baking supplies

Formaggio Kitchen
244 Huron Avenue
Cambridge, MA 02138
Tel: 888-212-3224
Specialty foods, baking supplies

Nordic Ware
Tel: 877-466-7342
www.nordicware.com
Baking equipment

Penzey's Spices
Tel: 800-741-7787
www.penzeys.com
Spices, extracts

Sparrow Enterprises, Ltd.
Tel: 617-569-3900
Fax: 617-569-5888
www.chocolatebysparrow.com
info@sparrowfoods.com
Chocolate, sanding sugar

Sur la Table
Tel: 800-243-0852
www.surlatable.com
Baking supplies, equipment

The Vermont Country Store
Tel: 802-362-8460
www.vermontcountrystore.com
Common Crackers

Williams-Sonoma
Tel: 800-541-2233
www.williams-sonoma.com
Baking supplies, equipment

Zabar's
2245 Broadway (at 80th Street)
New York, NY 10024
Tel: 212-787-2000
800-697-6301
Fax: 212-580-4477
info@zabars.com
Kosher cheese

BOOK DEALERS SPECIALIZING IN COOKBOOKS AND MANUSCRIPT COOKBOOKS

B. & S. Gventer Books & Ephemera
Bruce Gventer,
bgventer@bookfairs.com
D. Curto,
definite@bookfairs.com
P.O. Box 298
South Egremont, MA 02158-0298
Tel: 413-528-2327

Bonnie Slotnick Cookbooks
163 West Tenth Street
New York, NY 10014-3116
Tel: 212-989-8962
bonnieslotnickbooks@earthlink.net

Cooks Books
T. & M. McKirdy
34 Marine Drive
Rottingdean
Sussex BN2 7HQ UK
Tel: 01273 302707
Fax: 01273 301651

Kitchen Arts & Letters
Nach Waxman
1435 Lexington Avenue
New York, NY 10128
Tel: 212-876-5550
www.kitchenartsandletters.com

Liz Seeber
16 The Brow
Friston, Nr Eastbourne
East Sussex BN20 0ES UK
Tel: 00 44 (0) 1323 423777
liz@lizseeber.demon.co.uk
www.lizseeberbooks.co.uk

The Reynolds
352 Front Street
Bath, ME 04530-2749
203-443-8812
Fax: 203-443-2638
oldeport@TTLC.net

BIBLIOGRAPHY

Carlisle, Mrs. John G. *Kentucky Cookbook.* Chicago: F. Tennyson Neely, Publisher, 1893.

Malgieri, Nick. *Chocolate.* New York: HarperCollins Publishers, Inc., 1998.

Malgieri, Nick. *Cookies Unlimited.* New York: HarperCollins Publishers, Inc., 2000.

Nathan, Joan. *Jewish Cooking in America.* New York: Alfred A. Knopf, 1994.

Oliver, Sandra. *Saltwater Foodways: New Englanders and Their Food, at Sea and Ashore, in the Nineteenth Century.* Mystic: Mystic Seaport Museum, Inc., 1995.

Rombauer, Irma S., and Marion Rombauer Becker. *Joy of Cooking.* Indianapolis: The Bobbs-Merrill Company, Inc., 1967.

Rombauer, Irma S., Marion Rombauer Becker, and Ethan Becker. *The All New All Purpose Joy of Cooking.* New York: Scribner, 1997.

Sax, Richard. *Classic Home Desserts: A Treasury of Heirloom and Contemporary Recipes from around the World.* Chapters Publishing Ltd., 1994.

Tighe, Eileen, Editor. *Woman's Day Encyclopedia of Cookery.* New York: Fawcett Publications, Inc., 1966.

Williams, Richard L. *Foods of the World.* New York: Time-Life Books, 1971.

Acknowledgments

Although writing a cookbook can seem to be a solitary experience, it never is. *Heirloom Cooking with the Brass Sisters* was an exercise in collaboration. Although Blanche DuBois depended on the kindness of strangers, we have always depended on the kindness of friends and colleagues.

J. P. Leventhal, our publisher, continues to understand and share our vision of preserving the best recipes from America's home kitchens. His knowledge and encouragement continue to be invaluable. We thank Laura Ross for her insight and wise support, and we acknowledge the enthusiasm of Judy Courtade, Katherine Furman, and everyone at BD&L and thank them for their hard work. We are fortunate that Becky Koh, our editor, combined good common sense editing with a light hand.

Susi Oberhelman, our book designer, and Andy Ryan, our photographer, continue to be members of our extended family. They don't mind ironing a napkin or washing a dish, as well as being two of the most creative people we have ever met. Stephanie Lyness, who edited the recipes for *Heirloom Cooking*, brought her enthusiasm and valuable expertise to the team, while Candie Frankel, in an encore appearance as Copy Editor, continued to bring a fresh approach to what we wrote and helped to make it clearer and more complete. We are once again in awe of the optimism and professionalism of our publicist, Lisa Sweet, who arranged for two roundish ladies from New England to discover America. We welcome a new member to our team, our Food Stylist, Catrine Kelty, who shares our love of good food, creative presentation, and culinary antiques. She is a great cook, a hard worker, and knows how to keep us laughing during tough times.

We acknowledge the contribution of Judy Pray, who stewarded the idea and the proposal for *Heirloom Cooking* from its beginnings, and who offered valuable advice and guidance.

We thank Karen Johnson and Steve Axlerod, our agents, who made it possible for us to write a "kitchen table book," that we hope will be read, used, and enjoyed in your home kitchen. Their wisdom and guidance continue to assist us in honoring the women and men whose recipes and stories might have been lost, if we had not been able to act as their interpreters.

Barbara, Danese, and Dan Carey and the entire Carey and McCoy Families opened their homes to us. They continued to taste, lovingly criticize, and praise what we brought them. Losing Barbara suddenly, we all came together for comfort while sitting around the kitchen table sharing wonderful memories and cups of tea.

HEIRLOOM COOKING

Joan Katziff Kline, Lois Katziff, and Florence Tedeschi offered us family recipes and stories to fill in any of the blanks.

Finally, special thanks to two friends from New York City. Nick Malgieri, classically trained master baker, found the time to encourage two home cooks, while Bonnie Slotnick came up with intriguing scraps of handwritten recipes and valuable advice.

The following people generously gave us the encouragement and support, personal, as well as professional, that made it possible for us to write *Heirloom Cooking*: Jon Abbott, Anne Adams, Mark Alpert, Bonnie Asselin, Judy and Allen Azer, Richard Band, Sara Baser, Henry Becton, Sadie Martha Brass, Lynn Chase, Helaine Davis, Pamela Derringer, Laurie Donnelly, Margaret Drain, Lisa Ekus, Deb Fantasia, Mandy and Fran Finizio, Hilary Finkel-Buxton, The crew at The Fresh Pond Market, Leslie Gaydos, Aiden Gilbert, Brad Gregory, Mary and George Gueras, Ishan and Valerie Gurdel, Bill Gustat, Jeanne Hopkins, Anne Hosmer, Michael Jenike, Lee Joseph, Sherri and Jerry Kaplow, Kathleen and Sally, our Chocolate Angels, Norman Katziff, Anne Kemelman, Lawrence and Louise Kimball, Neal Kline, Jan Langone, Maria and Jim Levine, David Lima, Graziella Macchetta, Mimi MacKenzie, Rona Mael, Larry McCargar, Alexandra Myles, Meredith Nierman, Molly O'Neill, Dennis O'Reilly, Our Friends on the "L" and the WGBH Educational Foundation, Jamie Parker, Chris Prouty, Chris and Esther Pullman, Pamela Rajpal, Bev and Phil Reynolds, Mike Ripley, Leah Rose Rosenblatt, Debra and Mark Samels, Judy Scott, Laura Shapiro, Susan Sherman, Ken Shulman, Leah Steenberg, Holly Tarson, Donna and Eric Taub, Maureen Timmons, Rick Tompkins, Rachel Tortorici, Sue Truax, Lianne Welch, Larraine Yaffe, Anita Yeshman.

Conversion Chart

WEIGHT

I ounce	28 grams
¼ pound	114 grams
I pound	454 grams
2.2 pounds	I kilogram

VOLUME

I teaspoon	5 milliliters
I tablespoon	15 milliliters
⅛ cup	30 milliliters
¼ cup	60 milliliters
½ cup	120 milliliters
I cup	240 milliliters (¼ liter)
I pint	480 milliliters
I quart	I liter
I gallon	3¾ liters

LENGTH

I inch	2½ centimeters (25 millimeters)
12 inches	30 centimeters

OVEN TEMPERATURE

FAHRENHEIT	CENTIGRADE
212°F	100°C
225°F	107°C
250°F	121°C
275°F	135°C
300°F	149°C
325°F	163°C
350°F	177°C
375°F	191°C
400°F	204°C
425°F	218°C
450°F	232°C
475°F	246°C
500°F	260°C
525°F	274°C
550°F	288°C

SELECTED CONVERSIONS

BUTTER

I teaspoon	5 grams
I tablespoon	15 grams
½ cup (I stick)	115 grams
I cup (2 sticks)	230 grams
2 cups (4 sticks)	454 grams

FLOUR

I teaspoon	3 grams
I tablespoon	9 grams
I cup	120 grams

NUTS (CHOPPED)

I cup	155 grams

SUGAR (REGULAR GRANULATED)

I teaspoon	5 grams
I tablespoon	15 grams
I cup	185 grams

CONFECTIONERS' SUGAR

I teaspoon	4 grams
I tablespoon	9 grams
I cup	100 grams

Illustrations are in *italic*

HEIRLOOM COOKING

HEIRLOOM COOKING

Swedish Meat Balls.
lbs. Veal - ground (2 times)
¼ Lb. Pork " "
Onion chopped very fine
¼ Cup light Cream
Tablespoons, Flour ¾ Cup cracker
crumbs. Salt, pepper, pinch summer
savory 3/4 teaspoon Nut meg, Mix all
ingredients together form into small
Balls. Should make 40 or more. Brown
when all meat Balls
½ Cup white Wine
time, Rince out
Meats add

4.—
2 cups
2 cups
3 bay leaves
1 teasp. whole
1 teasp. whole
1½ teasp. sal
½ teasp. pepp
1 lemon sli

Heat
until

Here's what's cookin':
Lemon Stollen
Serves

¾ cup raisins
½ cup chopped mixed fruit & peel
cup currants
¾ cups flour
dry yeast
milk)
butter or margerine
sugar
t.
grated le
grated le

kissin' wears out
cookin' don't

Recipe from the kitchen of

From:
IONE ULRIC
Tel. BO
T

Pâté
1 lb chicke
1 tbs bu
mash i
until
ADD —
½ cup ch
cook
cut off fi
ADD
½ cup

ce
d
ater
s)
ause
mon
ka
re pepper
2 lbs dill weed
lbs fresh

Welsh Rarebit
2 tables butter
2 " cornstarch
2 teas dry mustard
2 teas salt.
1 teas red pepper
round steak
1 kernel garlic
1 cup sugar
Vermont

MY RECIPES

A Note from the Authors

We hope you enjoy reading *Heirloom Cooking with the Brass Sisters* and trying the living recipes we have selected from our collection of manuscript cookbooks. It's been a joy to share them with you and to share the stories we discovered when writing the book. We ask that you share with us the handwritten or oral recipes from family and friends that you've managed to preserve. We are always interested in trying new "old" recipes and learning about the people who created them. There are usually interesting stories connected to these scraps of paper and much-loved notebooks. We are always happy to meet and talk with you as we travel across America, but we hope you will contact us at www.thebrasssisters.com. We'd love to hear from you.

MARILYNN BRASS AND SHEILA BRASS